Fever of Unknown Origin

Fever of Unknown Origin

A True Tale of Medicine, Mystery, and Magic

Judith M. Ford

RESOURCE *Publications* · Eugene, Oregon

FEVER OF UNKNOWN ORIGIN
A True Tale of Medicine, Mystery, and Magic

Resource Publications
An Imprint of Wipf and Stock Publishers
199 W. 8th Ave., Suite 3
Eugene, OR 97401

www.wipfandstock.com

PAPERBACK ISBN: 978-1-6667-3838-4
HARDCOVER ISBN: 978-1-6667-9901-9
EBOOK ISBN: 978-1-6667-9902-6

06/02/22

This memoir is a work of creative nonfiction, which means it is truth, not fiction, but in order to tell that truth to the best of my memory (flawed as all memories are), I've had to recreate some dialogue, compress some scenes and might even have incorrectly remembered a fact here and there. Some names have been changed; the ones not changed have given me permission to use their names. During the years covered here, 1990-1997, I took notes, kept journals (as writers do when noteworthy or traumatic events occur) and I've relied heavily on those documents to make this the truest story I can tell. All dialogue maintains the essence of the feelings and the meaning of what was said at the time. Memory, after all, has its own story to tell.

"A dangerous illness fills you with adrenaline
and makes you feel very smart, I can
afford now . . . to draw conclusions."

—ANATOLE BROYARD, Intoxicated by My Illness

Contents

Acknowledgments

FEVER OF UNKNOWN ORIGIN was birthed and cared for by many helpers:

Debra Vest who midwifed the uneven beginnings of this story.

Mary Allen who provided encouragement, companionship, and expert editing. Without Mary the manuscript would still be living in my bedroom closet.

Natalie Goldberg who taught me how to sit still, how to mine my darkest material, how to be brave enough to write it.

My teachers at Vermont College of Fine Arts, who gave me the tools to be a stronger writer: Nance Van Winckle, Trinie Dalton, Brian Leung, David Jauss, Doug Glover, Jacquie Mitchard, Ellen Lesser, and Richard McCann.

Jessie, Rebecca, and Nic who patiently shared their time with this fourth child, Mom's book.

Chris, who believed in me beyond all reason, provided love and infrastructure, and supported my leaving home repeatedly to go to workshops, retreats and eventually, grad school.

My faithful friends who cheered when I finished the project, even though some of them never believed I'd get there.

My first readers, especially Chris, Amy, Freya, Jessie, Judith, Susannah, Nita, and Karen.

Prologue

Because I Could Not Stop

"Because I could not stop for Death,
He kindly stopped for me"

> —EMILY DICKINSON, "Because I
> Could Not Stop for Death"

July 4, 1990

IT's 7:00 A.M. AND already hot. My usual runs are four miles long but I've run seven and even eight miles a few times so a seven-miler isn't unreasonable for me to attempt. And I've decided that today—while I'm on vacation in Door County with my husband and three kids—I will run seven miles. Despite the heat. Despite the fact that I haven't been feeling very well lately. This run will be evidence that there's nothing wrong with me.

First I run past the bait shop where the resort rents out paddleboats and canoes and I notice that the black hand of the big round thermometer on the wall is pointing at eighty-five degrees.

The air is thick with humidity, no breeze, the trees are as still as photographs.

Just beyond the bait shop, I run up highway ZZ, about eight tenths of a mile, a slight incline. Not steep. And I start to struggle. My too-rapid pulse pounds in my ears. My trainer told me a while ago that it's normal for your heart to race when you start a run. Nothing to worry about.

1

Usually when I run everything evens out and an automatic rhythm takes over pretty quickly. But that isn't happening this time. Not so far.

I turn onto Mink River Road which runs alongside the Mink River Estuary, a large wetland full of reeds and sedges, edged in white cedar. Between the estuary and the road are fields of tall grass, stands of trees, and brush: sumac, scrub oak, purple thistle. There are houses here and there, set back away from the road down long driveways edged with maples or oaks, with pretty gardens (red poppies, purple asters, orange day lilies), trimmed lawns, clean, shiny doors and windows.

The road stretches out before me, wide open to the blistering sunlight. The tar along the cracks is shiny wet and oozing. There's very little traffic here. No pay phones, no gas stations. And, since it's only 1990, handheld smartphones aren't available yet. I'm on my own out here.

Every now and then I pass houses. Perfectly respectable houses. Why, I will wonder later, didn't it occur to me, when things got bad, to knock on one of those shiny front doors? I didn't even consider it. I've never been very good about asking for help. I wait a long time before I ask for directions. I like to think, though, that these days I'd ask for help if I were in any kind of real trouble. I think I finally learned that lesson during 1990, the year I'm on the brink of in this moment when I'm running. I hope I did. I think I did.

I don't ask for help today, on this 1990 fourth of July. I keep running, plodding on, one hot foot after the other, despite my racing heart, despite the heat, despite how sick I'm not letting myself feel. Because that's what runners do; we run through adversity; we keep going no matter what.

I haven't brought water. Hot day, three and a half miles before I'd be anywhere I could get a drink. Ordinarily three and a half miles would take me a half hour, not too much time to go without water. I don't like carrying water when I run. I want to be as light and free as possible. So no water with me now.

On Mink River Road I try every running trick I've ever learned. I shorten my stride. This takes some of the stress off my knees and back but my legs still feel stiff and achy. When I encounter the first hill I tell myself it's flat, keep my eyes on the ground to make the illusion easier to maintain. My brain says *flat* but my legs keep saying *steep*. Next I imagine a blazing sun inside my belly, pulsing energy into my legs and feet, fueling my muscles with fire and grace. No luck with that either. I experience no sign of grace and the only fire is the sun burning the part on top of my head and the hot highway scorching the soles of my feet.

I start taking walking breaks, one minute for every five minutes of running. Going at this pace it takes me forty minutes instead of twenty minutes to reach the old cemetery. Waves of heat rise up from the road making the gravestones look as if they were swaying in a light wind. I remember being here with my ex-husband and our daughter on a cooler day, back in 1983, the year we made one last misguided and unsuccessful attempt at reconciliation. As I take an extra-long walking break by the cemetery, I picture our daughter Jessie, five years old in 1983, running among the gravestones, grass stains on her sandals and knees. The sunlight lighting up her blond hair. The noise of the birds. All that shiny life alongside all those dead bodies and our dead marriage.

After the cemetery things get worse. My legs feel like bags of wet sand and I begin to feel a little dizzy. The Viking Restaurant is ten minutes away and the promise of air conditioning and water makes it possible for me to make it there. I enter through a waterfall of cool air just inside the restaurant and head straight for the ladies room. I turn on the tap full force and duck my head under it. Then I swallow a couple of mouthfuls of water. I catch a glimpse of my red face in the mirror. I look like someone who needs help. For a few seconds I consider asking if I can use the phone to call my husband Chris to come and pick me up, but I don't. I know that if I open my mouth to ask for anything, even something as ordinary as using a phone, I'll break down and cry. I leave the restaurant feeling a bit better, hoping the run back will be more doable.

I run easily for the first five minutes and then it gets hard again. My lungs ache as if I've been sprinting; my feet hurt; my legs feel heavy and weak. I slow to a walk and it's almost as hard to walk as it was to run. I decide to continue on rather than walk five minutes back to the Viking and call Chris. I think if I walk most of the way back I'll recover enough to run at least the final mile. If I can at least do that last mile I won't feel like such a failure.

It's eight o'clock by now and once in a while a car passes with a whoosh of hot exhaust washing over my bare shins like a cloud of poison gas. I get so concerned about being poisoned by the exhaust that after a couple cars go by, I start listening for them and stepping way off the road to let their fumes blow by me. It occurs to me briefly to ask one of these motorists for help, just as it occurred to me briefly to use a phone at the Viking. I reject the idea for the same reason: in order to ask for a ride, I'll have to acknowledge how broken down I am, how threatened I feel, and that would destroy what little self-control I have left. So I tell myself my situation doesn't merit flagging down a car. I can walk. I'm not dying.

I fix my eyes on the white line between road and shoulder. Chicory clings to the gravel bordering the white line. It grows in the cracks in the baked dirt beside the road. The meadow on my left ripples as the breeze rolls across it. I consider sinking into those green waves, the tall grass closing over me like water. But it occurs to me, if I leave the road, and if someone comes looking for me (and why would they?) they'll never find me. I keep walking in plain sight, in the open brutal sunlight, my gaze shuttling between the edge of the road and the curve ahead, beyond which lies the intersection of Mink River and ZZ.

As I walk on I think I see a bicycle gliding around the curve, coming toward me. As it draws closer I realize its rider is a child in cut-off shorts and a white tank top. It's my daughter—twelve-year-old, overly responsible, wonderful Jessie. I stop walking and wave at her. "I'm so glad to see you," I call.

She brings her bike to a stop two feet in front of me and starts scolding me for having been gone so long. "Chris said not to worry but Chris always says not to worry. So I decided to come and check on you." She tips her chin up; her bright blue eyes sparkle; her brown ponytail bounces. She's proud of herself for having found me.

"Thank you, Jessie," I say.

She peers into my face. "Are you alright? You don't look so great."

I don't want to tell her how bad I feel. I don't want to hear myself say it. So instead I tell her part of the truth, that my run hasn't gone well and that I'd like a ride back to our cabin. I ask her to go tell Chris to come pick me up.

"Sure," she says. Her concern shows in the quick and deliberate way she turns her body and her bike, the speed with which she rides away.

I watch her get smaller and smaller until she disappears around a curve. Absurdly, I feel abandoned. I walk across the road and sit on a large rock under an oak. My body feels as spent as if I've run a marathon. My head hurts, my eyes sting, and the quiet rash I've had for months on ankles and wrists is calling attention to itself from new locations, my chest and belly, between my shoulder blades. If I've actually been sick for months (have I been?) I've been doing a good job of not paying much attention to it. I pay attention to it now. I name all my symptoms, lay them out on the grass in the stark July sunlight: constant fatigue; the rash; the mind fog; the aching in my knees, wrists, and fingers; the intermittent pain in my chest. How on my worst days an overwhelming heaviness and sense of foreboding made me want to crawl under the bed with a pillow and blanket and hide. How on those days the edges of my vision would sometimes dim, as if someone had turned down the light in my mind as well as my eyes.

And what about my eyes? That's the newest symptom. A few days before we left for this vacation I woke up with eyes burning so badly I couldn't tolerate even dim indoor light. They stung and seeped all day long, oozing tears that ran down my cheeks, sliding out from under the sunglasses I wore that day while seeing my therapy clients. One of those clients was so disturbed by my appearance he didn't reschedule.

Sitting on that large rock, I see how the eyes and the rash are probably related to the fatigue, the muscle and joint achiness, the chest pain. I see the whole thing at once and it scares me.

I remember the next part as clearly as I remember the sensation of the air conditioning in the Viking, the apparition that resolved itself into my daughter coming toward me on the road, the way the sun burned the part in my hair at the top of my head.

As I sit there struggling to understand—and accept—what's happening to my body, I hear a car approaching, slowing down, stopping. I get up and wave. What I see is an old black English taxicab, like something out of a movie set in the 1930s. The car does a U-turn and brakes abruptly sending up plumes of dust and gravel. A noise like sleet.

The old black car is high-roofed and rounded and has a narrow rectangular rear window. The hood is long and low and sports a chrome hood ornament, something crouching, with wings. The car reminds me of a worn-down leather shoe with curved lines, a little scuffed. A man in a black cap sits behind the wheel, separated from the passenger area by a glass panel. My husband is sitting in the back. I pull on the heavy rear door and slide onto the cream-colored leather seat next to Chris. He opens his arms and in spite of the heat I lean against his chest, relieved.

"What's happening?" Chris asks.

"I don't know," I say into his shirt. "I'm so tired, I'm just so tired."

The old black taxi, a 1935 Studebaker, rolls smoothly into a gradually thickening fog. The sound of Chris's heart beating, loud and steady in my ear as I press my head against his chest, comforts me.

I don't even wonder why a British car out of a 1930s movie would have picked me up on a back road in Door County, Wisconsin, or where we're going in all this darkness and fog, where the darkness and fog came from on a blazing hot July morning. I don't give it another thought until years later, when I realize there was no way Chris would have come to get me in an old black taxi.

1

There is an Emergency

"I am invisible, and there is an
emergency rising from the mud"

—JOY HARJO, "Returning from the Enemy"

Family Therapy Conference, 1990

IT WAS EASY TO ignore in the beginning. The early symptoms were so
mild: tiredness, a rash, a subtle dimming of the senses. I was tired all the
time but after having been a single parent for nine years, working full-
time, I was accustomed to ignoring tiredness and other mild discomforts.
It would have been easier to admit I was sick if the disease had hit me full
force right away. Then, I imagine, I'd have known what I was up against
and would have asked for help sooner.

When the illness began I'd been remarried for two years. I was no
longer the only breadwinner but my salary was still as necessary as my
husband's. Between us we had two twelve-year-old daughters and an
eighteen-month-old son. When you have kids, you can't just fold when
you feel a little off. Same with being a psychotherapist: You show up for
clients even if you'd rather take a nap. And if you're in private practice,
as I was, you don't get paid if you don't work. You have to be really really
sick, for more than just a day or two, to stay home. And I wasn't sick like
that, not for the first six months.

In March, my friend Claire and I flew to Washington DC for a large family therapy conference held at the Omni Shoreham Hotel near Rock Creek Park. I woke that first morning to bright sunlight streaming in and inflaming the white walls of the seventh-floor room Claire and I shared above the hotel's circular drive. The room was quiet except for the muffled voices of arriving guests and the liveried valets who drove their cars away to a nearby guarded lot. Claire wasn't back yet from her run. She'd woken me up at six to ask if I wanted to go with her. I'd barely gotten the words "Not a chance" out before I plunged back into an irresistible sleep.

No amount of sleep, however, was going to refresh me. I'd been tired for months. In order to get up every morning, get dressed, let Nic's sitter in, get me and the girls off to school and work, I had to pretend I was my old, energetic self. This enactment had become so familiar that usually by the time I was in my car on my way to work I wasn't thinking about my tiredness. If I paused for more than a few minutes I found myself dragging. But mostly, I didn't pause. I met with my therapy clients, did paperwork, ate lunch, returned phone calls, untangled stalled insurance claims. I worked till nine twice a week; other days were over between three and five. Once I was home I'd read the mail, make dinner, spend time with the kids, and do the bedtime routines. All day long and into the night, functioning automatically, the way a dishwasher does when you push its buttons. Not questioning whether or not it feels like washing dishes, whether or not it might prefer to read a book. Every morning I pushed my own "on" button and went through my cycles.

Once in a while I had enough left over before bed to go to the back bedroom that served as my writing space and work on a poem or write a journal entry. But most of the time all I could manage was a quick review of the next day's appointments and a limp tooth brushing before sleep.

Now I lay in bed in that sunlit hotel room waiting to feel regenerated, waiting for whatever energy had been accruing inside me in one night's sleep to concentrate itself into a force that would propel me upright. The bed I lay in felt warm and comfortable and like where I wanted to spend the day. I wanted, just this once, to not press my "on" button. But I had a feeling that if I gave in that morning I'd stay in bed all weekend. I'd miss the whole conference. I'd miss the whole rest of my life. I told myself to get a grip and stop overreacting.

I took slow even breaths and calmed myself down. This was something I was good at, this ability to make my mind go blank, a kind of self-hypnosis that was almost as useful as keeping busy. Particularly useful for things like dental appointments, injections, waking up from a nightmare. I taught it to my clients.

I could have stayed there in self-induced numbness in that hotel room for a long time. But I thought Claire might turn up soon and she'd expect me to be ready to go to the conference activities with her. I had to get up, shower, and dress. I pushed the blankets off my legs and set my feet on the floor. My head was full of cotton balls. Cold sweat rose on my upper lip, chest, and back; my scalp prickled. I wanted to lie back down.

For months I'd been wanting to lie down whenever I ran across a surface large enough to accommodate the length of my body. When I walked through a department store I longed to get into the beds that advertised sheets and comforters. Even a bench at a bus stop triggered my urge to lie down. And any unpredictable event, like the babysitter canceling, my husband being distracted and distant over dinner, or more than one household appliance malfunctioning at the same time, made me weep with frustration.

Now I sat on the edge of my rumpled bed and listened to the waves of sounds rising from below. Car engines, doors opening and closing, threads of conversation snipped off as people entered the grand lobby with its crystal chandeliers, long sofas, and chubby armchairs. The broad corridors, the sunken lounge area, the lobby, and the rooms of the conference center were, I imagined, filling up with psychologists, counselors, and social workers.

My twelve-year-old daughter had told me once that she could recognize a therapist in any setting. The women, she said, all had this fashionably casual look. They wore soft clothes, skirts that draped or flowed, long shirts, scarves. Expensive blue jeans. Flat, comfortable shoes. Nothing tight or low cut. No hairspray. Just a bit of natural-looking makeup, lipstick maybe and mascara. Or, like her mother, no make-up at all. The men, she claimed, did a male version of the same thing. She wasn't surprised when I told her that one of my male colleagues wore elastic-waist pants that he bought in the women's section of a discount department store. What she didn't say was how profoundly un-sexy she thought we all were. I knew that was how we looked to her. We mental health people were nice enough, some of us overly so, but like butter knives we had no sharp points and we did not glint.

Jessie would have been amused, I thought now, at the atmosphere of good-humored helpfulness in the elevator on the way up to our room last night. Twelve of us squashed into one tiny elevator all offering to assist.

Can I push a number for you? Do you have enough room back there? I do, thank you. Ooooops, my floor, excuse me. See you tomorrow? A woman in the corner taking up less space than was humanly possible, holding a suitcase so close it seemed about to melt right into her chest. *Excuse me; did I bump you? No, no, don't worry. It's fine. Thank you.* A man stepping all the way out of the elevator to allow a woman to get out on her floor, placing a gentle restraining hand along the edge of the open elevator door which had shown no sign that it was about to close on anyone. I half-expected someone to say, "Nice job, Ray. You've made a lot of progress!"

So, okay, it was true. I wore comfortable clothes and flat shoes and a naked face too. I tried to be non-threatening. Unconditionally positive.

This was the second time I'd come to this conference. Four years earlier Claire had talked me into leaving my then eight-year-old daughter, Timmy our Golden Retriever, and my clients, to come with her, seducing me with talk of fine museums and Ethiopian food, teasing me about my propensity for overworking and not accepting my excuses.

That was before Nic was born. Before I married Chris. One of the things I remembered about that other time was how strong and healthy I felt then. And how in love. I'd called Chris every night when I was away. I'd only known him a few months. And I was besotted with him as he was with me. So, of course, I felt beautiful and fascinating and amusing. Chock full of stamina and rosy vitality. I ran three or four miles every morning back then.

This morning I couldn't have run if lions were chasing me.

Sitting on the edge of the hotel bed, pulling myself together, I tried to remember what workshops I'd signed up for. My brain engaged slowly, like a car starting up on a sub-zero morning. I was pretty sure I'd chosen an all-day workshop, something about using psychodrama for consultation. It had appealed to me when I was registering for the conference. Now nothing appealed to me except lying back down.

I stood up, stretched, and was once again aware of the post-pregnancy weight that wrapped around my middle like a cummerbund. I should have run with Claire, I scolded myself as I padded to the bathroom. On my way there I noticed Claire's discarded running clothes huddled on top of her Saucony shoes. She must have come back, taken her shower, and gone back out to hear the keynote speaker. I'd slept right through that.

My feet were soundless on the thick, off-white carpet and then the cool tiled bathroom floor. I stood in the shower and let the warm water stream down my face, hoping it would revive me.

A tap on the door; Claire let herself into the bathroom. The shower curtain billowed in. I shivered.

"So, you finally got up?"

"Sort of," I answered.

"I can't believe you slept so late. What a slug! Are you coming to your workshop? They start in about ten minutes."

"I guess so."

"Hurry up, then."

The bathroom door clicked shut; the shower curtain blew in at me again. I dried off; pulled on a pair of jeans and a t-shirt. Claire was sitting cross-legged on one of the two queen-size beds looking at something in her registration packet. She wore tight Calvin Klein jeans, an expensive V-neck t-shirt, and orchid Birkenstock sandals. Her hair, brown, highlighted with blond streaks, was short, curly, expensively cut.

Claire, contrary to what Jessie thought about therapists, was the kind of woman men turn to look at. The kind of woman they eyed across a room, sent a drink over to, walked over and sat down to talk with. She and I'd been friends for four years and now we worked together in a private psychotherapy group with eight other therapists.

"How was Paul Ehrlich?" I asked her. Mr. Ehrlich had been the keynote speaker.

"Inspiring," she said. "Made me want to minimize my consumption of products and become a better recycler. So what's the matter with you? You look terrible. Are you depressed or what? I thought you were going to go running with me."

Her question brought tears to my eyes. I sat down on the bed and got very busy sliding my feet into my sandals, adjusting the straps. I fastened the buckle on the right shoe, then, the left, patted the top of my foot a few times, and was finally able to look up at Claire dry-eyed.

"I don't know. Just tired lately. Did you know that this is the first morning I've slept late since Nic was born?"

"I can never sleep past six."

"That's because you're a mutant."

"Are you worried about your mother?"

"Maybe," I answered. But in fact, I realized now, I had been so preoccupied with my own discomfort that I'd forgotten about my mother's cancer. Claire knew that my mother had just been diagnosed with non-Hodgkin's lymphoma. It was early stage and not the most aggressive form, and since my mother was over sixty-five (not young), she was given the choice of either watch-and-wait or do one round of chemotherapy. She was leaning toward the chemo, even though she was worried it would make her lose her hair.

I had mixed feelings about this news. I knew I should feel sad for my mother or at least a little worried but I was inured to hearing about my mother's many illnesses. She'd been sick off and on for most of my life, with asthma, agoraphobia, and frequent spells of depression. She was a heavy drinker until she was in her early fifties and finally got sober for good, with the help of AA and multiple stays in alcohol rehab facilities. About fifteen years ago she was given a tentative diagnosis of lupus but none of her blood work had confirmed it. Still, the doctors suspected some kind of autoimmune illness. I suspected my mother scared herself unnecessarily over small symptoms. Made a big deal out of nothing.

When I was a child I worried a lot about my miserable mother. I did my best to be as perfect in school and at home as a kid can manage to be, in order not to burden my poor mom. But, of course, no matter how good I was my mother remained tired and depressed.

When I left home for college I found it hard to let go of my worry about her, until finally, with the help of a lot of therapy, I turned away. I cut her off for a few years. I learned that it wasn't—never had been—my job to save her.

She called me once, when I was in my thirties, and told me she thought my dad was putting arsenic into her food with an eyedropper, such small amounts she couldn't taste it. She told me she'd read about someone doing that in an Agatha Christie mystery. Luckily, by then I was in the habit of believing she was a hypochondriac so I could say, "No, Mom. I don't think so," and then let the whole thing go.

My only worry now, about my mother's cancer diagnosis, was that I'd have to somehow return to my childhood job of taking care of her. I didn't have the energy, the funds, or the inclination to step back into the impossible job of making my mommy better.

I began to rummage around the room, locating my notebook, a pen, my conference folder with its schedules and room location lists.

Claire went into the bathroom, leaving the door open, talking loud enough for me to hear her around the corner. "Are you sure it's true? Your mother's not just sick because you're out of town? This is interesting timing." She gave me a knowing look as she walked out of the bathroom, zipped her jeans, and stepped into her abandoned Birkenstocks.

"Oh, stop. Chris got the information from my father, who got it from the doctor. It's real."

Claire picked up her woven hemp bag from the bed. She put one hand on the doorknob and paused, watching me. In the space of our last few exchanges, I'd pulled the bedspread up over the untucked sheets and blankets on my bed, put last night's clothes in a drawer and tossed the clothes I'd slept in onto the closet floor. I picked up my conference folder. I stared at it, thinking about what else I might need to take with me. Kleenex, yes. And maybe a little money.

"Sorry. I'm a little scattered this morning."

When I look back at this now this now, I realize I should have sat down right then and there and told Claire the truth, cried if I had to, skipped the conference, and spent the day in bed. Yes, I was worried, but not about my mother's lymphoma. I was worried about the difference between how I'd been the last time I was in DC four years ago—running every day, full of excitement and energy—and this time. I couldn't decide if there was something going on that warranted worry or not. Was I over-focusing on minor symptoms the way my mother had always done? Or should I call a doctor as soon as I got back home?

"You're going to have to help them, aren't you?" Claire was leaning against the doorjamb now, her conference folder in one arm, her bag looped over her shoulder.

"My parents? Yeah, I guess so. They only bought life insurance two years ago because my brother and I insisted on it. They're like little kids about money."

"I wasn't talking about money. I know you can't help them with money; you don't have any. I meant they're going to need you to be with them, drive your mom to the hospital, other inconvenient things like that."

"I was afraid this would happen someday." I was standing still beside the bed, holding a twenty-dollar bill in my hand, as if I were waiting for Claire instead of the other way around.

"You knew *what* would happen?"

"My mother getting sick for real, me having to take care of her like I thought I had to when I was a kid."

Claire gave me a long look, shook her head, and sighed. "How about we talk about that later? We need to get downstairs now. Right now!"

"Sorry," I said. I walked through the door and down the hall behind my friend, my steps too intentional, driven by decision rather than instinct. The way people walk when they're drunk. The back of my neck was cold and wet; sweat trickled between my shoulder blades and between my breasts, gathered at my hairline.

Claire was heading for the stairwell, beside the elevator. Claire didn't cope well with waiting for elevators and with only two elevators and literally several thousand therapists in this hotel, the wait would be long. Besides, we were athletic women in our early forties who could easily walk the six flights down to the conference rooms. This morning, however, my legs trembled at the thought of all those steps. Worse still would have been to wimp out and wait for the elevator. I couldn't imagine suggesting it. Claire paused to give me time to catch up to her. She looked at me a little quizzically for a fraction of a second, or maybe I imagined it. At any rate, she continued to talk to me as if I were fine.

"You thought you'd escaped, didn't you?" she said in a teasing voice.

It took me a breath or two to realize what it was she thought I'd escaped from. The first thought that popped into my head was "No, I haven't escaped at all. I'm sick." But I didn't say that. I wasn't ready to say that.

What Claire was referring to, of course, was the conversation we'd been having as we left our room.

"I did escape from my mother. Mostly. I *so* don't want to go back there."

"You always have options," said my friend in her best chipper therapist voice.

"Oh, shut up," I told her.

2

Body, My Good Bright Dog

"Body my house
my horse my hound
what will I do
when you are fallen"

—MAY SWENSON, "Question"

July 9, 1990

SINCE THE DAY OF my failed run, I hadn't gotten any worse. I was still tired but the time off and the chance to sleep later in the mornings had made me feel a tiny bit better. My rash continued to come and go with the regularity of a bird in a cuckoo clock, but a combination of Benadryl and calamine lotion took an edge off the itchiness. I blamed my fatigue on the ceaselessly hot weather plus having spent that vacation in Door County with all three kids twenty-four hours a day for an entire week.

I had nine therapy appointments scheduled on July 9, the usual for a Monday, and since my fever was gone and Nic's favorite babysitter, my friend Barbara, was available, I couldn't see any reason not to go to work. By this time, I'd had considerable experience with working while achy and tired. I knew I could do it.

As I gathered papers, my purse, a sweater to buffer the office air conditioning, Barbara sat on the floor with Nic on her lap, trying to persuade
him that food was his friend.

Barbara, an oncology nurse, and I were the same age, forty-two. She
and her younger sister, Debbie, were my downstairs tenants in the duplex
I'd purchased to live in when Jessie was five. I was a single mom back
then, raising Jessie on too little money and too little time. Barb and Debbie, both single and childless, were delighted to watch Jessie whenever I
needed them. I had to persuade them to let me pay them even a minimal
babysitting fee; they'd have spent time with Jessie—and later with Nic—
for nothing. Barbara had nursed Jessie through a bad case of chickenpox
when I had to be at work. She'd spoiled Jessie with a daily Care Bear,
books, games, and mostly her love. When Nic was born she'd attended his
birth and became his main nanny for his first year of life.

She told him now that she'd read one page of his book for each
spoonful of Gerber's Apple Brown Betty he'd eat. He reached for the
book; Barb moved it out of his reach. "No, no, Nicko," she scolded. "First
a spoonful, then the book." Nic stuck out his lower lip and both of his
hands and demanded "Book!"

"Good luck," I whispered as I walked out the door.

As I drove to the clinic where I worked, I mulled over the exchange
Chris and I'd shared as we'd gotten dressed. He'd told me I should stay
home, that I was sick. I told him he should let me be the judge. He returned fire with "I don't trust you to judge. You both under- and overreact to sickness, never any moderation." I was offended and told him so.
There wasn't time for me to launch into the feminist lecture I wanted to
deliver, about how men have for centuries controlled women by claim-
ing to know what was best for them. In those days I rarely missed an
opportunity to stand up for womankind. Never mind that my husband
was not, had never been, that sort of a man. And I was annoyed because
some small part of me thought he might be right: maybe I should be
staying home in spite of the considerable bite that would take out of our
monthly income. Private practice means relying on hourly fees, paid either by insurance companies or the clients themselves. No sessions, no
payments. That annoyed me, too, that even if I'd wanted to stay home in
bed, I couldn't afford to.

So I did what married people have done for centuries: I aimed my
annoyance at my spouse. As he walked out the back door, I shouted after

him, "I don't get to stay home! I don't get sick time like you do!" He kept walking, mumbling something in a cranky tone.

I don't, of course, remember every detail about every client I saw that week, but I do remember a surprising amount. Because that week turned out to be more than a little unusual. Here's what I remember about Monday.

First session, 8:00 a.m.: A young woman—let's call her Ann—with an eating disorder. She was tall, so thin she was almost two-dimensional. Her long brown hair hung limp and tired around her pale cheeks and forehead. Enormous eyes in a bony face, narrow wrists barely supporting long-fingered, grown-up hands. We sat across from each other in soft armchairs as Ann described what she'd eaten since she last saw me, ten bagels and many ounces of ice water over ten days. I tried to hide my shock but she noticed and said, "What? At least I ate!"

All of this alerted me that Ann's illness had gained more ground. The week before she'd been having crackers and a bowl of soup for lunch in addition to the bagel. Last week she'd been scared about what she was doing; this week she was not. I'd seen this happen so many times. The semi-starvation had affected her thinking; I was going to have to convince her to be hospitalized. Even when I was feeling like myself, I didn't enjoy what I knew I was going to need to do next—cajole, persuade, manipulate—until she agreed to a voluntary admission. I'd probably have to involve her family before she'd give in.

My hip joints were hurting. I hoped Ann was too affected by her own physical condition to notice mine. I longed for the hour to be done. I'd been cold since I'd woken up that morning. I wrapped my arms around my chest and began to tell my client that her life was in danger, that she must go to the hospital. Her eyes widened and I watched a stubborn resistance take up residence behind them.

At eleven, I spent an hour with twenty-eight-year-old Vicki who was newly discharged from an inpatient treatment center for eating disorders where she'd relearned how to eat. Now she was buzzing with energy and a clarity of mind that she'd forgotten could be hers. She confessed that her new self was a little scary to her, that it was unfamiliar, "but," and here her face broke into a wide grin, "I wouldn't go back to the anorexia if you paid me."

"This one," I said to myself as I listened to her describe an evening she'd spent at a jazz bar with her friends, "this one is going to be fine."

I wasn't so sure about me being fine, though. Vicki's robust good health made my own lack of it stand out in comparison. Usually, on a day when I saw so many clients, I would feel more energetic, more engaged, as the day went on. Not this day. By lunchtime, I was dreading the three-flight walk down from my office to the first-floor kitchen where a peanut butter and jelly sandwich waited for me.

I decided (not easily) that I'd better skip my lunchtime run.

I started to shiver halfway through eating that sandwich, had to put it down, and clench my jaw to keep my teeth from clacking against each other. The chills didn't last too long, maybe ten minutes, and when they stopped, I felt hot. This unnerved me; the day before, I'd woken up without a fever, had chills at lunchtime and a fever of 102 by nightfall. I thought about the next half of my day, six clients. Told myself (again) that I could do it. I'd be done at seven and would go straight to bed when I got home.

I felt okay during my one o'clock session but by two, I was fading. I struggled through the three o'clock, but before I went into the therapy room with my four o'clock, I called five and six and rescheduled them.

I would like to report that I did that out of concern for myself, out of common sense. But no, not really. The increasing fever made it hard for me to think; I was afraid I might miss something important, do someone harm. I didn't want to hurt my clients. And I didn't want to be sued.

I drove home, feeling guilty about the people I'd rescheduled. I knew how much my clients usually looked forward to their sessions.

I took my temperature as soon as I got home. It was 103. And the red rash—which now was everywhere except my neck and face—itched like mad.

I curled up on the couch with a blanket and pillow. Nic, who, according to Barbara, had eaten like a small horse most of the day, was rosy with health and energy. He snuggled with me and together we watched a ridiculous video called *We Sing Silly Songs*. This was Nic's favorite, starring a man in a bear costume, wearing a pink tutu, dancing with a bunch of annoying smiley children in stiff party clothes. Nic lay against my side, giggling, singing toddler approximations of snippets of the grating songs until he went silent, asleep.

I felt better, again, the following morning. I went to work. By noon, I was shivering. My fever was 103 again by the time I got home at four. When I drove Jessie to a friend's house for an after-school study date, I had to concentrate hard in order to drive on the right side of the road and stop at the stop signs. I sent Chris to pick her up at six while I made grilled cheese sandwiches and heated up canned tomato soup for dinner.

My stepdaughter Becky, whose mother had dropped her off while I was cooking, watched the abominable *Silly Songs* video with Nic while I did the dishes. I went to bed before anyone else did. Chris read Nic his bedtime story. The long night's sleep did not revive me.

On Thursday morning I reluctantly cancelled the rest of my appointments for the week. I apologized and assured everyone that I would be fine by Monday. I scheduled thirty sessions for the following week, a hefty load for a private practice therapist.

Thursday afternoon, I took my high fever and strange rash to a Walk-In Clinic where a doctor assured me that my fever was caused by a sinus infection, in spite of the fact that I had no upper respiratory symptoms at all. He had no idea why I had a rash. He glanced at it, said, "Hmmf. I don't recognize that." He gave me a prescription for amoxicillin. To clear up my mythical sinus infection.

By Thursday night my fever hit 104. I was worried but I told myself that fevers are useful: their heat kills germs. And then they break and go away. Tomorrow, the fever would either be much lower or gone entirely. By Monday I'd be back at work.

And now, when I was obviously getting sicker and sicker every day, my fevers soaring into the stratosphere and my muscles weaker than I could ever remember them being, I did my best to ignore it all, to pretend it wasn't happening, as if by pressing on regardless I could make myself impervious, indestructible. Safe.

I was so not safe.

On Friday evening, when my fever hit 104 again, Chris announced that he was going to take me to the hospital.

"Why?" I asked. Chris gave me an "I don't think I need to answer that" kind of look. He folded his arms across his chest, planted his feet wider apart, and stared at me, waiting for me to get out of the bed I'd retreated to after dinner. I was snuggled up with Timmy, the dog. My whole body hurt and the fever was making it hard for me to think. I couldn't imagine getting up and walking to the car. It felt dangerous, it felt wrong.

"Let's wait and see how I am in the morning." I told Chris as I rubbed Timmy's ear between my thumb and forefinger.

"Uh uh," Chris said. He tossed a pair of shorts and a t-shirt on the bed. "I'm worried about you. If the people at the ER think you don't need to be at the hospital, they'll tell us so, and I'll bring you right home. Please."

"You promise you'll bring me home?"

"Promise."

I got out of bed and got dressed. Cooperating not because I thought he was right but more because it felt good to have someone else take over.

My feet carried me, half unwilling, through the hospital parking lot, from soft early evening into the abrupt glare of fluorescence. The lights in the ER were so bright I felt threatened by them, as if they could expose me, strip away the layers I'd been piling on, hiding beneath. What truth was I protecting? That I was, in fact, dangerously ill? Or that I was over-reacting? Wasting the doctors' precious time. Being a baby.

I stood a few steps behind Chris, like a child, as he handed over our insurance information. Telling myself that pretty soon someone would take my temperature, say something like "Oh my," and tell me to go home, take Tylenol, and rest until I felt better.

The ER wasn't busy, so as soon as my information had been entered into the computer, a nurse led me to the triage room, a windowless square space that looked like a regular patient room but without the bed. It had call-light cords, a panic button, lots of electrical outlets. And a large, cluttered desk. I remember the light being dim, but that doesn't make sense. It wouldn't have been dim. Maybe my mind has added dimness to the scene to reflect the dread I was feeling. Or the confusion.

The whole time I was in this ER I felt an odd sense of fracture, a feeling of having entered into something that was not me, not my life. Something that didn't belong in my story. I was not a sick person. And certainly not someone who would go to an ER for a simple fever.

I sat in a hard plastic chair in the triage room wishing I was back in my own bed with my dog. The nurse asked me about my symptoms. Each time I answered, Chris chimed in with a correction. "No. Not just three days. She's had a fever most of the time all week. She hasn't felt well for months."

I thought he was exaggerating. But I didn't say so.

I wondered why no one was letting me lie down.

"Can I go somewhere and lie down while you guys chat?" I finally said, thinking I was being funny. Another layer to hide beneath.

"Do you feel that bad?" the nurse took me seriously. He promised I could lie down soon.

Did I feel that bad, really? Yes, in hindsight, yes. The pain in my knees, elbows and hands made me want to sit very still, even though I'd gotten fairly good at ignoring it.

Because of the fever—and also the so-far-unidentified processes raging in my whole system—I felt weaker sitting in that hard chair that night than I can remember ever feeling before or since. But I wasn't about to put all that into words at this juncture. I was still telling myself that if I could just go home and rest, I'd be fine. It was taking longer than usual for me to be fine but I would be.

As I listened to Chris and the nurse, it was clear that the two of them thought the person they were discussing should be admitted to the hospital immediately. I had trouble believing that person was me.

I fought down the instinct to run to my car. Never mind that I couldn't have run more than six paces.

The nurse led me to an exam room that held two narrow beds, both empty. I took my shoes off and lay down on the nearest bed. The shivering was beginning again. Chris went to find blankets. This I took to be more proof that I shouldn't have left my bed. As if lying still would have made it impossible for the fever to find me. (This fever would prove to be expert at finding me, around the same time every day, for quite a while but I didn't know that yet.)

By the time the doctor arrived, I was huddled under three blankets, trying hard to hold still against the chills. It wasn't working. The shivering was even more violent than it had been at home, as if my body was showing off for the doctor. It was shaking so hard the bed creaked under me, its wheeled legs jiggling back and forth against the shiny floor. I hoped the doctor wouldn't notice.

Why, at this point, did I hope the doctor wouldn't notice? Why not give her every scrap of information she needed to help me? I was still trying to put a brave face on. *Things here are not as bad as they might appear.* If only I could muster enough strength to look closer to normal, then I could run away. Okay, maybe not run. Chris and this doctor would have to help me to the car.

I didn't like that people around me (Chris, the nurse, possibly this doctor) were acting as if the fear I'd been resisting for months was in fact reasonable. As useless as the Walk-in Clinic had been, no one there had said, "Oh my God, you really *are* in bad shape." What would I have done with that? Gone to the hospital sooner, maybe. Gone to the hospital and cut myself off from everything that made me feel useful and real. Which was exactly what I was afraid was about to happen to me now.

The doctor, a tall young woman with a kind face and brown hair pulled back in a low ponytail, asked me some of the same questions the nurse had asked. I gave her Chris's answers. She took my temperature. It was 104.5.

She held my hand and looked into my eyes. "You must feel just terrible," she said.

A whole bundle of my layers unwrapped themselves then and fell away. The lump in my throat kept me from speaking. I nodded, instead. For the first time since we'd gotten there, I was almost glad I came. The doctor asked intelligent questions about the life of the rash and discovered that the joints of my knees, elbows, fingers, and hips were swollen. She told me that because I'd had such a high fever for so many days she wanted to admit me. "To run more tests," she said.

"I'll send someone in to handle the admission process," the doctor said. The curtains around my bed billowed out in the breeze of her going.

"I can't stay here," I told Chris. The pitch of my voice rose as I ticked off my reasons: the income loss. Nic would miss me. So would the girls. We'd been planning to take them all to a water park the next day. They'd be disappointed. I'd be disappointed. The house was a mess. I hadn't brought anything with me, no toothbrush or clean underwear. Or a book.

What I didn't say out loud was that agreeing to stay in the hospital felt to me like the first step towards death. Like taking your clothes off and lying down in the snow when you're lost in a snowstorm and have hypothermia. The most wrong action you can take.

Chris sat down on my bed and wrapped an arm around me. "How about staying just tonight and tomorrow?" He asked, sweetly. The way I'd addressed Ann, my resistant anorexic client, earlier in the week. It occurred to me then that I might be being an idiot. That it was possible going home and going to bed with Timmy *wasn't* the best thing for me.

How in the world had this happened to me?

"Well, Jude? Will you stay?" Chris asked. His voice so soft, so calm. All I wanted to do was lean on him and go to sleep

"I'll stay," I said, making the decision as I spoke. "But only for tonight and tomorrow."

Once I gave in it didn't feel at all like a step towards death but rather a flicker of hope. A hope, perhaps, as misinformed as my mother's belief after her stroke two years from now that the random twitching of her left hand was a sign of recovery. Wrong, but bracing, nonetheless.

As soon as I agreed to stay, I imagined myself sliding into a sparkling white hospital bed, all comfy and clean and warm, and my body immediately setting itself to rights. Like when you bend just the right way and your spine pops and crackles and you go, "Ahhhhh."

I would spend the entire next week in that hard hospital bed. There would not be one moment that was an "Ahhhhhh."

3

I Feel Very Sick. I Feel Awful.

"I feel very sick. I feel awful. There's no reason to be afraid, but I am. Sometimes I'm not here, and I don't like that. Because then I'm far away and all alone."

—PAUL BOWLES, *Sheltering Sky*

July 13-14, 1990

AFTER CHRIS WENT HOME that night, I found myself even more aware of how bad I was feeling. My head was hot with fever and I was so tired I could barely change my position on the hard narrow mattress that made a crackling noise every time I moved.

At first, this new bed felt like a very sudden, very wrong place to be, but of course it hadn't been all that sudden and it definitely wasn't wrong. I grudgingly accepted that Chris was wise to bring me here; the wrong thing would have been to spend one more night in my cozy bed at home with Chris asleep on one side of me and Timmy on the other, with my fever climbing higher with each passing hour. It was right to be here in the hospital alone in this narrow bed, in this lonely room.

In truth, for months, I hadn't felt like I belonged anywhere, not even inside myself. Every morning this past week before Chris made me come to the hospital, I'd woken up with a uniquely heavy tiredness and a weird change in my vision—as if I were seeing through dark lenses. I'd felt like I was in a dream, an awake dream.

There's a diagnostic term for that feeling: *Depersonalization,* a weird sense of wrongness. I'd felt it as far back as the Family Therapy Conference. The *DSM* (*Diagnostic and Statistical Manual,* the bible of all mental health practitioners) describes depersonalization as "tiredness, a fuzzy-headed, fogged-in feeling."[1] Wikipedia says that depersonalization is: "an 'alteration' in the perception or experience of the self so that one feels 'detached' from, and as if one is an 'outside' observer of, one's mental processes or body . . ."[2] The world has become less real, vague, dreamlike, or lacking in significance.

What does one do about feeling detached and depersonalized? I know what I did: Whenever I could, I turned away from what I was feeling, tried to ignore it. I'd discovered that talking about anything other than myself helped me ignore how strange I was feeling, helped me feel less afraid. Talking to my clients about their discomforts, for example, was so much better than thinking about my own. Every time I was alone and quiet though, my mind would slide into what my body, my intuition, was telling me and I'd be swamped with a sense of unidentifiable danger, a feeling of dread.

They warn you about the *dread* feeling in public education pamphlets about heart attack and stroke. You should go to the hospital if you have chest pain or a headache, accompanied by a feeling of dread. Now that I was in the hospital I found that the feeling of dread had come right along with me, gaining strength from the pastel walls, the smell of rubbing alcohol, and the voices that called through the PA system.

As I lay there waiting for someone to come check my vital signs (again), I remembered something my mother said to me when I was twenty-one. By then I'd been living alone (without my mother's approval) in an apartment for two years. My mother called me one day to tell me she'd had a dream about me. She'd thought about whether or not she should tell me and decided she'd be a bad mother if she didn't. "I dreamed," she told me, "—it was so real this dream—that you were older, in your thirties, and you came down with this terrible, chronic disease. I was so worried about you." A catch in her throat. At the time, I had two reactions: one was annoyance. This felt like my mother clinging to me; it

1. Endicott, et al., "Anxiety and Dissociative Disorders," 259.

2. "Depersonalization," *Wikipedia, the Free Encyclopedia,* http://en.wikipedia.org/wiki/Depersonalization.

felt like intrusion. This kind of pessimism and over-focus on illness was typical of her and I hated it. I'd worked hard to curb that same tendency in myself. But my other reaction was stronger: On some deep level I'd had an inkling that my mother's dream might well be an accurate prediction. I was in my forties now instead of my thirties, but otherwise it looked like my mother's dream had come true.

Remembering this now as I lay in my hospital bed, I felt a thrill of recognition and a sense of deep sadness.

Could I have done something to prevent this happening? I had this colleague—let's call him, Jim—who'd recently explained to me that he'd unconsciously invited a case of bronchitis because he'd needed to learn a lesson about patience. Bronchitis, according to Jim, was actually a gift from the Universe. My take, as I'd explained to Jim, was that he was finding meaning in a random event. "That's what we humans do," I maintained. "We ascribe meaning to random events to help us adapt in response to our experiences."

The bestselling book that year, *The Secret,* promoted beliefs similar to Jim's: for example, if you walk around afraid that you'll lose your job or fall off the roof, the Universe (whatever that is) hears that as a request for exactly that learning experience and makes it happen to you. As if just by being afraid you'd posted an ad: *Wanted: one painful lesson, as soon as possible.* On the other hand if you focused on what you did want and were unambivalent in your desire, it would come to you. And if it didn't, it was because you'd had mixed feelings about your desire.

The faulty logic of that kind of thinking irritated the hell out of me. I didn't like Jim's implication that everyone who gets sick asked for it in some way or needs it for some reason. Classic case of blaming the victim. It seemed such a heartless and misguided—even dangerous—perspective. As irritated as I felt when Jim talked like this, I also felt a little sorry for him. How frightened he must be, I thought, to have to try so hard to control the uncontrollable. "Jim," I wanted to say to him, "Jim, sometimes shit just happens!"

I didn't notice right then, lying in the hospital, that I was thinking sort of like Jim, wondering what I'd done to make this bad thing happen to me. I wasn't aware of how desperately I needed to find a rationale. It wasn't an intellectual exercise, this search for a reason, nor was it just my manic tendencies, my wish to understand everything and to always keep moving forward; it was an existential imperative. I mean, I couldn't stand the not knowing.

This first week in the hospital—the first of what would turn out to be several weeks—I was too sick to think about any of these things for very long. Every morning my fevers started near 100, never lower, then rose and fell, off and on, all day and into the night. They spiked up to 103 or higher (that's what the medical people called it: *spike)* and then rolled downward a few degrees before spiking again.

I'd feel very cold when my temperature would begin to rise. My teeth would chatter and my body would shake. When I could remember to ask, the nurses would bring heated blankets and pile them on top of me. Their warmth was comforting but couldn't touch the iciness at my core. When the fever would get as high as it was going to get, it would settle in for a while. The chills would stop, replaced by waves of heat. My heart would race and my muscles would tense in a way I couldn't voluntarily release, as if my body was getting ready to respond to some external threat. There was no way to rest when the fever was at its highest. After a while—a few hours, usually—I'd begin to sweat copiously and the fever would go down a few degrees, enough to leave me the clarity of mind to be amazed at what I had just experienced. The respites were brief, half an hour to an hour, barely enough time to rest before the next siege. Each time my fever rose I was supposed to call the nurse's station so that someone could come draw my blood. I averaged eight blood draws every twenty-four hours.

Even more annoying than all the needle pricks was the persistent rash which felt like an attack of tiny biting ants. Calamine, Benadryl— both of which had eased some of the itching weeks earlier—no longer had any effect. Nor did the stronger antihistamines prescribed in the hospital. The rash and the fevers together made it impossible for me to relax, much less fall asleep.

Every day, every night, all week long, the same cycles, the same intolerable discomfort.

My fever reached 105 my second night in the hospital. I thought that meant I was going to die. The nurse pulled the thermometer out of my mouth, told me the number, and then left the room, as if it were no big deal. It seemed like a big deal to me. Shouldn't someone be doing something about 105? I considered phoning the doctor who'd admitted me (Dr. Chan) and filling him in. But it was nearing midnight, I hadn't even met the man yet, and I had neither a phone book nor a business card with his number on it. There was a squadron of nurses at the end of the hallway, I told myself, why not just get out of bed and go tell them to help me. A brave thought, an ambitious thought. But I wasn't sure I could make it that far.

All right then. I was going to have to weather 105 on my own.

As my face and the top of my head burned with fever, my mind wandered half-dreaming into memories of other times of intense heat: a heat stroke at day camp when I was six; the smell of scorched cotton when my mother set a too-hot iron down on the collar of one of my father's white shirts; a summer day when I was sixteen and new to southern California and spent a full day at Newport Beach. I got so burned I couldn't sit in a chair, couldn't go to school for two days. The many mornings when I was a toddler and woke with fevers and infected eyes, my lids glued shut with crusty discharge. My father coming with a cool washcloth to wipe my eyes and cool my head.

How wonderful it would be if my father and his washcloth could come now and wipe my fevers away.

As I lay in bed with my 105 degrees, I thought about something my father told me when I was ten and had Asian flu, with a fever nearly as high. "Fevers," he'd said, "can make you feel like you're going to die—but you won't."

I remembered that long-ago illness as a week-long blur of fever and restless sleep. When finally I began to feel better, I was bored. I wasn't allowed to go back to school or even to go outside and play until I had a few more fever-free days; people were dying from this flu, my parents told me, so we needed to be careful.

One day my father told he had a surprise for me. "Go watch out our front window," he said.

He posed in front of the window like a prizefighter, bunching up his nonexistent muscles, showing off his imaginary strength. Then he kneeled down, gathered a fistful of wadded-up snow and rolled it all over the yard until it was as tall as my waist. Then he did the same thing again. And again. He stacked the three snowballs one on top of the other. He turned to smile and wave at me, gesturing at his creation as if he were a magician who had conjured it out of nowhere. I shrugged and mumbled the word thanks into the window glass.

My father furrowed his brow. Clearly he'd expected a better response. He stood with his chin in his hand, staring at his creation, thinking. Then he snapped his fingers and pointed upwards (indicating the light bulb of an idea).

He ran into the house, not bothering to take off his dripping galoshes. "Wait'll you see this!" he shouted as he dashed outside again, carrying some things in his arms. He worked for ten minutes, his body blocking my view of the results. Then he stepped aside, gesturing once again: Ta-da!

I laughed and clapped. My father had built me a snow lady. She had molded white curls on either side of her face, an old black felt hat with a torn veil tipping over her forehead, red Kool-Aid lips, charcoal briquette eyes, and, shockingly, breasts under her sculpted white blouse. He'd wound a red scarf around her neck. There was a puffy little bird made of snow sitting on her shoulder.

Remembering the snow maiden (my father's term for his creation), I picked up the phone receiver, stuck my finger in the round-numbered dial of the heavy phone and dialed my parents' number, hoping it would be my dad who'd pick up. It was. He sounded pleased that I'd called.

"How's my favorite daughter?" he asked. (I was and am his *only* daughter.)

"No better, I'm afraid."

"Those doctors figure anything out yet?"

"I wish."

"Well, you tell 'em if they don't hurry it up your old man is going to have a word with them."

"They'll be so scared."

"You bet."

"How's Mom doing?" My mother had been diagnosed with lymphoma when I was in DC at that family therapy conference. She'd had radiation treatment and three infusions of chemo.

My dad's voice stayed cheerful. "She's doing pretty well, I'd say. Considering."

"The chemo's not making her too sick?"

"Not yet. They say it takes some time before that happens. She has another treatment tomorrow afternoon. I might stop in and visit you when I bring her. She doesn't much like me hanging around while they drip that stuff into her."

"It'd be great to see you."

"Wish I could make this all go away for you."

"You and me both. Hey, Dad? Do you remember that fever I had with the Asian flu when I was ten?"

"I do remember it. That was a real bad flu, that one."

"And you built me a snow maiden."

"I did. That's right." He chuckled.

"Thank you. That made me feel so much better." I choked up a little and hoped he wouldn't notice.

"Hey, nothin' to it back then. Not so simple now. For one thing, no snow."

I hung up thinking, *yeah, not so simple now.* I sank down into my overly solid pillow and stared back up at the ceiling, wishing I could float up there, thin myself against the white pocked tiles, go numb, disappear. The way I'd learned to do when I was a kid and afraid or in some way miserable. I'd stare at an empty wall, hold my breath, pretend to exist only in the blank space between my breaths, making myself go half-dead (as I called it in my head) so that nothing bad could reach me. In this self-induced trance state I could function, sort of, but couldn't feel anything. I got so good at this dissociation technique that in my twenties it started happening without my consciously summoning it. Something overwhelming would happen and I'd be full of emotion and then, click, no feeling at all. I'd had to learn to recognize the triggers and consciously stop myself from going numb.

It had been a lot of years since then. I decided to find out if I could still do it. I held my breath and focused on the spaces in between. I did this for maybe three minutes. But instead of going numb I became more aware of my discomfort as a surge of heat rose up like wildfire from my chest and swept outward to scorch the palms of my hands and the bottoms of my feet. There was no escaping this.

I managed to drift off into a brief light sleep. I dreamed I was alone walking down a dark road. Up ahead, the road seemed to be glowing with a hot red light. In fact, I saw with horror, it wasn't just light; the road was filling with fire and molten lava. The flames were swirling toward me, filling the street from curb to curb. Terrified, I turned and ran toward what looked like a person in the distance. He was beckoning me to come to him. As I got closer, the heat of the fire at my heels, I saw he wasn't a man at all, but a small fiery demon, with horns and a forked tale. Just as I felt the first wave of heat that preceded the flames, I woke up. The fire was inside me then; my whole body was hot.

❧

I don't know how much time passed after the dream before a nurse came to my room bearing ice packs.

"These should help make you a little more comfortable," she said as she tucked cold damp plastic containers of ice tight against my body at my neck, my armpits, the insides of my elbows and knees. The coolness made the itching subside. The fever remained but with the ice it was somehow easier to tolerate.

I lay on my back, not moving, partly because moving hurt but also so I wouldn't dislodge the ice packs. I lay like that, motionless and miserable, all night, a night that elongated like a nightmare hallway. The more I longed for its end the more it seemed to stretch away from me. Sounds seeped through the walls and under the closed door of my room. Someone coughing. Footsteps against a tiled floor, a brief murmur of voices. A door opening, then closing. Then silence for a while, but a silence full of the sub-audible vibrations of medical machinery.

I couldn't remember a time I'd felt more helpless.

It rained later that night. Evening storms are common in Wisconsin in the summertime. After hours of trying to sleep, being mostly awake, I got out of bed and pushed my window open. I stood before it, feeling the wind and watching the flashing sky. There was something so vital, almost death defying, about the rain and the wind, the smell of the wet pavement three floors below. When I went back to bed with those smells and sounds rolling over me, I slept much better. While I slept, though, someone came in and closed the window. When I woke, the only smell in my room was that of the antibacterial liquid soap, the only sounds the floor polisher and the weeping of the woman in the room next door.

The following morning, day three, Dr. Chan, the on-call doctor who'd recommended my admission, came into my room. He was a short, middle-aged Chinese man with a British accent. "We will crack this mystery and then we will see what we can do to make you feel better," he assured me. He had, he told me, a few hypotheses, one of which was that I might have a disease called ankylosing spondylitis. Ankylosing spondylitis, he informed me, caused severe inflammation in the spine and bone spurs that fuse the vertebrae together. It also caused fatigue and sometimes fevers.

Dr. Chan sent me downstairs to get an x-ray of my spine to confirm the diagnosis. For one day spondylitis was the best guess. But the next morning, day four, Dr. Chan announced that some of my blood work was odd. A certain kind of white blood cell was overly abundant and my red blood cell count was low. He needed to call in some other specialists: a dermatologist who would do a biopsy of my rash, an infectious disease person who would look for rare microbes, and an oncologist who'd do a bone marrow test. Ankylosing spondylitis just couldn't account for all of my symptoms.

We were back to the generic diagnosis I'd had the night I was admitted, "fever of unknown origin."

The idea of yet another bunch of doctors asking me all the same questions and presumably taking more of my blood was disheartening. I was beginning to think no one anywhere was smart enough to figure this out. In the meantime, while they were trying, I wanted something to be done about my fevers.

"Not yet," Dr. Chan said.

"They're awful."

"I know. I'm sorry."

"When I was a little girl my father told me a fever can't kill you. Was he right?" The words got out of me before I had time to think about them. Dr. Chan answered me in the same dry way he always did.

"Yes," he said, "your father was right."

"Even when it's 105?"

"Even then," the doctor said, but he wasn't meeting my eyes.

4

A Minute Fiercely Burning
Particle of Being

"This fiery motionless particle set itself unaided to
resist destruction, to survive and to be in its own
madness of being, motiveless and planless beyond
that one essential end. Trust me, the hard unwinding
angry point of light said. Trust me. I stay."

—KATHERINE ANN PORTER,
Pale Horse, Pale Rider

July 15, 1990

EVERY DAY FOLLOWING MY admission, I lost more pieces of my life. Or
so it seemed to me. Nothing this bad had ever happened to me before. I'd
had losses, sure, and pain. There'd been boyfriends who'd left me, a kidney
stone. Childbirth without an epidural, twice. Leaving my first marriage,
believe me, hadn't been any piece of cake. But I'd never been this inex-
plicably and totally sick before. Never feared for my life in so immediate
a fashion. Being this sick was as novel to me as a trek in the Himalayas
would have been. I was fascinated by my own disintegration. I watched it
closely, minute by minute. I took notes.

I imagine this narrowness of mind, this preoccupation with oneself, happens to anyone who is sick enough to be in a hospital for more than a day or two. My mind wasn't busy with its usual concerns. It occurred to me that I was experiencing anhedonia, a mental health term that's one of the defining characteristics of depression. I'd written it many times in session notes. I'd never understood it as well as I did from my hospital bed. Anhedonia, the absence of pleasure. You would think the absence of something would feel like nothing. But it doesn't. It's painful not to engage with anything or anyone. To not want to.

I lost all my appetites. It wasn't surprising, given the high fevers, that I had no appetite for food, but it wasn't just food; I didn't want to take in anything else, either. Like music, I couldn't bear listening to music. Before this illness, I'd been all about music, turned it on in the car, at home while I cooked, did dishes, took a bath. I'd loved music ever since I was little. "I'm a Little Teapot" and the "Brownie Song" ("There is something in my pocket, it belongs upon my face . . .") evolved into *The Music Man*, *My Fair Lady* and *Camelot*. I could sing the entire score of over a dozen Broadway shows by the time I was twelve. In my teens, it was The Beatles, of course. The Stones. Simon and Garfunkel, The Beach Boys. When I was in my late thirties, I started taking voice lessons. So, it was logical that, once people knew what was happening to me, they sent me tapes of music they thought I'd like. While I appreciated their intentions—in a detached kind of way—I found all the music equally annoying.

Couldn't read anything worth a damn, either. I couldn't concentrate on written words. I also didn't want anyone to touch me. I'd have predicted, if anyone had asked, that if ever I was critically ill, I'd want Chris to lie full-length right next to me, like the young husband did with his dying wife in the movie *Love Story*. But, as it turned out, I didn't want anyone, not even Chris, anywhere near my rash.

I lost track of my writing, too. I had Chris bring me my notebook and a couple of pens. I was occasionally chronicling what was happening to me (silly me, I thought I would forget), but most of what I wrote was bare facts, as dull and lifeless as I was feeling.

I stopped calling my parents and most of my friends. There were only two people I called with any regularity: Chris, and Doris, the office manager at Therapies East. I'd wait until the end of each day before I called her and asked her to cancel the following day's appointments. Against all evidence, I kept thinking there was a chance that I might suddenly get better and be able to keep some of those appointments.

All evidence pointed, in fact, to my losing more ground every day, without any sign of recovery or even an hour's clemency. That whole first week was an ongoing tale of worsening symptoms. My spleen became inflamed, my liver panel came back abnormal and there was fluid building up around my heart. When none of the blood tests came back positive, the infectious disease specialist came to my room to offer her condolences. "I was hoping for an answer for you," she told me. "It may turn out in the end that we'll never know what caused your sickness." She seemed comfortable, almost cheerful, about this notion.

My white blood cell count remained elevated, each day more so. And I became anemic. I began to dread Dr. Chan's twice-a-day visits because he always brought more bad news.

By day five on Three-East of Columbia Hospital, it was obvious even to me that I couldn't feign wellness anymore. So, instead, to keep myself steady and to fend off my fear, I relied on controlling anything I could. I'd been instructed to call my nurse whenever I felt my fever spiking. The nurse was supposed to come immediately to take my temperature and if it was sky high, she or he was to alert the phlebotomists to come draw blood right away, the assumption being that a rise in temperature often meant a surge in viral or bacterial activity, thus, more micro-beasties available to snag and identify.

Despite the effects of a high fever (confusion, sleepiness, a muddy brain) I was able to remember to alert the nurse every time I felt my fever rise. Sometimes it took a while—too long in my opinion—for the nurse to come, but once she had taken my temperature, I called the blood lab myself. I didn't believe she would do it promptly enough. People didn't seem to be paying enough attention. Even when my fever was over 104, no one would bring me the ice packs unless I specifically asked for them. It wasn't easy for me to remember all of this. It seemed it was even harder for some of the nurses, even though, presumably, they were operating *without* fevers.

I tried to watch out for myself, as much of the time as I could. If the Internet had been available at that time, I'd have been surfing medical websites like crazy.

A part of me longed to sink down into the capable charge of someone reliable (but, that had rarely ever in my life seemed like a smart thing to do) and in the hospital, I thought it could be suicidal. I wasn't consciously thinking about all the times I'd seen my mother go limp in the face of her own illnesses, but, looking back, I'm sure my resolve was at least partly driven by my fear of behaving like her.

I trusted no one. I questioned everything.

The concentration required to keep all of this going, particularly with a high fever, was rather like driving a car when you can't see through the windshield, like in a snowstorm at night when the road is ice coated. Every instinct, every skill has to be focused on getting through it and home safe.

I was trying my damnedest to get myself home safe.

One morning in the middle of that first week, I woke up to find myself surrounded by a pack of six anxious medical students, writing things down on their clipboards. They were talking to each other quietly. I caught a few words, like "febrile" and "the patient," and "inflammatory process." They hadn't noticed I'd opened my eyes and was staring at them.

"Good morning," I said, in a not-nice tone. "Did you guys need something? Or is this where you usually get together in the morning? Am I in your way?"

Several of them looked startled. As if the bed had suddenly developed lips and a tongue and had spoken. One young woman, with red braids and thick rosy lips, giggled nervously and squeaked, "Good morning, Mrs. Ford." Then there was an uneasy silence. Until the attending physician walked in and rescued them. He explained to me who they were and that, because my disease was rare, he'd chosen me to be a "teaching case" for them.

I wanted to say, "How about I teach your students some manners, then." But I restrained myself.

"I'm sure you won't mind," the attending added.

"I may well mind."

"This is a bad time? We'll leave you alone for now. I'll check back with you later." He ushered his flock out the door before I could inform him that as long as I was in the hospital all my times were likely to be bad times.

The medical fledglings had barely cleared my door when a woman from the lab appeared wanting four more vials of my blood. Guessing, correctly, that the students had placed the order, I refused to let her near me. She looked flustered but put her vials and her rubber straps back into her tray and left my room.

When Dr. Chan made his morning visit I told him I didn't want to be a teaching case. "I won't have students in my room," I blustered. "They will not order tests or blood draws or so much as a Kleenex for me."

"I completely understand," Dr. Chan said. "I'll take care of it." He was much nicer to me than I deserved or expected. Perhaps he understood how important it was for me to hang onto control of something, anything. I couldn't say "no" to my fevers; I *could* keep the medical students out of my room.

It was later that same morning, I think, that I again asked Dr. Chan for some reassurance.

"Am I going to have to be here much longer?" I asked him. "I really need to get back to my clients. I'm losing a lot of income."

"Mrs. Ford," he said, sternly, "you're seriously ill and we can't treat you until we know what's going on. Once we have a diagnosis, we can talk about when—or if—you're going back to work. I'd say you should clear your calendar for several weeks at the least."

I stared at him like one of those big-eyed waifs painted by Margaret Keane and sold at truck stops. I'd heard him say "if." *If I go back to work.* I started to cry.

Dr. Chan, his face softening, drew the vinyl armchair closer to my bed and sat down. "What is it, Mrs. Ford? Are you worried?"

"Of course, I'm worried." I choked out the words. "You just said I might never work again. Some of my clients really need me. My children need me. Even the dog needs me. I'm worried about money. God, I miss my kids!" I was sobbing by the end of this, sitting on the edge of the bed, my face in my hands, my hospital gown slipping down over one shoulder, gaping open in the back.

"How many kids do you have?" Dr. Chan asked, after I'd stopped gasping and sniffling.

I pointed to the pictures Chris had tacked to my bulletin board. Jessie, twelve years old, with braces on her teeth, freckles across her nose, and my stepdaughter Rebecca, eleven and a half, her long strawberry blond hair blowing across her cheek. And Nic, twenty months, sitting in the grass in his Oshkosh B'Gosh overalls, an incongruously troubled expression furrowing his brow, more like an adult than a toddler. "It's my little boy I'm most worried about."

"Ah. Yes. I have little ones at home, too. Your children can come see you here any time, you know."

"I know." I didn't have the presence of mind to explain to him that as long as I was this sick, visits with my kids would do me no good. They'd be scared if they saw me like this and I'd be helpless to reassure them.

I wanted us to be the way we'd always been, when I was taking care of them, not them taking care of me.

"Don't you think your clients will understand? Won't they wait for you?"

"Maybe. I don't know."

"My father was a psychiatrist," Dr. Chan told me, folding his hands over one bent knee and looking dreamy. "When he got sick with terminal cancer, he kept his practice running right up to within a week of his death. His patients really stuck with him."

Terminal.

"Do you think I'm ever going to get well?" I blurted.

The doctor stopped looking dreamy. He put both feet flat on the floor and straightened up. "I don't know, Mrs. Ford. It depends on what this turns out to be. I do think you'll feel better than you do now." He stood and picked up my chart. As he walked to the door, he said, "I'll see you this afternoon. Try not to worry about your family and your clients. They're all hoping you'll do whatever you need to do to get well and come back to them."

After Dr. Chan left I sat for a long time staring at the empty vinyl armchair, letting the information sink in. *I may never get well.*

5

Blue Devil

"How did you beat this blue devil of yours?"
"I showed him I could endure him and
made him respect my endurance."
"How?"
"Just by enduring. Endurance is something that spooks
and blue devils respect. And they respect all the tricks
that panicky people use to outwit and outlast their panic."

—TENNESSEE WILLIAMS, *Night of the Iguana*

July 17, 1990, night

TIME GOES SLOWLY IN hospitals. Being separated from your life makes you feel oddly adrift, unsure of who you are—or were—and unsure of your place.

I was uncomfortable every minute of that first week, because of the fevers and the rash, but also because I was scared and always tired, unable to relax into sleep, unable to relax at all.

The night that Floria was my nurse I was already feeling pretty lousy. Barbara had brought Nic to see me that afternoon and the visit hadn't gone well. She'd phoned me at lunchtime, telling me she thought Nic needed to see me. All morning, he'd come to her again and again, taking her hand and pulling on it, saying, "Go find Mommy?" Again and again, "Go find Mommy?" Barbara thought they'd better get in the car and go find Mommy.

When Nic walked into my room that afternoon, he didn't even look at me. He headed straight for the green sofa near the window. I sat up in my bed, held my arms out and called to him, "Nic! Come see Mommy!" He didn't seem to hear me. He climbed onto a sofa arm, curled himself into a ball and rolled down onto the cushion. He repeated the climb-and-roll a couple times. Then spotted the cord to the overhead light, wrapped his fingers around it and yanked. The light turned on. He pulled again and it turned off. He giggled.

"Nicker-bean," I called to him, using his infant nickname. I was sure he wouldn't be able to resist it. He didn't even turn my way.

Instead, he went to Barbara, pulled her over to the light cord, put it in her hand and said, "Turn on light, Bobwa."

Part of me was jealous and sad. Another part of me was relieved not to have to get up out of my bed and pretend interest in Nic's game. Another part, the therapist part, understood exactly what was happening. I knew how attachment worked. Nic was doing what little kids do; he was erasing me, replacing me with a surer bet, a familiar grown-up who wasn't going to disappear for five days, as I had done.

While the light turned off and on, off and on, I thought about another hospital room, the room Nic was born in, how his brand-new eyes had locked onto mine in those first few seconds. Falling in love with another adult is wonderful enough. Falling in love with a baby can't be matched. It's total fusion, a visceral "I'd-stand-in-the-path-of-an-oncoming-train-for-you" kind of deal.

I'd broken that deal and Nic was doing what he had to do to survive my betrayal. I knew the damage wasn't going to be irreparable, but neither was it going to be an easy fix. I wished I could talk to him about it, tell him that that I didn't *want* to be away from him, that I couldn't help it. I wanted at least to tell him I'd be coming back. But, what if I made that promise and never came back?" It was sensible of Nic to bond with Barbara. I shouldn't mess with it.

On one level, I understood all this. On another level, I didn't get it at all. I'd only been gone for five days. I suppose he'd already had his doubts about me since I hadn't had much energy for him for months. Still, *I* was Nic's Mommy. Not Barbara. *Me.* What I wanted to tell him most of all was not to give up on me. Please.

After a few minutes, Nic tired of the light cord game. He turned and bolted out of the room. Barbara followed him and brought him back in her arms to say good-bye. "Wave bye-bye to Mommy, Nic."

Nic didn't want to wave. He squirmed in Barbara's arms and said, "Go home now."

I managed not to cry but it wasn't easy. I ran my eyes all over my son, memorizing him. His squirming, his unwillingness to look at me, his soft pink cheeks, his big blue eyes, the way his blond hair fell over his forehead, the roundness of his small bottom, covered by red sweatpants. The way he kicked his small, sandaled feet against Barbara's thighs.

The entire visit was over in ten minutes.

After dinner that night—I only ate the red Jell-O—I tried to find something to distract me from the many ways I felt lousy. I dreaded the nights. My fevers were worse at night and I felt more alone. I hated turning out my light and trying to sleep. I put off the moment as long as I could.

This Tuesday night, the fifth night of my hospitalization, I first tried reading the book that Chris had brought from home. *Oldest Living Confederate Widow Tells All: A Novel*. It took over 700 pages for the widow to tell all. The book was too heavy for me to hold, even with both hands. My fingers hurt from holding the pages open and I didn't remember one word of what I read. I gave up and buried the *Widow* in the drawer of my bedside table.

Next I tried TV. Of the four available channels, three were showing reruns of situation comedies. I switched to the fourth, which turned out to be the patient information channel. The screen filled with a still photo of the chapel on the first floor, colored sunlight streaming in through its stained-glass windows. Nondescript organ music oozed up out of the transmitter's tinny speaker. A voice, treacly with generic compassion, informed me that if I needed spiritual comfort, I could ask my nurse to call the chaplain.

I turned the TV off and picked up the volume of *Reader's Digest Condensed Books* that I'd found in the family lounge down the hall. Ordinarily, these collections of predigested stories wouldn't have appealed to me, but just then, they were about all my mind could handle. The story that I'd picked out to read was about a woman who taught developmentally delayed children. Lots of short sentences. Nothing lyrical. I liked it. I read for an hour.

When I closed the book, the clock on my bedside table told me it was 10:00 p.m. but I could have guessed the time from the diminishing of the noises outside my room. Fewer voices, fewer footsteps, the voices I did hear were slower, quieter.

The floor polisher roared past my room and back again, erasing the quiet. As the noises diminished, my anxiety began to rise. I didn't like being in my room. I could feel people had suffered and died here. It was easier not to think about the room's history when the lights were on and the door and window were open.

I was not yet sick enough to believe I was dying on that particular Tuesday. And yet, I had this unshakable intuitive sense that whatever was wrong with me was something calamitous.

I'd built myself a tight, predictable life. I'd placed myself in charge of as much of that life as I could. Not leaving any gaps through which a nightmare could poke its nose. Once I landed in the hospital, there were lots of gaps, nothing *but* gaps. Who knew what horror might slither in?

I clung to solid comforting things: the fresh air through my open window; the voices that drifted in from the hallway; the neon-generated path of light that reached in from that hallway at night, crossed the gray tiled floor, bent itself up the shadowed wall to the square bulletin board and settled in puddles across the photographs of my children, making disembodied pieces of them shine out at me. Jessie's cheekbones, the soft down along Becky's hairline, Nic's untamable white hair, reminiscent of a baby owl.

I tried to imagine where Nic was right then. I pictured him in the pale blue summer pajamas that snapped together at the waist, asleep in his crib, on his stomach, with his legs bent underneath him. His bottom, thick with its nighttime diaper, the highest object in the bed, like a big round watchtower over his back, the roundness of his fuzzy head. His fists closed and resting beside his face. His cheeks rosy from the warmth of the summer night. I summoned up the smell of his skin, his hair, the sweet infant scent of Nic. This made me miss him all the more, of course, but it also placed me for a few minutes back into my safe life.

Hard to hold any image long in a hospital. Everything interrupts. I often heard the person in one of the rooms near mine coughing. I'd learned from one of the nurses that this person was a teen-age girl with pneumonia. Her door was always closed and had a big yellow sign on it that explained the precautions you should take if you were going to go in. Face mask, gauze booties, and a paper surgeon's smock to cover your clothes. She wasn't getting well as quickly as a young person should, the talkative nurse had told me. People were worried about her. Were her parents there with her, I wondered? Did she feel abandoned, too, like Nic did?

Like I did.

Thinking about the girl next door made me think of Jessie. I wondered if she, too, would give up on me. Jessie had been twenty months old when I left her father, same age Nic was this summer. When the impact of my divorce might have stunned me into immobility, Jessie was my reason to keep going. It was for her that I filled our new house with plants, a canary, and a hamster. For her that I went out and marketed my psychotherapy services, even though I hated everything about marketing and had to force myself to do it.

Jessie and I had grown so close over the years that we knew each other's feelings without words, even across miles. Jessie was twelve and we still read together every night before bed. We'd been in the middle of *A Tree Grows in Brooklyn* when I'd gotten sick. I wondered if we would ever get to finish the book.

Then there was Becky, Chris's daughter from his first marriage. I never knew what Becky was thinking. Long before she met me, she'd gone underground, gathered herself together and hidden away inside herself. I was sure there were good reasons, but I didn't know what they were. I couldn't read her the way I read Jessie. She wouldn't let me. Maybe she was glad to have me gone. To have more access to her father. Maybe she missed me. Either reaction—or both—were equally possible.

Even as I studied the kids' pictures in the glow of the hallway light, I told myself they would be all right without me. I didn't believe it but it helped a little to entertain the possibility.

After ten, the hospital switchboard was closed to incoming calls. No one's voice was going to travel through the wires to rescue me from myself. I didn't usually make outside calls either. Chris came every day to see me; I didn't have anything much to say to him by 10:00 p.m. Didn't have anything much to say to anyone. Didn't want to call and worry my parents or my kids.

As I was thinking about whether or not it was too late to call my mother and if I could manage to sound chipper enough not to alarm her, I started shivering again. At first, the chills came hard and fast, just like they did the night Chris brought me to the ER. After twenty minutes or so, they began to subside, which, I'd learned, meant my fever was about as high as it was going to be for a while. I tossed the blankets off and lay uncovered in the oversize t-shirt (a souvenir from a recent running event) that I preferred over a hospital gown, my whole body blazing hot again. Even my hands and fingers were red. I hadn't realized that hands could flush with fever just like faces.

The nurses rarely came quickly enough to take my temperature when I told them it was rising. They were supposed to keep a record of when the fevers peaked and then they were supposed to call the lab to come draw my blood. I didn't trust them, so I'd asked Chris to bring me a thermometer. I kept my own record and sometimes I called the lab myself to have them come draw my blood.

This time my thermometer read 106.

106.

Why did 106 seem so much worse than 104 or 105? It did, way worse. Maybe it was because of this story I remembered from one of the *Little House on The Prairie* books by Laura Ingalls Wilder. A little girl in a log cabin with a very high fever; did she lose all her hair? Or go blind? Did she die? I thought she went blind. I couldn't remember.

I pressed my call light.

"My fever's 106," I told the voice that answered. "Could I have the cooling blanket the doctor ordered for me?" My friend Barbara worked a few floors above in the cancer unit of this hospital and she had suggested to Dr. Chan that this new device, the cooling blanket, might be helpful.

"I'm sorry but we're doing report right now. It will be a while." Said the bodiless, heartless voice on the intercom.

"Please come as soon as you can. I feel really bad," I said. I *didn't* say what I was thinking. I didn't say, "I'm scared I'll go blind. I'm scared I'll die."

Thirty minutes later I tried again. Amazing, kind of, that I was conscious enough to be this persistent with so high a fever. By this time I was very used to having a fever. Also, the adrenalin, generated and maintained by my fear, was keeping me cogent.

I demanded to speak to a nurse immediately. In a few minutes, the new night nurse assigned to me, Floria, spoke through the intercom. "Can't you wait a minute? We're changing shifts and I'll be there when I can." She sounded angry.

I caught my breath. I could hardly believe I'd heard her correctly.

"You get in here now!" I shouted back at the small grill in the wall. "I've waited more than half an hour. Do you have any idea how high my fever is?"

Floria didn't answer. She'd cut me off. In a few minutes, she appeared, armed with the cooling blanket and the machine that operated it.

Floria was a tall, angular, Black woman with tight, short hair. Everything about Floria was tight. Her mouth, the cords of her neck, the way she held her hands and fingers.

"You have to understand," she said without making eye contact as she pushed my body roughly onto its left side and lay down half the vinyl blanket, "that we got other things to do. A fever ain't no emergency." She rolled me over on my opposite side and laid down the other half of the blanket.

"Floria," I said, with considerable effort. "I don't have to understand anything at all. I'm the patient. I'm feeling terrible and I made a reasonable request. Patients should take priority over report."

"You sure got yourself an attitude," she threw back at me. She flounced out of the room.

And out the door with her went all my bravado and lucidity, but not my fear. That continued to ratchet up.

I thought of one of my clients who, at the age of three, could read maps. When she bragged about her skill to her father, he left her by the side of a country road and told her to find her way home. She had no idea where she was. That was her punishment for bragging. For acting important. For having an attitude.

I had an attitude. Floria was my punishment.

A small metal machine sat next to my bed and was attached to the cooling blanket by a narrow hose. It hummed like an old refrigerator as it pumped what I guessed was a viscous liquid into the chambers of the cotton-covered vinyl blanket. The blanket was rapidly turning icy under my body. This was not a nice combination, the heat of my fever and the cold plastic beneath me. I felt as if I had an all-over sunburn and was lying naked in crushed ice. My brain didn't understand the conflicting signals. All my muscles tensed up, trying to pull away from the cold.

"This is good for me," I told myself. "This will save me."

I watched the clock. Its hands held still. I held still, too and worked on relaxing my muscles so the cooling blanket could do its job. I pictured myself floating, levitating just above a snowfield. I imagined air currents rising up and over me. "It is a hot day," I told myself. "I welcome the cooling breeze." I worked hard at these images for fifteen minutes.

But my body didn't welcome the cooling breeze. My body knew I was lying. It remained braced against the threat of systemic frostbite.

"Fuck this," I thought.

I rolled over to the edge of the bed and pulled the stiff blanket out from under me, letting it slip to the floor. Immediately the heat at my core overflowed and washed outward to my fingers and toes.

I pushed my call light and asked for my nurse to bring me ice packs. A half an hour passed; Floria didn't come. I pushed the call light again. "Please send Floria to my room."

"I'll tell her again," said the ward secretary.

Floria finally appeared looking disgusted. "You wanted this damn cooling blanket thing," she snarled. "It ain't my fault you don't like it."

"It's really uncomfortable. I had no idea it would feel like that. Could I have the ice packs, instead? I can tell my fever hasn't gone down yet." I was trying to be nicer. If I was nicer, wouldn't the evil Floria be nice back?

"And why should I go run around like that for you? How do I know you ain't gonna just throw those on the floor, too?"

"Because I won't," I told her. And then it dawned on me. Floria didn't care if I died or went blind. Floria cared about not working hard. Floria cared about control and I was entirely at her mercy. There was about as much point in trying to outwit Floria as trying to outwit an oncoming hurricane. And yet, it felt like my life depended on doing exactly that.

"Floria," I said in a soft, tense voice, "everyone else has gotten the ice packs for me and I've used them happily. You *will* get them for me. If you don't, I'll call my doctor at home even though it's after midnight. I'll explain to him that you're refusing to follow his orders."

Floria left. She returned with the ice packs, tossed them in a heap at the foot of the bed and walked out again without a word. I did my best to place them where the other nurses (the good nurses, the kind nurses, the ones I now longed for) had put them before: armpits, back of the neck, backs of the knees, insides of the wrists. Then, lying very still so the icepacks would stay where I'd put them, I tried again to rest. My heart was pounding, whether from fear of the fever or fear of Floria, I didn't know. Everything felt scary. The deadly room, the dim light, the flattened-out air, my hot skin, my racing heart.

I let myself sink down into the fever, losing my sense of where and who I was. The images that rose up behind my eyelids—the chair beside my hospital bed where my visitors always sat, the four-poster bed Chris and I shared at home, the double bed of my childhood covered with the quilt made by my great grandmother—all of these were coated in shadows in my mind, as if darkness had fallen all over them like dust, in layers, for centuries. I slept then, lightly, restlessly and, in a dream, a path appeared, dimly lit. It would save me, I thought, but when I'd taken two steps onto it, it vanished. No other path appeared.

The next day I woke clear-headed, a little surprised to find myself intact. My fever seemed to have dropped two or three degrees overnight. I expected it wouldn't soar again until midday. That was the pattern I'd learned to expect.

Now when I think about my behavior with Floria, it reminds me of my mother. My mother and her bedside bell. A round silver bell with a button on top, the kind you might see on a check-in counter in a motel alongside a sign: *Ring for service.* When she was sick in bed, she'd ring for service. She'd tap that little bell, sending its *ping* throughout the house in search of one of us. She assumed we all would serve her. And we did. When I was a kid, I prided myself on being good at answering the bell. I liked feeling essential to my mother. I stopped enjoying being essential to my sickly mom when I hit my teens and started to hate that damn bell and everything it demanded.

I think I get it now. Just as I was with Floria, my mother was afraid for her life. She was afraid whether fear was warranted or not and when she hit that bell, she got an infusion of being in charge. When she badgered my father, she knew she was alive. Two years from now she would find herself in a nursing home in a wheelchair and she'd push her call-button to summon an aide every few minutes for the same reason, to resist her own destruction. To take up space. To assure herself that she remained.

6

All This Must Go

"What you held in your hand,
what you counted and carefully saved,
all this must go so you know
how desolate the landscape can be"

—NAOMI SHIHAB NYE, from "Kindness"

July 18, 1990

WEDNESDAY MORNING, A FEW hours after the breakfast I didn't eat,
Barbara brought Nic to visit again. I'd only been in the hospital six days
but it felt like a lifetime. Maybe that was because I was sicker every day;
maybe because I was not a patient person. Maybe because, like Floria
said, I had an attitude. Whatever the reason, every additional day I spent
in the hospital felt like a week. Every day I felt more in danger. As if simply being here was putting me in harm's way. I woke each morning with
a longing to go home, a reflex to get out of bed and run for the elevator.
Once I'd sat up and walked, accompanied by my IV stand, the few steps to
my bathroom and brushed my teeth, I'd used up all the energy I had. I'd
lie back down in bed, drained, and think about my clients, my children,
running, walking the dog; I knew I couldn't manage any of it. Still, the
impulses kept coming, tugging at me. The way amputees feel itching in
their missing limbs; my whole life had become a missing limb.

Along with Nic, Barbara also brought me a helium-filled balloon, shiny yellow Mylar with a big red grin and blue dots for eyes. She tied the maniacal face to my bed-tray while Nic climbed up and leaned on me. I buried my nose in his sweet-smelling hair and tried not to hold onto him too hard. After a few seconds, he spotted the light cord in the corner, squirmed out of my arms, and slithered down to yank it. My bed felt emptier than it had before he'd been in it.

"Hey, look!" Barbara distracted me from the lump that was rising in my throat. She held a shabby, brown teddy bear by its ears. She danced it in front of me. "Jessie thought you might need this," she said, as she set the bear on my lap.

Poor old bear, flat from being hugged and slept on, and the fur around his nose was mostly gone. Every animal of Jessie's early years had suffered a similar baldness about the nose and mouth. She'd had a habit of plucking out bits of plush from their faces and rubbing the "fuzzies" against her upper lip while she sucked her two favorite fingers. This teddy also had a large Band-Aid across a torn seam on his right side.

"Uh oh, there you go again." Barbara handed me a tissue from the box beside my bed. "I told Jessie it would make you cry."

"Thank you, Barbara," I said into the teddy's crumpled head. "For everything you're doing."

"Glad to do it," she told me as she sat down in the chair and entertained me with stories of the things my husband was forgetting to do and the sorry state of my house. I sighed. Ah, yes. Here was the reminder I needed of why I couldn't just get up and go home; all the chores that had overfilled my time, expanding way beyond my energy, even before I'd gotten sick.

Barbara's stories about Chris and the mess my house was in entertained me, but only because she was a central character in them. She was in my house almost daily, making sure nothing irreparable happened to the furniture or the walls, the kids or the dog.

The visit was short; Nic got bored with the light cord and nothing else in the room interested him. He walked to my bedside and informed me that he had to "go home now." He took Barbara's hand and pulled her toward the door.

"It's okay," I told her. "Let's try again tomorrow." She waved and was gone.

It was still morning; my fever hadn't risen very high yet and my rash was a little less itchy. As long as I lay still, my joints didn't hurt all that much.

When these brief reprieves occurred, I'd look around my room as if I was seeing it for the first time: The bland green walls, the nearly empty spiral bound notebook and the Kleenex box on my bedside table, the TV pinned up high on the wall, the glowing rectangle of the window. It was summertime out there, beyond my window. July.

Lying in my hospital bed this morning, I stared at the sunlight that bounced off the rooftop of the School of Architecture across the street from the hospital. I imagined the sidewalks three stories below, busy with university students in shorts, children walking to College for Kids classes, maybe a group of toddlers strapped into a large cart, pulled by a day care worker. Or a boy on a skateboard in saggy cut-off jeans, navigating through the pedestrians. Cars slowing and stopping for the traffic light, waiting, starting up again. The roaring of a passing bus, the sound of foot-steps, conversations, laughter, the sticky sound of hot tires rolling against asphalt. I imagined all these sounds, all these moving people. I longed to hear and see and smell all of it even though where I was this morning, in this motionless quiet room, imagining was really all I could tolerate.

Resigning myself to another boring hospital day, I returned to the question of how I'd gotten sick, as I always did whenever my symptoms didn't occupy the forefront of my mind. What had I ignored? What cue had I missed; what, if I'd paid attention to it, would have prevented all this? The only thing I could think of was that maybe I'd gone back to work too soon after having Nic. I'd started seeing clients again when he was only a month old, returning to my office sleep-deprived and distract-ible. It had felt important to keep hold of my professional self. To keep my practice alive. To keep myself alive and awake, not lost in the haze of housewife-and-motherhood. Wouldn't I have done myself more damage if I'd stayed home and let myself get depressed and bored? But then, may-be I'd worked too many hours. Should I have done more yoga? Maybe run less often? Or more? Gotten more massages? I kept reviewing the same facts over and over, thinking I was missing something. It frustrated me that I couldn't come up with a plausible theory. Made me feel stupid, too, and a bit ashamed. The way I used to feel in advanced algebra in high school. The only class I ever failed.

I tried to do relaxation techniques, deep breathing, connecting to my intuition. Hoping, I suppose, that what my intellect couldn't figure out, my unconscious mind would know. I told myself to relax and let go. I named each part of my body and instructed myself to relax it. "I'm relaxing my foot; I'm relaxing my ankle." And so on. One of my therapy supervisors, Emily, had taught me to empty out my mind this way, to make room for more intuitive information. I could hear her voice in my head: "You know the answer. Just let it come." But now, here in the hospital, nothing came. The spaces I'd cleared remained alarmingly empty. And silent. As if all the phone wires had been cut.

I was hugging Jessie's bear when a nurse came in to do a routine check of my vital signs. She noticed I'd been crying and asked me why.

"Because nobody knows what's wrong with me or what to do about it," I told her.

"Your doctors will figure it out," she said, with a sweet smile. "They're working on it, and they'll figure it out." The nurse was young, fresh from nursing school, it looked like.

"I hope so," I mumbled before she slid the thermometer under my tongue. She seemed so innocent; I didn't want to tell her that I didn't share her faith in western medicine. *If the doctors were able to figure this out, they would have done it by now*, I thought. I couldn't imagine that a homeopath, body worker, naturopath, shaman, curandero, or wizard had the answer either. It could be, it occurred to me, that nobody was going to know what was wrong with me. Maybe it wasn't knowable.

I found that last thought oddly reassuring. If it wasn't knowable I didn't have to keep trying so hard. I didn't have to feel like being sick meant I'd failed somehow. Maybe there'd never been any way for me to avoid this illness. Maybe it had been waiting inside me ever since the day I was born. Biding its time. I couldn't figure out what I'd done to make myself sick because I *hadn't* made myself sick. Maybe my mother's dream had been right. This had been pre-ordained, by my genes or something else.

I began, finally, to relax a little.

When the nurse slid the thermometer out of my mouth and wrote my temperature in my chart, I didn't ask her to tell me the number. For the first time since last Friday, when I came to the hospital, I didn't care.

As the nurse closed my door and the hallway sounds faded away a memory rose up in my mind: the first time I climbed the big elm tree at the back of the vacant lot across the street from my childhood home. The tree was over thirty feet tall. I was four and a half feet tall and ten years old. That morning I'd bragged to my doubting big brother Dick that I could climb to the top of this monster. Now I had to prove it.

The day was hot and humid. I stood below the tree and looked up at the patches of blue sky that appeared and disappeared between the trembling branches. My heart pounded in my throat, and my knees threatened to buckle. I forced myself to stand tall and still, the way I imagined a warrior would. My hands were wet as I grasped two of the tree's lower branches and hauled myself up. Dick yelled to me from below to not look down, don't ever look down. I anchored my eyes on the branches just above my head. Dick had taught me to hold on tight with my knees and one hand, right up until the moment my other hand and foot found safe purchase. Then I should let go with the other hand and foot and move up fast. Then I should do it again. He didn't need to tell me not to pause in the middle. I knew that if I did, I'd freeze.

Eventually, I was so close to the top of the tree that the only branches above me were thin wispy ones that couldn't hold my weight. I lodged my butt in an intersection of branches and, disregarding my brother's advice, I looked straight down the trunk to the ground.

My head spun. And the most wonderful feeling rose up into my chest, right alongside the terror. It was a good thing I was old enough to know for certain I couldn't fly because otherwise I'd have tried it then, leaned forward, spread my arms, tightened my body and slipped out into the blue sky. The physical experience of looking down and feeling my life teeter on an edge, knowing that I could, in an instant, either soar or fall and be smashed to bits, shook me so awake that the sunlight on the rooftops below me glittered like diamond dust. The chatter of the nearby robins and sparrows rose so loud in my head my eardrums ached. My damp hands prickled from the bark beneath them. I could feel my pulse in the veins of my legs where they gripped the tree. Everything else disappeared. Including all my efforts to control my world, my determination to be a good girl, to be the perfect daughter, to find a way to cure my mother of her constant tiredness, her asthma, the sadness and disappointments that made her go silent for days, the cocktails that changed her by suppertime most nights into someone I didn't like.

Right that moment there was only the solid tree and the transparent sky and myself more alive than I could ever remember being.

Why was that memory coming back now, I wondered. And then it was obvious: the freedom of not being in charge of my fevers or my treatment was very like the freedom of not needing to fix my mother or myself. True, lying in bed and not knowing what was happening to me or what would come next wasn't exhilarating like being on top of a tree but the relief was similar: I wasn't in charge and was not required to be more than I could be.

7

Steep Places

"Sometimes we need both hands to climb out of a
place. Sometimes there are steep places, where one
has to walk ahead of the other. [. . .] If I can't keep
up, if you're far ahead, look back. Look back."

—ANNE MICHAEL, *Fugitive Pieces*

July 19, 1990, Thursday

ON THE AFTERNOON OF my seventh day in the hospital, Dr. Chan came
to my room to talk to Chris and me about what to do next. My fevers had
continued their intermittent soaring, new patches of rash had replaced
some of the scabbed-over areas, the joints of my knees, wrists and ankles
ached. The phlebotomists were still drawing my blood four or more times
a day, continuing to monitor red and white blood cell counts and to test
for antibodies. None of the counts had improved; in fact, most of the
numbers were worse. I'd tested positive for two viruses, Cetamegalo and
Epstein-Barr, but all that meant was that I'd had those viruses in the past,
not that they were active. I continued to feel exhausted, itchy, and uncomfortable. And hot, when I wasn't shivering.

The diagnosis Dr. Chan proposed was not, as I'd hoped, something
easily cured. He wasn't certain, but he thought I might have a rare disease
called adult-onset Still's disease, also known as AOSD.

Dr. Chan stood at the foot of my bed holding my inch-thick hospital chart, listing the symptoms of Still's: extreme fatigue; waves of high fevers that spike and then lower, repeating several times a day; a salmon-colored skin rash; enlargement of the spleen and liver. Sometimes fluid accumulation around the lungs or heart. The only symptom on the list that I didn't have was that last one. That would come later.

Dr. Chan gave Chris an article from a medical journal. "Adult-onset Still's Disease: Experience in 23 Patients and Literature Review with Emphasis on Organ Failure."[1]

I still have that article. I reread it just a couple days ago and even now I don't understand how the doctor could have thought it was a good idea to give it to us that day. Or ever. Though couched in sterile medical vocabulary, the article is chilling. Here's an example: "There was a total of eight deaths in all of the reported series. Causes of death included disseminated intravascular coagulation, acute abdomen complicated by congestive heart failure, status epilepticus and shock . . . sudden and unexplained death . . . and acute liver failure." I don't even like reading this stuff now, so many years later.

Chris glanced at the first page of the article and then rolled it into a tight tube and clutched it in his hand. The doctor explained that Still's is a chronic disease with periods of flare-up mixed with periods of remission. No way to predict how long either phase would last. His voice droned on and on—I stopped hearing him. Chris had tuned out, too, and was tapping the rolled-up journal article against his palm, tap-tap-tap, tap-tap-tap, tap-tap-tap. Like some impotent Morse code signal, an SOS no one would ever respond to. Just before Dr. Chan left the room, he told me he wanted me to reduce my stress level and make my health my top priority.

Chris followed the doctor out into the hall.

My room felt as if all the air had been sucked out of it. I lay in my bed in that stillness trying to imagine what my life with this disease was going to be. I thought first about my work. How was I going to manage a therapy practice if I was going to periodically be this sick? I couldn't invite a client to trust me, to share secrets, show me their worst parts, and then say, "Oh by the way, my colleague, Naomi, is going to be seeing you for the next month until I feel better; you can start all over again with her, okay?" The only clients I'd have left would be the ones with too little self-esteem to expect decent treatment.

---

1. Reginato, et al., "Adult Onset Still's Disease," 39–57.

I thought about my kids next. They weren't going to understand that sometimes I could be their usual mom and sometimes no mom at all. I couldn't tell toddler Nic, for example, that I was too tired to make his lunch. How often could I tell twelve-year-old Jessie, eleven-year-old Becky, that I couldn't help with a homework assignment, couldn't come to a swim meet or a parent-teacher conference? I imagined myself as sick as I currently was for the rest of my life, in my bedroom, day after gray day. I pictured the girls perched on the edge of my bed chatting for a few minutes after school, anxious to be done with me and away.

That's when I seriously considered suicide. I didn't think I could face being a half-assed therapist, an unreliable mom. Or worse, an obligation. Someone like my mother on her bad days, a fragile sick person with a silver bell on her bedside table.

Chris came back in and stood over my bed, looking down at me. Although he tried to hide it, I could see he was as scared as I was. We'd only been together two and a half years at that point. We'd had some difficult things to deal with, for sure, but nothing matching this. I searched his face, expecting to find there a closing-down, a pulling-away. I wondered if he regretted having married me.

I loved Chris more than I'd ever loved anyone, as much as I'd loved my mother when I was in a little girl, in spite of (or because of) my worry about her.

I remember the first second I laid eyes on him. We'd been matched by a video dating service and had talked briefly on the phone to set a meeting time and place halfway between each other's neighborhoods.

After a year and a half of rarely interesting, sometimes bizarre, and usually dead-end arranged rendezvous, I'd learned not to have my dates pick me up at home. I always drove myself to the meeting places so that I could drive myself back whenever I wanted to. I had a repertoire of a hundred different ways to say, "I have to go now."

The night I met Chris, my car was parked half a block away, and I only had an hour available before I had to pick up eight-year-old Jessie at a friend's house. I got to the Coffee Trader a few minutes before him. I spotted him outside the window of the café. He was leaning into the winter wind, his trench coat flapping, thick glasses speckled with melting snow.

Could that be him, I wondered, scarcely daring to believe it. He was tall and good-looking in a bookish kind of way. Unlike most of the men the dating service had picked out for me, he looked like he might actually be someone I could be attracted to. Despite a voice in my head that warned me not to count on anything, when Chris walked to my table, wiping his glasses on his shirttail, smiling, I was a goner. It happened that fast.

When I returned home the following evening, after our second date, I announced to Timmy, the golden retriever, that I'd just met someone who was going to be in our lives for a long, long time. I remember Timmy edging out of the room as I hopped around the kitchen, doing dishes, singing, the Steve Winwood song, "the finer things keep shining through/ the way my soul gets lost in you."

My pleasure didn't stay that uncomplicated. A week later, I was doubting my reaction, telling myself I was impulsive and immature. I'd had two dates with Chris Ford; I didn't really know anything about him. He might turn out to be as depressed and angry as my first husband, as unpredictable as my mother. From the time I'd left my first marriage until I met Chris these eight years later, the only person I'd let anywhere near my heart had been my daughter.

I tried to play it safe. Over the following months, I learned as much about Chris as I could. How did he feel about his previous wife? What was his stand on reproductive rights? Did he like his job? How did he feel about his mother? I looked under every rock, doing what I thought was a covert psychological assessment. Chris told me years later that he'd known exactly what I was doing and had put up with my distrust, had even been amused by it, because he understood that I was afraid. He was, too.

That first year we spent as much time together as we could fit in between our careers and our parenting. (Our daughters were both eight when we met). Beginning with the night after our second date, Chris called me every day, without fail, for an entire year. Day after day, month after month, as regular as a sunrise, he kept showing up until finally I came to believe that he always would.

"Hi, honey," he said now with tenderness as he pulled a chair close to my bed and sat down.

"I'm sorry," I said.

Chris looked up confused. "Sorry for what?"

"For being in the hospital. For being so sick. It wasn't supposed to turn out like this."

"Silly woman," he said. The chair let out a soft puff of air as he leaned forward, picked my hand up off the white blanket, and kissed it.

8

Hatch Out the Total Helplessness

"Prayer is an egg.
Hatch out the total helplessness inside."
—RUMI

July 20, 1990

THE FOLLOWING MORNING I lay in bed studying my maddening rash. The only part of me still unspeckled was my face. My spots had a life cycle; they started as small as pores, hot red pores, then grew larger and less distinct, sometimes blending into one another to make intensely itchy football fields of dots. Next they crusted over like chicken pox lesions. Then they flaked off, leaving apparently unfazed skin behind. When I moved my legs under the sheet now the fabric caught here and there against my skin. The spots there were in crusty phase. Next, I noticed my hands. There was a whole new crop of fresh, red, pinpricks on the backs of my hands. I was staring at them when Tom Riley, the phlebotomist, walked in with his rattling tray of vials and needles and rubber straps.

"Hello, phlebotomist," I greeted him. I considered sharing with him the information I'd been gathering about my rash but decided he probably wouldn't be as interested as I was.

"Hello, Mrs. Ford. Let me have another go at those arms of yours." I held out both my arms, elbows down. Tom poked at a few veins, made his choice, and wrapped a rubber strap tight just above my elbow. I didn't feel the needle as it slipped in. Tom was an expert. The plastic tube attached to the needle immediately turned dark red. Without disturbing the needle's position in my skin (wiggling it would hurt), Tom slid a glass vial on to the tube, watched it fill, removed it, and snapped an empty one into place. He did this six times. I felt a vague sense of accomplishment every time my blood flowed into a vial.

"What's it like on the outside today?" I asked Tom.

"Hot. Damp. And overcast," he reported as he tilted the sixth full vial back and forth and laid it onto my tray table. "But I'm not complaining. What's it been like here on the inside?" He pressed his thumb against my arm and slid the needle out. Stuck a strip of gauze and then adhesive over the oozing spot.

"It's been mostly cloudy here. With a tornado watch," I told him. "Threatening. Very threatening. Not good picnic weather."

"Mmmmm. Sorry." Tom pasted a Snoopy Band-aid over the gauze and tape at the needle site. Yesterday it was Mickey Mouse. "See you in a couple of hours," he said as he lifted his tray and turned to go. "Maybe the inside sun will be out by then."

"I wouldn't count on it."

Tom's rubber-soled shoes made spongy sounds against the floor as he walked out.

A few hours later Dr. Chan returned. "I don't think you've got Still's," he announced. "The consensus in the medical community is that Still's might not even be a real illness. It appears to be a catch-all term for inflammatory illness for which we have no other answer. I'm just not satisfied with that."

I received this news with a combination of relief—*I don't have that horrible disease!*—and confusion. *What do I have then?*

"We'll keep exploring," the doctor said, and he left the room.

What he didn't know—what I couldn't know—was that in the future Still's disease would gain acceptance as a disease in its own right, with a consistent set of symptoms (matching almost all of mine) and treatment protocols. It would take my visiting two other rheumatologists and finally, in 1997 the Cleveland Clinic, before I got what I was longing for in the summer of 1990, a definitive diagnosis, agreed upon by all three doctors. adult-onset Still's disease.

The room was abruptly quiet. I looked over at my telephone and then remembered it was a weekday. My friends were all at work, as was

Chris. The kids were in their various summer programs. No one would be calling me for hours and hours. I didn't know what to do with myself. I briefly considered meditating; I'd had some training. I was afraid to try, imagining that if I closed my eyes and counted my breaths, all that would happen was more emptiness, no access to my higher self or inner healer or whatever you want to call the core of yourself where you store things up for the winter.

I knew my breath smelled bad. The inside of my mouth felt scummy and sour. *I should get up and brush my teeth.* But brushing my teeth wasn't easy. It took planning. I'd have to get out of bed carefully so I wouldn't jar or pull on my IV line. Then I'd have to unplug the IV machine and pull it along with me into the bathroom. Last night standing at the bathroom sink, I'd gotten so dizzy I thought I might fall. I worried now that I might feel dizzy like that again. And if I got up to brush my teeth, I'd see my face. I didn't like how my face looked, my skin stark white in contrast to the red dots on my neck. My cheekbones standing out like misplaced elbows.

I decided to postpone the tooth brushing.

I sighed and settled back against the pillow to wait for the breakfast that I wouldn't want to eat. I turned on the TV and watched *The Today Show* until an aide arrived with a wheelchair to take me down to x-ray. They were going to do a CT scan of my abdomen. To check my liver, I guessed, and to see whatever else they could see in there.

In the x-ray waiting area I sat in the wheelchair wrapped in a hospital gown and robe longing to lie down. After about ten minutes a technician wheeled me into a room and gave me a large beaker of sweet contrast fluid to drink. It tasted vaguely (only vaguely) like thick flat Coke. I lay down on the narrow bench of the CT scanner and the technician warned me to lie completely still. As if I felt like moving. I actually fell lightly asleep as the giant humming doughnut of the scanner passed over my body in slow motion.

Later that afternoon I was hit with a sudden bout of intense abdominal cramps. I surprised myself with how easily I managed the IV stand as I rushed to the bathroom. There the cramps continued until I was utterly emptied out. I returned to bed feeling shaky and cleansed. When Dr. Chan came to check on me a few hours later, I asked him if the contrast fluid caused diarrhea.

"No. I've never heard of that happening." He told me he'd send a gastroenterologist to see me the next day. Another doctor for my team. He or she would be as clueless as the one before, I was sure of it. I was losing faith. Before I got so sick, I thought doctors could always provide answers and cures, medicines that would make quick work of any germ.

The thought of good medicine sent me back. In my memory I was six years old, standing at my father's side in Schwartzmann's Pharmacy, leaning against his gray wool-covered knee. The shelves were tall above and all around me and full of things I didn't recognize. There was a smell in the air, a dusty dry mixture of something warmly spicy like cloves woven into whiffs of iodine and the hot fudge at the soda fountain. The winter wind rattled the plate glass window behind the cosmetic counter. My father's black galoshes dripped melted snow onto the black and white linoleum floor. He patted my head reassuringly. My head was hot with fever. When we got home, my father spooned a liquid sulfa solution into my waiting mouth. To my delight, it was flavored chocolate-mint, like a Brach's mint candy bar.

My father had always wanted to be a doctor.   When I was around twelve, I discovered a box of letters he'd written to my mother when they both were in college. In them he described his passionate wish to go to medical school and his doubts about being able to afford it. His parents couldn't help much and his job at Rennebohm's Pharmacy barely covered his undergrad tuition and lodging. After a couple pre-med years and another couple of years majoring in engineering, he married my mother and got a full-time job. As an electronics engineer, not a doctor.

Years later, when I was busy with my therapy practice and three children and everything in my life seemed to be conspiring against my becoming a writer, I thought I understood the dimensions of my father's loss. I asked him if he regretted not having become a doctor.

"I used to," he told me, his voice matter of fact, his eyes not meeting mine. "But I think things turned out all right this way." He looked up then and grinned. "I got a great daughter out of the deal."

Perhaps it *was* best that my father was a doctor only in his own house. All his patients were people he loved. And we got our very own private lay-physician, available twenty-four hours a day and always glad to see us. If he'd had a real medical practice, he'd probably never have been home. We'd have missed out on the best parts of Bert.

My earliest memory of my dad's doctoring is of him coming to my crib in the early morning, barely dawn. I don't know why but around the age of two I had these frequent eye infections and I'd often wake up unable to open my eyes, my eyelashes glued to my cheeks with a dried-on discharge.

I remember the thin morning light, a blur of grey and pink, on the inside of my closed eyes and how I panicked when I couldn't open them. I was too little to know I could wipe my lashes free with my fingers. It was terrifying to be unable to see. So I sat there, crying, helpless, until my father came with a warm washcloth. He wrapped his arm around my shoulders. I stopped crying as soon as I heard his voice. "It's okay. Everything's okay. Daddy's here." The washcloth darkened the muted light behind my pasted lids as my father stroked downward, gently, lash by lash. Finally when he'd wiped off every lash, he told me to open my eyes. The light was blindingly bright. He smiled at me and lifted me out of my crib.

All my experiences with illness, from childhood until now, had ended similarly, with kind doctoring, good medicine, and quick recoveries, even my frequent bouts with bronchitis or the kidney stone I had when I was thirty-seven.

Now, in my hospital bed as I drifted off into another feverish and restless sleep, I realized I'd never again have such faith in medicine or in my own body. No warm washcloth or kind words could wipe away whatever this illness was. And my sweet, sickly, doctoring father needed doctoring now even more than I did.

Later that morning, after the morning blood draw and partway into my dispirited breakfast, Dr. Randall, the gastroenterologist, appeared. He was tall and thin, with a wide face and dark brown hair. He looked a little like my brother Dick. He took my hand and said "Mrs. Ford. I'm Greg Randall. Dr. Chan asked me to talk with you." His voice was deep and pleasant.

I made no effort to remove my hand from his as I described the attack of diarrhea.

"I know you've been through a lot of tests already, and you must be feeling pretty terrible," Dr. Randall said. "But I think it would be worth our while to do a colonoscopy. That's a procedure in which we insert a lighted tube into your rectum, move it into the lower part of your colon and take a look at your intestinal lining. It's not a big deal. You might feel a little discomfort but no real pain. Takes only about ten minutes. Frankly, I don't think we'll find a thing, but since we still don't know what's making you sick, it makes sense to do it."

"What would you be looking for?" I asked, not liking the sound of this test at all. That word discomfort, I knew, was code for pain that wasn't bad enough to warrant an anesthetic but which, nevertheless, was not something any halfway normal person would voluntarily choose to experience.

"Well, sometimes people who have some kind of rheumatic disease, as we are guessing you do, can also develop inflammatory bowel disease, colitis or Crohn's disease."

"I know what Crohn's is. My brother's had Crohn's since his twenties," I told the doctor. I remembered visiting Dick a year ago after he'd had a section of his intestine removed. His entire adult life had been structured around managing his Crohn's disease. Since his bowel resection, he'd been well almost all the time. He'd gained enough weight to finally look healthy and his cheeks had a roundness that I couldn't remember seeing since he was twelve.

"I don't really think you have colitis or Crohn's. But we'll just make sure." Dr. Randall let go of my hand and stood up to leave.

"Dr. Randall? Can I ask you something?" I hesitated, not sure what the question should be. There were so many and most of them unanswerable. Like, when would I get out of here? I was often scared these days but unsure how scared it was reasonable for me to be. Probably not as scared as the young man down the hall who had testicular cancer. Or the woman in the room next to his whose groans and sobs traveled down the hallway in the night and squeezed under my door, making my heart race with the instinct to go to her. I didn't have cancer and I was not in agonizing pain. So far all I had was FUO, Fever of Unknown Origin. Or maybe Still's disease. I was still thinking about that one. My fevers had been coming and going for two weeks by now—which was pretty awful—but not fatal. And I'd only been in the hospital for eight days.

Suddenly, I felt small, greedy. Privileged. A woman with an attitude.

Dr. Randall stopped and turned back to look at me. "Well, try me. What's your question?"

I pressed forward before I could stop myself. "Do you think I'll ever get well?" I tried to sound flip, casual. As if I were kidding. As if we both knew the answer was obvious. As if I'd never doubted it for a minute.

But Dr. Randall took me seriously. He came back to my bedside and took my hand again. "I can answer that. Yes. Of course, you will."

"How do you know?"

He chuckled. "Because of the nature of your symptoms. You'll be well again. You can count on it. I'm the same age as you; that means I've been in my field as long as you've been in yours. I know what I'm talking about. You should believe me. I'm telling the truth."

"Thanks. I don't believe you, of course, but I really need to hear it. Keep telling me, every time you see me."

"Happy to," he said and left.

The colonoscopy, which Dr. Randall scheduled that same day, revealed nothing at all. As I left the procedure area in yet another wheelchair pushed by yet another hospital volunteer, Dr. Randall wished me luck and added, "Remember. You're going to get well!"

I wasn't sure Dr. Randall had facts to back up his earnest reassurance, but I tried to believe him. For the first time in a week, my fear shrank back a little.

When I returned to my room, I decided to do something proactive. I would call information (no cell phone and no phone books in hospital rooms in 1990) and ask for the phone number of one of my old therapy teachers, Dick Olney. I thought Dick might be able to help me get well.

The next day, Dr. Chan arrived before sunrise to tell me I could go home that afternoon. I stared at him, sleepy and unbelieving. I'd been longing to go home, but I hadn't imagined that when I went my illness would be coming with me. The doctor said he'd give me a prescription for high-dose aspirin. He wanted me to continue resting in bed, especially when I had a fever.

Here's what I imagined I was going home to: unwashed dishes, moldy bread on the counter, unopened mail in heaps on the dining room table, the kitchen floor covered in crumbs. Unmade beds. Three somewhat deprived children.

Here's what I *couldn't* imagine: resting in bed, fever or no, before I'd cleaned up my messy house. I also couldn't imagine having the energy to wash one dish or even locate the broom.

I remembered a short story I'd read decades before about a very busy woman, a wife and mother, who died on her feet but was so busy taking care of the house, the kids, the dog, her job, that she couldn't find the time to lie down and be dead. She just kept doing task after task after task, thinking she'd deal with being dead as soon as she had some free time.

"You're still quite ill, Mrs. Ford," Dr. Chan told me, probably in response to the stricken look on my face, "but there's nothing the hospital can do for you now that you can't do at home."

This made no sense to me at the time. It was 1990; long hospital stays were relatively common. The only reason I could think of for Dr. Chan to send me home was that my case was hopeless. I was going to die and he wanted me to be more comfortable doing it.

Dr. Chan left to fill out the discharge papers. He needed to run one more blood test; I would be discharged after lunch.

9

For Help and Health

"Who would be born must trust the bridge untried
Fling piteous wagers in that mad gambling
Nor ever ask, will this frail bridge suffice?"
—DICK OLNEY

AFTER CHRIS WENT HOME I lay in bed thinking about Dick Olney. I'd known Dick for almost twenty years. I wasn't sure if the picture I had of him in my mind now was how he'd looked when I first met him or how he'd looked two years ago, the last time I'd seen him. In my memory he'd never changed much, except for a few new wrinkles and thinner hair.

I met Dick when I signed up for his experimental writing class when I was twenty-five and about to get my bachelor's degree. I was in my seventh year of college. I'd re-enrolled at the University of Wisconsin-Milwaukee after three years of being a dropout, and first, I majored in speech pathology, then English, then general liberal arts. I finally landed on elementary education with a minor in English.

Dick was in his late forties when I was twenty-five. He was tall, with broad shoulders and big hands and feet. His face was long, with a great beak of a nose and cheeks grizzled with whiskers, his graying hair parted and combed to one side. He had a deep bass voice, soft but not quiet. A voice that made you want to listen. A voice I'd been willing to follow ever since I first heard him speak in that writing class.

The class was unconventional to say the least, designed to crack us open, to expose us to our deep personal truths so that our writing could be real. Or at least the syllabus had said something like that. In reality, the class turned out to be more like a therapy group. It was 1972; encounter group techniques, with an emphasis on catharsis and role-playing, were showing up in all kinds of venues back then, from businesses to psychiatric hospitals to classrooms. Many of us had heard about groups like this and so were willing to follow this unusual teacher even though we didn't know where we were going.

On the first night of the class Dick had us push the tables and chairs to one side and arrange the pillows he'd brought against the walls. From that night on we never sat in chairs, only on those cushions. We shared weeks of intense personal exploration, role-playing, pillow pounding, shouting, crying, and comforting. Dick was solid: confident, gentle, and skilled. Willing to offer a warm supportive hand on your back as you wept. Willing to wrap his arms around you when you felt like you were flying to pieces. Not one of us quit in spite of the high emotion and the dearth of writing assignments. By the end we were a family.

A few years later, after I'd begun graduate school, I joined Dick's group training sessions for psychotherapists. I also became his therapy client. He was my first—and one of my most important—mentors. He taught me his unique ways of working with and empowering people who came to him for help. He showed us all, clients and students alike, how to tune into the messages of our own bodies; how to listen to our own interior wisdom; how to accept ourselves right here and right now, no matter what our current condition might be. He called his method "Self-Acceptance Training."

Dick thought of himself as a guide, offering direction and safety, but also said that every time he worked with someone he explored and learned right alongside his client. At the end of every session, he would thank the person for including him in his or her exploration.

When I became a therapist myself I incorporated much of Dick Olney's Self-Acceptance Training into my work and I often used his trance-induction techniques to help my clients access unconscious strengths and resources.

It would not be exaggerating to say Dick changed my life. He believed in me in a way that no one else ever had. Or, as he would say, *I* changed my life; he only accompanied me. He was my champion and my stand-in father, stronger than my real dad and just as loving. I stayed in his therapist-training group for three years; then I started adding more traditional therapy methods to my repertoire.

Lying in bed in the hospital, I thought about Dick's emphasis on staying in tune with your body, being awake and aware, and I realized how very far away I was from that. Ever since the strange rashes and fatigue started months ago, I'd turned away from my body as much as I could. Maybe—it occurred to me now—in order to recover, I might have to let myself feel the enormity of what was going on in me, become awake and aware. But I was too tired, too scared, too worn down. I needed Dick to help me be brave enough, strong enough, to get all the way back inside this sick body.

I sat up in bed, dialed information, and wrote down Dick's number. I called him and left a message, asking him to come and help me find my way one more time.

At noon on the day of my discharge Dick strode into my room. "Hello, Judith," he said, warmly. "How good it is to see you."

He sat down in the chair beside my bed and peered into my eyes, as if he could read there everything I might be hiding even from myself. His own eyes were clear and bright, despite the way the lids now hung heavy over them, the pouches beneath.

It seemed incongruous to have him here. Dick, the source of so much strength in my twenties, beside my bed in that room where every object—the shiny bare floor, the IV stand, the chimes that sounded in the hallway, the very walls—seemed to be sapping my energy. Even before Dick spoke a word I felt more hopeful.

He picked up my hand and leaned in closer. "What's been happening with you, my dear?"

I told him about the long slow emergence of symptoms, how eventually they'd landed me in the hospital, how no one knew how to help me. I told him my immune system seemed to be operating overtime, damaging my organs in an effort to defeat something that was probably not there. "If I were stronger," I found myself saying, "maybe I could convince my body to stop fighting itself, but I've never felt weaker in my life."

He nodded. "Mmmhmm. So you want now to relocate that strength?" I nodded yes. Then he began talking in that irresistible, rhythmic voice of his. "Remember a time when you felt just as strong as you need to be right now."

I recognized the beginning of a trance induction, the rhythmic pattern, the soft voice. I didn't know that since I'd last seen Dick he'd been studying with Native American medicine people. He'd gone on vision quests in the deserts of New Mexico and in the Wisconsin woods—real vision quests, outdoors in the real world, with no food or water for three days and nights.

I did my best to follow Dick's instructions without knowing exactly what he had in mind, without asking him a single question. I was forty-two, way past the age of following anyone blindly. But this was Dick. Before I'd known how to trust myself I'd trusted him. I would have gone anywhere he led me. And he knew that.

"Your body knows," he said. "When in your life have you felt the opposite of your current weakness?"

My eyes, which I didn't remember having closed, popped open. "I don't know. I can't think of any time like that. I can't do this. I'm too sick."

He went on as if I hadn't said anything. His own eyes remained closed. In the same tone, the same rhythm, he said, "If it's been long, then think back to long ago. Go as far back as you need to."

I closed my eyes again, sliding back underneath his voice, into the familiar trance. When Dick asked me again when I'd felt the opposite of weak, I remembered. I'd felt strong often: Working with clients. The first time I ran eight miles. My weekly modern dance class. Hiking in the Colorado Rockies. The time I walked to the bottom of the Grand Canyon.

Dick asked me to go there now, back to the Grand Canyon, and so that's what I did, seeing it all as if I were there again, living it. The long hike down the Kaibob Trail. The weight of my backpack, a gallon canteen of water slung over each of my shoulders. The DNR signs along the way that warn you to drink your water, "NOW." The pink trail dust, soft as talcum powder, on the canyon floor. The rattlesnake, the same pink as the trail dust, that slithered into the brush. The ravens that slid up and down on the air currents overhead.

It didn't seem odd to me when Dick suggested that I, myself, was a raven and then, a little later, when he suggested I was a pink snake. This was the most fun I'd had in weeks, imagining I was something other than sick, feeling strong and playful, instinctive and untroubled.

I was so deeply into the experience I was surprised when I heard Dick's voice calling me to wake up as if he was calling to me from very far away. I didn't want to wake up. But even as I resisted I lost the feel of the hot sun, the sensation of having wings, the sensation of sand sliding against my belly. Instead, I became aware of the texture of the sheet against my skin, the weight of the blanket, the light in the room filtering through my eyelids.

When I opened my eyes I saw that Dick's eyes were still closed. He was repeating something over and over in a metronomic voice, saying I was going to get well, stronger and better, with every passing hour. He said it again and again: "more and more well, stronger and stronger."

Then he said what sounded like a prayer. "*O Mitakuye Oyasin.*" He repeated it three times, followed each time by these words, "We come only for help and health." I learned later that this was addressed to the spirits he believed were guiding us. The foreign words were, I think, in a language spoken by the Tewa Indians in New Mexico or maybe the Ho Chunk tribe in Wisconsin. The words meant something like "we are all one," or "we are all connected."

Dick sat silent for a few minutes, eyes still closed, and then began to sing. "Comes now the sun, comes now the light, comes now the sun, comes now the light. Into her heart, into her heart." His voice was off-key but he sang with conviction. I couldn't help but wonder what a nurse or doctor might think if they walked by my room. It felt almost sacrilegious to be doing something so entirely non-medical in this medical setting.

I thought I heard him whisper something that sounded like, "Grandmother, she is yours now," right before he opened his eyes.

"Hello," he said to me. "How are you feeling?"

I was feeling relaxed, I told him. And peaceful. I didn't tell him that I thought I might recover after all, because I didn't realize I was thinking that until after he left. I slept soundly for at least an hour then until a nurse came with the wheelchair that Chris would use to take me to the car. It was time to get dressed and go home.

10

A Literal Hairpin

"Are there known techniques for surviving a literal
hairpin turn in the midst of a life span—early or late—
without forgetting the better parts of who you were?"

—REYNOLDS PRICE, *A Whole New Life*

July 21, 1990, eight days after admission

IT DIDN'T TAKE LONG to pack my suitcase; some dirty underwear, the
t-shirt I'd been sleeping in (I hated those flimsy hospital gowns), toothbrush, shampoo, maybe some hand lotion, Jessie's worn teddy bear, a few
books, mostly unread, and that notebook I'd intended to write in but had
only managed a few pages. The last things I packed were the photos of
my children. I sat down on my unmade bed, worn out from packing,
and stared at them. Since it was late afternoon, my fever was rising and I
was shivering, trying not to, but shivering anyway. I wanted so much not
to be shivering anymore. These harbingers of fever were more powerful than the optimism I'd felt briefly in Dick Olney's presence, making
it near impossible to continue to buy into the myth of wellness. Or even
better-ness.

As I sat with my black-and-white-paper kids in my lap, my favorite nurse, Carol, came in to say good-bye. I sat up a little straighter and
smiled a greeting.

She sat down next to and a little behind me, her weight creating a dip in the mattress. She was about my age, heavier and shorter, with thin curly, brown hair, and a face that was what my mother would have called "plain," not unattractive, but ordinary. Carol never wore make-up and was always dressed in white pants and a white, short-sleeved top made of a shiny synthetic fabric. The shape of the uniform, combined with her big, cushy chest, gave her the look of a large unadorned white box. A box with sensible white shoes sticking out at the bottom, from cuffs that were hemmed a little too high.

Carol had worked at Columbia Hospital since she was twenty. She knew where everything, and every*one*, was located. She knew who could be pushed and who couldn't. Which doctors would yell at her if she called them in the middle of the night on behalf of a patient and which ones would thank her. If one of her patients was in pain, Carol would give them their pain meds a little early, if it was safe, and she'd sit with that patient until the drug took effect. When Chris had arrived after visiting hours one night (visiting hours ended at ten in those days), Carol had pretended he was invisible. Sometimes he'd stayed till midnight.

I wished all the nurses on my unit were like Carol. Sitting beside me on the bed, she emitted a soothing warmth.

"How are you doing?" she asked me. And before I could summon up a socially appropriate and falsely cheerful response, she clarified, "I mean, how do you feel about going home?" She craned her neck to look at Nic's picture "Cute kid. I bet you miss him."

"I do miss him," I told her, "but I'm not sure I'm in any shape to take care of him."

"This isn't what you expected, is it?" said Carol. "You're supposed to be able to come here and get fixed. And *then* you leave. It feels all wrong to leave when you're not fixed and no one knows why."

"It would help if someone could tell me I'm going to be well again. It doesn't work when I tell myself."

"I think you'll get well." Carol put a hand on my arm and went on, "It's going to be rough going home, though. Probably not much there has changed, but you're going to feel as if *everything* is different. Because you're different."

"What do you mean, different?"

"I mean, you know some things now that you didn't know before. That you wish you didn't have to know. You'll never again be the same person you were before you got sick."

For a minute or two, I couldn't speak. An unnatural stillness seemed to have erased the usual hospital noises. Along with my voice. I hadn't expected this insightfulness from Carol. She was good, even wonderful, but I hadn't realized she was also wise. I turned so I could look more directly at her. I couldn't hold her eyes for more than a few seconds, my own welling up with tears. I ended up staring at the white, plastic buttons on her uniform and her nametag, "Carol Nelson RN."

She kept talking. "The people around you who haven't had experiences like this don't know what you know. Like, that you can't ever predict or control what's going to happen to you next. And death is real to you now in a way that it wasn't before, isn't it? You can never again *not* know these things. You know them."

"How did you know I feel that way? That's right." I whispered through my tightened throat. Carol gathered me into her arms. I gave up pretending. I cried hard, really hard, like a baby, with noisy gasps and sniffles.

"I just knew," she said.

11

A Demented Woman

"I imagined [my illness] as a love affair with a demented woman who demanded things I had never done before."

—ANATOLE BROYARD, *Intoxicated by My Illness*

July 21, 1990

CHRIS PUSHED MY WHEELCHAIR (required by the hospital) out the hospital's front door into the hot, humid city air and I was startled by the bright sunlight and the sudden noise. While I waited for him to return the wheelchair to the parking valet, I leaned against the rough bricks of the hospital wall, marveling at the vivid green of the trees that shaded parts of the visitor parking lot, the little explosions of light where the sun struck glass and chrome on the parked cars. The shininess of the black tar oozing up through a crack in the asphalt driveway.

The sounds were even more intense. A nearby tree full of bird chatter, a bus shredding the air as it accelerated from a stop sign. Car engines, air conditioners, footsteps, and loud voices. I wanted to close my eyes, wrap my arms up over my head, stop my ears.

You wouldn't think that spending just eight days indoors would have done this to me. But it had. During the first few days that I'd been hospitalized, I'd consciously tried to stay connected to the outside world. I'd called my office twice, called the several clients I was most concerned about to reassure them that I'd be back, and, whenever I could get away with it, I'd kept my hospital room window as wide open as it could go. The fresh air, the traffic noise, the occasional outdoor voices that reached me through the screen reassured me that I wasn't permanently cut off from the world. I wouldn't care about any of that later in the summer, when I was way sicker, but that first week, feeling so abruptly imprisoned, I'd cared a great deal.

As over-stimulated as I felt standing in the summer heat waiting for Chris to pick me up, I was also elated. *Oh yeah!* I thought, or something like that. *This is making me tremble but I love it.*

By the time Chris parked the car in front of our house (a ten-minute drive from the hospital) I was exhausted. I crept up the stairs to our second-floor flat, hanging onto the banister, and sat down on the first piece of furniture I came to, the old red sofa.

"Nic! Mommy's home! Hooray!" Barbara shouted. She clapped her hands and hopped from one foot to the other, showing twenty-two-month-old Nic how she expected him to feel. Nic looked up at her impassively from his spot on the floor and then turned to study me. He quickly dismissed me, turning back to the toy-filled laundry basket he'd been in the process of emptying onto the living room rug. Showing me the same disregard he'd shown when he'd visited me in the hospital.

Months later, I'd work hard to glue him and me back together again. But that day, I didn't feel even a shred of the heartbreak I'd felt during his visits in the hospital. It seems odd to me now that I didn't care about his reaction that day when I first came home. I'd always been the kind of parent who delighted in every physical aspect of my babies. The smell of their necks and scalps, the warmth of their fat fingers in mine, the fuzz that substituted for hair in their first couple years of life. I understood why women of my mother's generation would sometimes say, "Oooh, you're so cute! I could just eat you up!" I knew the feeling. But not that day. The only thing I felt that day as I watched Nic, taking in his pink-cheeked face, his brow furrowed in concentration, his diaper-thick overalls, was admiration that he'd been so successful at latching onto another adult, Barbara, when his own mother was clearly not dependable. Smart boy. Good for him.

I sat on the worn couch near the door, feeling its scratchy fabric glue itself to the backs of my sweating legs, watching Nic's activities for the same reason I would later watch hours of daytime TV in bed; I was too tired to do anything else.

Nic upended the basket and spread the rest of its contents out in a single layer on the floor. Barbara sat down beside him. Nic put a blue plastic doughnut in her hand. "Blue, round," she said. Next he handed her a little square Golden book. "Ooooooh, the Grover book! Let's read that!" she exclaimed with an enthusiasm I couldn't remember ever having.

I had no inclination to get off that sofa despite its scratchiness until I noticed, fifteen minutes later, that I'd stopped sweating and had begun to shiver. It was mid-July, temperature near 90, humidity almost as high, no air-conditioning, second-floor flat. And suddenly I was freezing. I knew that meant a fever was building.

So I roused myself and went to bed. For the first few seconds, lying between the soft, clean sheets with the smell of fresh-mown grass wafting through the window, I felt relieved to be at home. The robin's egg blue of the bedroom walls, the warm dark oak baseboards and window frames, the four-poster bed, soothed me. The things on the walls. A picture of our house, done in needlepoint by my mother; a framed wedding picture taken in 1987, Chris in his thick dorky glasses, me with my big curly hair. On the wall above our bed in an oval frame, a poem written by my friend Marty, a wedding present. "Four individuals," it began "asked about/ miracles today in our presence/indicating the desire for swift/ change by virtue of chance resurrection." Swift change. Chance resurrection. I could have used a miracle that day, that summer. A swift change. A little resurrection.

The few minutes of pleasure I felt being in my own bed, a short-lived interval of hope, soon gave way to the same old garbage, the ache in my knees and fingers, the shivering, the dull despair.

As I lay there hating what my body was doing, I thought about how strange it was that my high fevers were always preceded by chills. Months later, I'd research this phenomenon. Here's what I found out: When your immune system identifies a threat such as a virus or a bacterium, it produces something called pyrogens (*pyro*, as in "fire"). Pyrogens signal the hypothalamus, the body's thermostat, to increase your temperature, because heat kills viruses and bacteria. To create this heat the hypothalamus uses the same mechanism as the one that warms you when you're outside ice-skating: blood vessel constriction and shivering. That eventually creates heat. Before the shivering heats you up you put on layers of sweaters or crawl under blankets. Which also heats you up. Once your temperature is high enough to help fight off the threat, shivering stops and you experience the full force of the fever. What I still don't understand—and no one has been able to explain it to me—is why, without an outside trigger like a virus or a bacterium, my body responded with fevers, fevers that could spike all the way to 106.

I don't remember if I wondered about any of this that summer, but if I had I couldn't have wondered for long. The fevers blunted my thinking, made me slow and stupid.

I turned the electric blanket to "high" and pulled the heavy lamb's wool quilt up to my nose. The scabby skin of my shoulders and upper arms caught on the cotton quilt cover every time they brushed against it. There were a few minutes of ease as the chills stopped. Then the fever hit its peak and I threw the blankets onto the floor.

I reached for the remote lying on the bedside table and turned on the new TV Chris had bought for our bedroom. An extravagance, given all the money I was losing by not being able to work. But I was grateful now for his impracticality as I tried to empty my mind into the vacuum of *Let's Make a Deal, Family Ties,* and *The Brady Bunch.*

I lay on top of the sheet in just a t-shirt and underwear, a breeze from the open window blowing over my dry, hot skin. The flat sound of the TV filled the room along with Nic's and Barbara's voices rising and falling, floating through the walls, twittering like birds. Timmy bounced onto the bed at some point, arranging his large, furry self against my side, his chin on my shoulder or my chest.

Whenever I was sad or sick, Timmy had a way of looking at me, searching my face, with what seemed like deep and accurate compassion. He would become my constant attendant the next two months, as my symptoms shifted and worsened. He'd lay his chin across my feet when I sat in a chair; he'd follow me to the bathroom, curl up on the bathroom rug and wait, cuddle close whenever I was in bed. Always watching me with those shining black eyes, like pools of deep living mud.

1 2

Water Buffalo

"I love people who harness themselves,
an ox to a heavy cart,
who pull like water buffalo, with massive patience,
who strain in the mud and the muck
to move things forward,
who do what has to be done, again and again."

—MARGE PIERCY, *To Be of Use*

THE MORNING FOLLOWING MY release from the hospital and every day thereafter, for the next three weeks, I called Dr. Chan, as he had instructed, to report on my condition. Between those phone calls I was mostly in bed, watching TV or trying to read. I took the high doses of aspirin that Dr. Chan had prescribed and now and then I made an effort to play with Nic. After three days, my ears began to ring. I could barely hear Nic talking—or anything else besides the high C that droned in my head. It was a side effect of the aspirin, Dr. Chan told me. He changed my prescription to another non-steroidal anti-inflammatory medicine called Indocin. The next step, he said, would be Prednisone. He wanted to avoid that as long as possible because of the side effects. Things like heart damage, glaucoma, diabetes, deterioration of the hip joints. And in a few very unfortunate patients, psychosis.

I was all for the Indocin. And at first it seemed like the miracle I'd been longing for. After my first dose my temperature fell to 98.7 within a few hours. It was the first time it had been that low for two weeks. My knees and fingers were still swollen and I still felt tired, but not having a fever was wonderful. I didn't expect it to last so I took immediate advantage. I got out of bed in the middle of the morning, went into the living room and watched *Sesame Street* with Nic on my lap. I carried on long conversations with Jessie and Becky. I stayed up until after lunch. By late afternoon I was shivering again, my fever rising (no doubt in response to hordes of pyrogens rallying my hypothalamus). I retreated to my bed with Timmy.

The next few days were similar. Little or no fever in the morning, rising fever in the afternoon, sky-high fever at night. I felt somewhat like myself—a diminished version but myself—in the mornings. One morning Nic came into my room with a book, pushed it into my hands and said, "Read Nic." So I gave it a whirl. What could be hard about reading a toddler's picture book with only three or four lines on a page? But I couldn't muster my former reading style, the animation, the funny voices. After a few minutes Nic took the book out of my hands, closed it, and walked out of the room without a word or a backward glance. He wouldn't bring me another book until September.

On the fifth day post-hospital my mother-in-law, Betty, came to babysit Nic. And me, too, I supposed, in spite of the fact that I didn't need much. My appetites for stimulation or food were virtually nonexistent.

My weight had continued to drop. On the day Betty arrived I weighed 114, ten pounds less than before I went to the hospital. The Indocin continued to moderate my fevers though. By the end of that week, my highest temps in the evening were only 100. I'd stopped having chills and no new red rash was appearing. I didn't feel great but at least I was alert. I could make it all the way to the end of a thirty-minute TV show or a magazine article. I began to think that maybe I'd turned a corner.

On Friday, a week after my discharge, I decided to go to work for a few hours a day. Although I still felt weak I assumed the Indocin would keep doing what it was doing and that by the next Thursday, the day I planned to go to the clinic, I'd be in great shape.

One morning when my fever was low I called Doris, our clinic's billing person and office manager, and asked her to schedule ten of my former clients on Thursday and Friday. There were several people I was particularly concerned about. One of these, Sarah, had revealed in her

last session that she'd been repeatedly sexually abused by a group of pe-
dophiles when she was a child. Like many victims of abuse, she'd been
threatened that if she ever told anyone, she or someone she loved would
be killed. She'd kept her silence for nearly thirty years, until she whispered
those few sentences to me. She'd left the session feeling both relieved and
terrified. That had happened just a few weeks before I landed in the hospital. I knew Sarah would need to hear my voice in order to believe I
was sick, only sick, not hurt by her abusers. When I told her what was
happening to me she was suspicious. "How do you know for sure they
haven't poisoned you?" she asked.

"I know because this illness began long before I met you."

I didn't know for sure that that was true but I was beginning to remember symptoms, bone-deep fatigue and months of low fever, that had
scared the shit out of me ten years before these current symptoms. Every
few days for two years back then I'd felt exhausted and achy, with a chronic
sore throat and low-grade fevers. Not every day though. There were days
when I felt totally normal, relieved, believing the illness was over. But it
wasn't. It came back over and over until finally, after many nights of extra
sleep, a healthier diet and some healing imagery, the illness didn't come
back anymore. Until now. So much worse now, could this be the same as
that mysterious illness ten years ago? I saw six different doctors back then
and one of the doctors finally diagnosed it as chronic fatigue. And maybe
that was right. Whatever that illness was I hadn't thought about it for ten
years. Until now.

Not only did I not think much about this history while talking to
Sarah; I didn't think about the connection of the old illness and this new
one until many years later when I learned more about Still's disease.
Those earliest symptoms? Still's disease in its earliest form.

Sarah took me at my word, that my illness had begun long before I
met her, but I knew she'd need to quiz me for more details next time we
met, before she'd accept that my being sick wasn't—on an energetic level
at the very least—her fault.

The other clients on the list I gave Doris were all people who'd been
in therapy with me for a long time, working on complex issues, making
steady but slow progress. They relied on me, these long-termers, and I felt
as guilty being away from them as I did about not being available to my
own kids. These people needed me.

And on some level I needed them, too. I hoped seeing my clients
would pull me back into my usual self. I was beginning to think that I

would never be any more well than I was right then, clear-eyed mornings leading to sick afternoons. If that didn't change I'd have to learn to work with it. Why not start now? Besides, we needed the money.

Although that seemed like unassailable logic at the time, I see now in hindsight that going back to work right then, before I'd had even one full day of being energetic and pain-and fever-free, was unwise, if not insane. That kind of unwise, insane-but-determined decision was (probably still is) typical of me. Press on regardless.

When I told Dr. Chan my plan, he was pleased but warned me to go straight to bed as soon as possible after work. Every day, no exceptions.

The day before I was going to return to work I decided to begin a daily walking routine to regain some of the strength I'd lost from being inactive for the past three weeks. I pulled on a t-shirt and a pair of shorts (at least an inch too big in the waist, hanging off my bony hips), put on my running shoes and stepped outside. I made it past two houses and then I started to feel peculiar. I kept walking and trying to focus on my senses, hoping that would make me feel solid, real. Awake and aware. I made an effort to feel the hot sun on my bare arms, to notice the dappled shadows cast by the ash trees on the road. I focused on the sound of the cicadas screaming in the humid trees; I lingered on the scent of lilies in a neighbor's garden. It didn't help for more than a second. Everything around me—the leaves, the lilies, the trees, the sunlight—felt unreal and wrong. Or maybe I was unreal and wrong.

It was as if I was in a movie set or in a dream. It wasn't like the trance state I'd experienced with Dick Olney or the self-hypnotic state I could put myself into when I was upset. It wasn't soothing at all. I felt separated from everything. My legs didn't feel normal; their movements were abrupt and floppy, as if my body was a wooden doll and I was a puppeteer pulling strings to make my arms and legs rise and fall. It took every ounce of concentration I could rally to get all the way around the block without sitting down on someone's lawn.

The only time I'd ever felt anything similar was in my early twenties when a friend's boyfriend gave me some very strong hashish. I'd expected it to bring me pleasure. I'd expected enhancement of my senses, the kind of relaxation and expansiveness that pot can produce. But instead I just felt peculiar. And not in a good way. After eating an entire package of Oreos and a bag of potato chips, I sat in my living room watching the clock, caught in a distorted alternative universe. The only thing I could do was crawl through the expanded minutes until my body cleansed itself of the chemicals. Which it did after a few hours.

I thought about that hash experience as I crossed the lawn trying to hurry to my front door, hoping no one was watching me. Maybe this weirdness was a chemical reaction like the hash.

When I got inside I looked up Indocin in my very own copy of *The Physician's Desk Reference*. Among the list of possible side effects of Indocin were: "mental confusion, psychic disturbances and muzziness." Muzziness. Yup. That was it. I called Dr. Chan and asked him if the muzziness would go away in time. He'd never heard of muzziness and couldn't predict. "Give it a few more days," he said.

13

Press on Regardless

"The antidote to exhaustion is not necessarily rest.
The antidote to exhaustion is wholeheartedness."

—DAVID WHYTE, *Clear Mind, Wild Heart*

THE NEXT MORNING MY friend Barbara buckled Nic into his car seat and drove us all to the old Victorian building that housed the clinic I'd been working at for two months. Leaving my former clinic and moving in with Therapies East Associates had been rather like leaving a bad marriage to go live with a lover. Painful, guilt-producing, exciting, and rectifying. And so newly begun that when I went into the hospital I still hadn't finished hanging pictures or organizing my files in my new space.

Barbara stopped the car in front of Therapies East. The practice owned its location, a gray house with dark red trim and two large baskets of pink fuchsia plants hanging over a white rattan bench on the front porch. The morning sun glinted off the front windows. The sight of all that color and light made me happy to be back despite how tired I still was. My legs trembled as I walked to the door. My knees were swollen and aching. I turned to blow a kiss to Nic. He wasn't looking at me but Barbara was watching to make sure I made it up the front steps. I put on a reassuring smile for her and waved, meaning, "Go home now. I'm fine." She waited until I walked inside.

Yesterday I'd made arrangements to switch offices with Madelyn, whose office was on the first floor, next to the waiting room, instead of on the third floor where my office was. I walked into the billing office, located in what used to be the dining room of the old house, feeling suddenly shy, as if I didn't belong there. I imagined my new coworkers thinking of me as someone prone to collapse; I imagined they regretted inviting me to join them in the practice. The office manager didn't give me time to linger on my lack of market value. She launched into questions before I'd set my briefcase down on the table.

"Doris," I said, "I've told you how wonderful you are, haven't I?"

"A few times." She smiled back. "But I can always hear it again." Doris was a few years older than I was and treated us all as if we were her adolescent children. She was bossy and warm and essential to the success and good reputation of the clinic. She held out a stack of pink "While you were away" slips and said, "You don't look like you should be back yet but since you are, here are a few people who want to talk to you. Do you want me to call your other clients and start scheduling them for next week?"

"Yes." I handed Doris a list of names and numbers and my appointment book. As I left to collect my waiting client and lead her to Madelyn's office, Doris already had the phone nestled against her ear, calling the first person on my list.

In that first session I struggled to listen to a young, single mother, Carolyn, who'd followed me here from my previous practice. Carolyn was tall, blond, and slender, and as tough as they come. A year ago she'd brought her seven-year-old son to see me because he was difficult for his teachers to manage. In the intake, she'd told me she was a lousy mother for Jack because she couldn't remember a thing about being a kid herself. I'd seen Jack just long enough to identify his superior intelligence and attention deficit hyperactivity disorder and to help his mother get him into and adjusted to a special needs classroom. Jack had quickly calmed down. His mother, however, had begun to have nightmares, then memories, of repeated sexual abuse by a neighbor.

Carolyn and I had been through a lot together. I wished I could be honest with her now and just tell her, "Look. I won't charge you for this hour. You just sit there and be client-like and I'll see if I can remember what it is I'm supposed to do with you. If it doesn't work we'll both go home."

But of course I said nothing of the kind. I struggled to hear her with more than my auditory nerves, with the thoroughly and expensively trained inner hearing that gets so ingrained in an experienced therapist that it's impossible to turn it off. I looked for that skill now. It wasn't there. Throughout the hour I smiled and nodded at Carolyn. I hoped I didn't look as stupid as I felt. Carolyn looked back at me suspiciously but kept talking. Carolyn was good at talking. I didn't need to say much; she filled the minutes on her own.

Those minutes seemed to stretch for days. When the session was finally nearing its end—just five minutes left—I was suddenly overcome with intense abdominal cramps. I took a deep breath and reached for my appointment book.

"You think you're ready to handle this?" Carolyn asked as we scheduled the next week's appointment. I hadn't told her I was still sick; I'd had Doris call and cancel her session the week before though, and Carolyn was no dummy.

"Of course. I'm just a little tired today."

Carolyn looked at me doubtfully as I ushered her out. I dashed for the bathroom the instant I was out of her sight. I barely made it. Diarrhea again, just like I'd had in the hospital. It went on and on. Each time I stood up I was gripped by cramps again. I was cold and shaky, drenched in sweat. I closed my eyes, leaned my head against the cool, tiled wall, and practiced Lamaze breathing. When this didn't help, I whispered the Buddhist *Heart Sutra*, a chant I'd used in the last stages of labor with my daughter.

"*Gate, gate, paragate parasaṃgate bodhi svaha.*" Over and over, leaning against the wall.

My body quieted. I started to feel better. "I'm okay," I told myself. "I'm fine."

The day proceeded this way. I spent each session mentally running after the trailing ends of my own insubstantial thoughts. More than half of them eluded me. I let my clients do most of the talking. At the end of every hour I rushed to the bathroom, which blessedly was right next to Madelyn's office. By noon I was spent. My fever was starting to rise. I sat alone in the clinic's kitchen choking down a peanut butter and jelly sandwich and telling myself not to cry. This was only my first day back, I told myself, and tomorrow was bound to go better.

I was wrong about that last part.

The night following that first day back to work I was awakened at 1:00 a.m. when something grabbed hold of my intestines and twisted. Timmy padded behind me to the bathroom and settled himself in the doorway. More diarrhea. (It's an interesting sidelight—interesting to me, anyway—that I can't to this day spell diarrhea correctly. Every time I type it a wavy red line appears beneath it, courtesy of autocorrect. Of course, being a therapist and an adept speller, I think this might mean something about how I feel about diarrhea.)

I sat on the toilet for an hour in the middle of the night. Puzzled. Worried. Exhausted.

I tried my relaxation breathing and my "gate-gate"s. I begged God, whose existence I was uncertain of, to help me, to save me, to let me go back to bed. Nothing helped. Then, there was a pause in the pain. I waited a few seconds. A few more. The worst, I thought, might be over. I pulled myself up, gripping the edge of the sink. I reached down to flush and straightened up again in shock. The toilet bowl was full of blood. My stomach lurched. I grabbed the sink again. I told myself this wasn't as bad as it seemed. I looked again. It was actually worse. I was going to die. What else could this mean?

I averted my eyes and flushed away the evidence. When I looked again the water in the bowl was clear. "It wasn't really that bad," I told myself again. "It's just because of how often I've had diarrhea." But I'd read too many medical books. I knew the blood was not a good sign.

14

Bloody Bites

"Many carnivorous animals devour their prey
alive; the usual method seems to be to subdue the
victim by drowning or grasping it so it can't flee;
then eating it whole in a series of bloody bites."

—ANNIE DILLARD, *Pilgrim at Tinker Creek*

I WALKED BACK TO bed, running my hands along the hallway wall to keep my balance. Chris woke up when I pulled the blankets back and slid under them.

"Are you all right?" He mumbled

"I don't know. I had diarrhea again."

"Mmmmm." A long pause. "Okay, now?"

"I don't know. I hope so." Another long pause. "It was full of blood."

No response from Chris. He'd fallen back to sleep. I lay beside him with the dog's head and front paws across my knees. I imagined invisible rays of canine healing emanating from Timmy and wrapping around my middle. For a few seconds, I pretended to be comforted by this but I wasn't. No way was I going to be able to sleep. I was hyper-alert, the way I would be if there was a newborn in the house again.

Within ten minutes, I was back in the bathroom. I paged through the few magazines that sat on the square brown basket next to the toilet.

Discover, Health, Time. Nothing in them held my attention. I picked up a dog-eared copy of Annie Dillard's *Pilgrim at Tinker Creek.* I had to read every sentence two or three times before I could make sense of it.

"Many carnivorous animals devour their prey alive."[1]

I found these words strangely soothing. My mind floated off into Dillard's world of brutality and death while my body went on emptying without me.

Two hours later I was able to get up from the toilet. This time I didn't look before I flushed.

I went back to bed with my head full of the habits of giant water bugs and praying mantises. I fell asleep but only for an hour. I woke at four and ran for the bathroom a third time. Again the toilet bowl filled with blood. I didn't need to look. I felt it, I smelled it. I was bleeding out. A distant part of me was telling me to take action, to save myself. But all I could think to do was repeat the phrases I always used when I was scared. *Don't overreact. Breathe. By morning, this will be over.* And wisdom from my mother: *Nothing is as scary by day as it is in the middle of the night.*

I could hardly get a full breath around my growing horror.

I was still talking to myself as the marbled glass of the bathroom window faded from black to gray. The birds started up. Early morning, five o'clock or so. Still not daring to go back to bed, I read a little more Dillard. "We wake, if we ever wake at all, to mystery, rumors of death, beauty, violence."[2] The effort of holding the book open tired my hands. I set it down on my lap, draped one arm across the lip of the sink and rested my head there. The book fell to the floor. I dozed off. Just before seven I woke up, took a shower, and got dressed for work.

1. Dillard, *Pilgrim at Tinker Creek*, 8.
2. Dillard, *Pilgrim at Tinker Creek*, 4.

15

The Angel in My Blood

"I think I'd kill to stay alive,
at least myself,

and if you can't accept that
you don't know the angel in my blood.

—MAX RITVO, "Name My Time of Death"

I MADE IT THROUGH the following morning in the same desperate way I had the day before. That afternoon I called Dr. Chan and reported my symptoms. "It seems to have stopped now," I told him. He didn't sound worried but recommended a colonoscopy and the bone marrow test. I made the appointments quickly without thinking about what any of it might mean.

I went to work for one more very long, exhausted day. That night too I woke up over and over with my skin itching and my bowels driving me to the bathroom. Nevertheless, I scheduled fourteen clients for the following week.

On Monday morning between therapy appointments I went to see the dermatologist to see if my rash could be identified. The dermatologist, a squirrel-like little man, with coarse, gray hair; piercing, dark eyes; and twitchy body movements, told me he didn't recognize it. He recommended cortisone cream and Benadryl pills, both of which I'd already been using to no effect. I left disappointed, thinking he was rather stupid.

On Tuesday afternoon, I had that bone marrow test, which revealed nothing abnormal.

On Wednesday Dr. Chan agreed I should stop taking the Indocin since it made me feel so unlike myself. Within hours the muzzy feeling lifted.

On Thursday, I had a very uncomfortable colonoscopy. Uncomfortable—actually, very painful, despite large IV doses of Versed—because by that time my entire colon was inflamed. It looked, Dr. Randall told me, like someone had scraped the lining of my colon against a gravel road.

"I'm reasonably sure you have ulcerative colitis," he announced once I was dressed and ready to go home. "A few of your symptoms still puzzle me—your rash isn't typical and your systemic symptoms came before the colon inflammation; usually it's the opposite. Everything else fits, though. And this is good news. Colitis is treatable."

Dr. Randall told me I'd need to stay in bed until my symptoms improved, until my blood work returned to normal, the inflammation of my spleen and liver subsided, the diarrhea stopped and I had no more of those spiking fevers. He was going to prescribe Prednisone which, he assured me, would bring the fevers down almost immediately.

"And," he added in a scolding tone, "you have to eat. You're losing weight you can't afford to lose. Eat lightly but eat."

I changed out of my hospital gown and robe, back into my familiar shorts and t-shirt and met the doctor outside the changing room. I had one more question for him.

"What if all this doesn't work?"

That's when he told me that if this approach didn't work he would remove my colon.

I stared at him. *Did I hear that right? He's saying I might have to have my colon taken out?*

"You mean, have a hole in my belly with a pouch to poop in?" The words spilled out of my mouth before I could think of a more delicate way to say this.

Dr. Randall sat down on a nearby vinyl sofa, looked me in the eyes and with a very serious tone (meant to soothe me, I imagined) said, "A colectomy does mean an ostomy. But it also means a complete cure. Not only a cure for the diarrhea," the doctor continued, with the enthusiasm of a car salesman describing the sunroof, the anti-lock brakes, the leather seats, the cruise control. "A colectomy would mean no more rash, no anemia, no fluid around your heart, no more enlarged spleen, no abnormal liver function."

I was finding it difficult to join him in his joy.

"What if I don't want to have my colon removed?"

"Stop worrying about the what-if's, Mrs. Ford. You're going to get well, I promise. It won't happen quickly, but it will happen."

The next morning I wrote a letter for Doris to send to my clients, telling them my diagnosis and that I would be returning to work when I was fully recovered.

16

No Short Cut, No Invisible Path

"The only path to Nirvana
(. . .)
No short cut . . .
no devious way . . .
no dubious method
and no invisible path"

—SATHYA NARYANA, "The Path to Nirvana"

I DID MY BEST to follow Dr. Randall's instructions: "Go to bed. Rest." The go-to-bed part I could do but not the resting. My body no longer knew how to rest, my muscles constantly tense in a futile effort to escape the colon cramps, the weakness, the misery. I hadn't eaten anything much for weeks. I couldn't remember why I used to like food. I felt myself diminishing with each passing hour. I imagined turning into smoke, water vapor, a shadow.

Nic came to crawl around on my bed now and then. I appreciated him as one appreciates a painting or a sculpture. I liked his white-blond hair, his huge blue eyes, and his riveting intelligent gaze, incongruous in so small a person. He was interesting, even beautiful. After three or four minutes of climbing on Mommy, Nic, sensing my detachment, would leave for more responsive terrain. I was usually glad to see him go.

On the morning of the fourth post-colonoscopy day, my friend Claire called to see how I was doing.

"It's hard to keep going," I told her. "I don't see what the point is."

"I asked my psychic about your illness yesterday," she informed me. "And she said your illness was an allergy to a drug, an antihistamine. Selfdine or Feldane? Are you taking something like that? She said you should stop."

"Seldane? I haven't taken it in months. I think they took it off the market."

"Well, all I can say is that's what she said. She said you'd been contaminated."

"I feel contaminated."

"My psychic said you'll get well when you really want to."

"What the hell is that supposed to mean? Don't tell me stuff like that. I hate it."

Claire paused for a few seconds. I didn't fill in the silence. I didn't have the energy right then to say any more about how I felt about that belief (common among some of my colleagues and friends, including Claire) that sick people choose to be sick and can choose not to be sick. Claire and I'd had several prickly talks about this over the years. She remained a staunch believer that our minds create everything that happens to us and that we invite bad things into our lives in order to learn from them.

"I heard an interesting story in yoga yesterday. A Zen teaching story. Wanna hear it?" She went on as if I hadn't just been irritable with her.

I didn't want to hear it. I wanted to put the heavy phone down and close my eyes. I expected more of the woo-woo trash I hated. I believed in science. I believed in happenstance, random events. I believed that illnesses, like accidents, are neither optional nor desired. Nor deserved. Suffering is also not optional. We almost never get a choice. Random shit happens all the time.

But here's the tricky part which occurs to me as I write this: Despite my marriage to science and rational thought, I've also always practiced my own form of preventive magic, consisting of healthy habits and an extreme faith in my own goal setting and determination. Staying in motion. Before my illness I believed not only that I could stay in good health by doing all the right things, but I also believed I could choose to learn, do, or accomplish anything I wholeheartedly wanted.

I'd started practicing this personal magic in my thirties after my first child, Jessie, was born, and committed even more fully to it after my experience with that mysterious illness I had in 1979–1980. I'd continued it right up to now, 1990, when I was the sickest I'd ever been.

Besides my overblown faith in my own intelligence, my stay-healthy habits included things like eating lots of vegetables, sleeping eight to nine hours a night, exercising daily, locking my car doors. I took vitamins. I tried to be kind to all sentient beings. I did my best to think positive thoughts and to let go of anger. And sometimes I repeated affirmations while I swam or ran. "I am healthy and strong." "I have within me every-thing I need to accomplish my goals."

My form of magic had failed me; I'd gotten terribly sick even while living so well. I didn't realize, while I was sick and in the hospital, how angry I was—outraged, actually, and stunned—that I had no agency at all over my illness, could not in any way influence its cure. It was a big shock to be confronted with how quickly and unpredictably I could lose my grip on everything that mattered to me. I'd thought I held the reins, but what in fact I'd been holding onto were wisps, fog and smoke, pretenses to power. The hard truth was that I'd been operating in a bubble of illu-sion because I couldn't tolerate knowing how vulnerable I was, we all are, at every minute, imperiled by the unseen and the uncontrollable.

I wasn't thinking about my health magic or my vulnerability on the day Claire wanted to tell me her Zen story. All I knew was that I felt ter-rible and although I wanted to hear her voice—she was a good friend—I just didn't want to have her lecture me.

"Sure, go ahead," I said. "Tell me a condensed version."

Claire started telling me a story about a young Buddhist monk who wanted to reach Nirvana without having to mess around with multiple reincarnations. He'd heard he could accomplish this by traveling to a certain temple, entering a dark room there, and crossing that room to a door on the opposite side. His heart's desire, Nirvana, would be behind that door. The catch was that the room was filled with a thousand demons who would harass him as he crossed the room.

"He should have given it up and gone home, that's what I'd have done," I said.

"No, you wouldn't have and neither did he," Claire said. "It turned out that the demons were the embodiments of the monk's deepest fears. He made it through the room by remembering the demons weren't real, by keeping his feet moving, and by staying focused on his heart's desire: Nirvana. In other words, the lesson of the story was, you will succeed if you keep your eye on your goal and never waver."

This advice sounded familiar but I didn't try to figure out why right then. I see now how this tip resembled my motto, "press on regardless," my belief about the power of keeping moving and holding fast to my goals. Being as depleted as I was right then, I'd totally forgotten about focus and persistence. So instead of seeing the similarities between the monk and myself, I defaulted to being offended.

"Are you trying to tell me my illness isn't real, that it's a creation of my own mind?"

"Well, it's worth thinking about."

"Uh huh," I said, wishing she'd hang up now and leave me alone. I'd been sick for nearly six weeks. Stories weren't going to help me. Nothing short of a megaton medical miracle was going to help me. (Interestingly, as it turned out, it might have been some form of a miracle—or an act of grace—that ended up helping me. But I didn't yet know that.)

"I don't believe," I said, trying not to sound pathetic, "that I have any power at all over the demons in this body."

"Jude, I just don't want you to give up. I want you to keep your feet moving, get through this and come back to your life. I miss you."

"Me too," I said. "I miss me too."

17

Rolling Loose

"Time is a hurdy-gurdy, a lampoon, and death's
a bawd. We're beheaded by the nick of time.
We're logrolling on a falling world, on time
released from meaning and rolling loose"

—ANNIE DILLARD, *Holy the Firm*

Sometime in August

EVERY DAY I, LIKE that determined young monk, kept my feet moving, but not towards my heart's desire. My feet rushed me to the bathroom over and over again. I tried to rest even while pinned to the toilet. I half-slept there when I wasn't reading Dillard. Back in my bed I ate a spoonful of soup and a bite of the toast Betty always made for me. I didn't want any of it, but I knew I needed it so I made a weak effort. The ever-present Timmy was a willing garbage disposal for whatever I couldn't swallow.

On the morning of the fifth day after the colonoscopy, Betty stood in the doorway of my bedroom and announced, "I've been working this out in my mind and I asked myself, what do we give babies when they have diarrhea? We give them rice and applesauce, is what we do. So, I'm going to make you some rice dishes, all different kinds, some with applesauce and a few raisins maybe, some made with chicken broth, some plain. Brown rice, of course. It's better for you."

Betty was very pleased with her plan. "How's that sound to you? Could you eat rice, do you think?"

I hesitated, not wanting to hurt her feelings. I didn't want any rice dishes, yet eating rice seemed to me about as sensible as eating anything; soup, toast, crayons, wallpaper paste, parings, toothpaste. "Sure," I said, "It's worth trying."

While Nic napped I heard Betty in the kitchen across the hall, humming to herself as she turned on the stove burners. Click, click, click, click, click, click. She didn't turn the dial down, so the clicking kept on. Click, click, click, click, click, click. Like a dripping faucet, like someone drumming their fingers against a desk, no, against my forehead. I wanted to scream "Turn the damn dial!" Yet how could I fail to appreciate the effort Betty was making to help me? I was an ingrate. Knowing I was an ingrate made me even more impatient. The pots clattered. The burner clicked. I heard the hissing sound of something boiling over. I imagined the mucky mess that must be accumulating. I imagined a growing pile of dirty pots and utensils mounting in the sink. No one would wash them because no one would be as bothered by them as I would be.

This was how it had always been in this house, I said to myself. I didn't want to clean up after everyone, but the mess bothered me so I had to do it. And given how weak I was at that point, I couldn't do it. And no one was going to step in to fill the gap.

I was riveted by the clicking of the burners and by my imagined kitchen catastrophe. I wished someone would come home and distract Betty from her mission of mercy. But neither Barbara nor Chris would be home from work for hours.

My colon gripped. I stumbled through the bedroom door and peeked quickly, fearfully, into the kitchen on my way. No Betty. A pot was boiling hard, the gas turned up high beneath it. Puffs of white steam popped out from under its rattling lid. The sink was as deeply piled as I'd feared. Rice water had spattered down the side of the stove and onto the floor. There were sticky-looking pools of it inside the three unlit burners.

I heard Betty in Nic's room, chortling at him as she changed his diaper. He giggled at her. I crept into the kitchen and turned down the burner. The clicking blessedly stopped. I wanted to do more but my colon wouldn't let me. I made it to the bathroom just in time. And I was lucky this time. I was able to go back to bed in only twenty minutes.

Lying in bed, not resting, I continued to think about the mess in the kitchen and worried about the unwashed clothes in the basement. And the unstacked newspapers and unwatered plants. The mail strewn across the dining room table. All those things I used to do to keep our home running called to me like unfed infants.

The night following Betty's rice-making, as I lay awake next to my sleeping husband, I thought I heard thunder, just barely, under the rumble of the window air conditioner. Then a flash of lightning lit up the window. Raindrops ticked against the glass and the metal top of the air conditioner. More thunder, then harder rain for over an hour. Chris snored occasionally. I stared into the dim bedroom and wondered again if I might be dying. The dog stretched in his sleep and pushed his spine tighter against my leg. I stroked his silky ear.

Tomorrow Chris would begin his new assignment at Children's Court. For two years he'd paid his dues by doing the unexciting work of collecting child support for the district attorney's office. Now finally he was on the verge of doing trial work. Because this change was so important to him, I was trying to put extra effort into being cheerful. I wanted him to go to his new assignment without carrying a giant load of worry about me.

Actually, I was getting sicker every day. I'd called Dr. Chan every morning since the colonoscopy and reported my symptoms to him as Dr. Randall had instructed. This morning, Dr. Chan asked if I was eating. Had I lost more weight?

"No," I'd told him, not sure if this qualified as a lie. I hadn't weighed myself. I'd been afraid to. I could see how thin my arms and legs had gotten, how my belly sank in and my ribs stuck out. I didn't want to think about what this meant.

"I still have diarrhea every night," I told Dr. Chan this morning. "And it's still bloody."

As usual, he took in this information and made no comment. He didn't ask any more questions and he didn't suggest that I go back to the hospital. This puzzled me some, but because I was trying so hard not to be as sick as I was, I decided I'd take his inaction as a good sign.

Right now, in the middle of the night, I saw a different truth. As if, after bushwhacking through brambles and close-knit trees, I'd managed to climb up high enough to see the whole messy area. What I saw, what stood out stark in the midst of the wilderness, was that I was not getting better. And the sicker I got, the harder I was trying to hide it from Chris, from Betty, from my friends, from my children, and from myself. It made some sense not to scare my kids, but why was I pretending to Chris or the doctor? Why to myself? How stupid was that?

Not stupid, I tried to reassure myself. *Just trying not to overreact.*

But lying beside my peaceful snoring husband, I thought I could feel my life seeping out of me with each of my own exhalations. The part of me in charge of both reassurance and its close cousin, denial, told me to relax. *Tomorrow will be better.*

I'm not going to be better tomorrow morning, I argued back. *If things keep going like this, I'm not going to make it at all.* But was that really true? I'd never come anywhere near dying before so how would I know? But I did know.

I said the words to myself again, to get a better feel for whether or not they were true: *I'm dying. Should I call someone and say, hey, I think I might be dying. Take me to the hospital. What if I was wrong? It would be this big melodrama. I'd feel like such an idiot.*

There was no way I was going to wake Chris up and say, *honey, I'm dying.* It would have wrecked his first day at Children's Court. I *could* get through another day or two. I was in a routine that worked: staying near the bathroom, lying in bed, dozing, staying half-conscious as much as possible. I could keep doing that; I could manage for a little longer.

And then what? Dr. Randall had said to stop worrying about "what-ifs."

Stop worrying.

I watched Christopher sleep. I laid my hand on the crown of his head. *I wish I could spare you all this,* I said to him, in my mind. *I'm so sorry.*

18

Sickness

"Sickness, sometimes I think you are my Jerusalem;
my holy land, the country to which
I have always belonged."

—TONY HOAGLAND, "Bliss"

CHRIS GOT UP EARLIER than usual. Smelling of soap and looking handsome in a navy-blue suit and maroon tie, he leaned over the bed and kissed me on the forehead. "Mmm," he said. "You're a little cooler this morning. How was your night?"

"Not too bad," I lied. "I wasn't up quite as often. Have a good day in Children's Court today."

"Call Dr. Chan," he said over his shoulder as he left.

As soon as I heard the door close behind him, I got out of bed. The cramps had already started. I took a few steps towards the bedroom door and the room began to whirl. I grabbed the bedpost to keep from falling. The bathroom was only thirteen feet away but with the floor pitching, it felt like a hundred. I held my index finger up in front of my face and focused on it, a trick learned in childhood ballet classes, to quell the dizziness of doing a series of rapid turns called chaînés. My finger, thank God, stayed still while the room continued to whirl. For a few seconds, Finger and I were standing on a fixed platform inside a centrifuge. And then the walls settled into their places and I was able to walk to the bathroom, do my thing, and get back to bed where I began shivering like I had in the early days of this illness. Like I did when my fever was routinely soaring up over 104. Why was this happening again? And why in the morning? Even in the hospital, the highest fevers always came at night. What did this mean? Dying?

For just a few minutes, I didn't feel scared about dying. I didn't feel anything. In fact, once I stopped shivering I felt calm. The edges of my vision blurred and darkened. My muscles relaxed and the chatter in my head ceased. It had been so long since I'd felt this calm, as if I were suspended over the edge of deepest sleep.

Maybe, I said to myself, *if I give in to whatever this is, everything else will fall away and there will be no more pain.* My eyelids closed. My head grew heavy against the pillow.

For a few seconds I let everything go, the misery, the worry, the effort to understand what was happening to me. No more struggle to think, to talk, to do anything at all.

Suddenly a surge of fear flashed through me. My eyes popped open. *What in the world was I doing?* Jessie was due home from summer camp that afternoon. I'd been sending her letters for two weeks telling her I was better. She probably thought I was fine. I couldn't let Jessie come home to a dead mother. I looked over at Timmy, asleep at the foot of my bed, and said out loud, "I can't die today."

I pushed myself up on my elbows. My vision blurred again. My heart beat wildly. What had I done by relaxing like that, letting my guard down, giving in? Had I set in motion a process that I couldn't stop?

I sensed something lurking in the room, something evil hidden under the surface of the bedroom walls, between the molecules of the bookshelf, the rocking chair, the green pottery lamp on the bedside table. My vision was narrowing. I'd never fainted before but I was pretty sure that was about to happen, and then I was going to die. Like those people in the old movie *The Invasion of the Body Snatchers*: you close your eyes for a split second and, you're gone; the alien pod people take over your body. I'd been terrified of body snatchers since the movie at the Starlight Drive-in movie theater with my parents when I was seven years old.

I lay in my bed, holding very still, as if I were on a narrow ledge with a fatal drop on both sides. I tried to get through these current awful minutes as I'd gotten through other kinds of awfulness, by being still, by slowing my breathing, by trying not to feel, and by waiting. I expected I'd soon feel better, less endangered. After a few minutes I realized, with a jolt of adrenaline, that this time it wasn't working. Another jolt of adrenalin and I was out of bed before I'd actually decided to be. The darkness rushed at me. I sank to my knees and crawled to the door. I stopped, dizzy again, thinking maybe I could lie on the floor until I felt better.

No. Wait. If I lie here, the snatchers will find me! I thought. *I should scream for Betty.* But what help would Betty be? She wouldn't be able to get me off the floor.

I grabbed hold of the door frame and pulled myself upright. I wobbled and lurched out of the bedroom, through the dining room, into the living room. Betty was sitting in a rocking chair reading to Nic who was sucking two fingers and looking drowsy. She stopped mid-sentence and stared at me.

"Well, hello," she said, keeping her voice calm and steady. "Are you going to join us for a while?"

I couldn't answer. It was taking all my concentration to cross the living room. I intended to settle slowly onto the couch. What I did was more like stumbling into it and falling hard against its cushions. As soon as I was supine, my eyes closed. The strange, dizzy darkness flooded my head. *Stay awake, stay awake. Keep your eyes open.* I forced my eyes open.

"Betty," I said. "I don't know what's wrong. I feel terrible and I can hardly see. I think you should call the paramedics."

"I don't think I know how to do that," Betty said. She set Nic on the floor beside her chair and handed him the book she'd been reading to him: *There's a Monster at the End of This Book.* Nic patted the book's cover. "Gwovuh is a monstuh!" he told me, cheerfully.

"Get me the phone," I told Betty.

The ambulance arrived within five minutes. By the time Betty opened the door for the two white-coated young men, my vision had cleared and I felt better. I told them I wasn't sure I needed them anymore. But instead of being upset with me for calling in a false alarm, the taller of the two men lifted my wrist to take my pulse while the other asked me for more information. I told them about my weeks in the hospital, my colitis diagnosis, that morning's dizziness.

"I think we'll take you to the hospital and have them take another look at you," said the tall man who was taking my pulse. They made a chair of their hands. As I moved to sit there, I caught a glimpse of Nic in his grandmother's arms, clutching a lock of her thick grey hair, sucking hard on his fingers. My vision darkened again. I swayed against the shorter paramedic's chest.

"Whoa. Easy now," he said "Put an arm around each of us. That's it. We gotcha. Hey. Looks like you've got company."

I opened my eyes. There was twelve-year-old Jessie, her backpack slung over one shoulder, walking into the room with her father. She saw me and stopped dead.

"The back door was open," Paul, my ex, said. "What's going on?"

"She was dizzy this morning," Betty said. "She's going to the hospital so they can be sure she's okay."

"Hi, Jessie," I said, trying to make my voice sound normal. I rested my eyes on the usually welcome sight of my daughter. She was tan and freckled from her weeks outdoors. Her face was expressionless. She hadn't moved since she first caught sight of me.

"Hi, Mom," she said quietly. "I guess you're not all better."

As the paramedics carried me down the stairs and out to the ambulance, I knew that this moment was going to stick in my daughter's memory forever and there was nothing I could do to erase it.

19

There Was a Door

"At the end of my suffering
there was a door.

Hear me out: that which you call death
I remember"

—LOUISE GLUCK, "The Wild Iris"

No NEED FOR SIRENS, we rode quietly to Columbia Hospital. It was noon when we arrived. I gave my recent medical history to the emergency room physician who looked skeptical, either because he didn't believe me or because he wasn't familiar with the systemic effects of ulcerative colitis which was, at this point in the story, my diagnosis according to Dr. Randall. Whatever the reason, the ER doctor didn't seem to know what to do. He had a nurse start the inevitable IV line. She hooked up a glucose solution, on the assumption, I suppose, that I might be dehydrated. I napped off and on; no one came into my curtained cubicle for hours, or if they did, I slept through it.

When I opened my eyes, still in the ER, at three in the afternoon, I could tell my fever had dropped. My vision was normal and my head was clear. The morning's creepy feeling was gone. I sat up, and no darkness tried to snatch me. The doctor discharged me, suggesting that perhaps

I had an inner ear infection. I knew he was wrong, but I was too tired to argue with him. He prescribed an antibiotic. As soon as he left the room I crumpled the prescription paper and threw it into a nearby waste receptacle. *He's an imbecile,* I thought, *just like the dermatologist.*

I was disappointed to be going home. Maybe I should have been glad; I supposed it meant I wasn't actually on the brink of death. I waited for the nurse to bring me the discharge papers to sign, feeling like a wounded soldier stitched up and sent back into battle. I wondered what I had to do to get to stay. *One of two things is true,* I told myself: *either I was dying this morning or I'm losing my mind.*

I signed the papers. The nurse informed me that my brother had come to take me home. Dick, four years my senior, had suffered for most of his life with Crohn's disease, a close cousin to ulcerative colitis. He and his family lived about twenty miles away from me but we rarely got together. Not from any animosity but rather because we were very different from each other, in personality, interests, habits. Still, we tended to show up for one another in emergencies. I knew Chris had kept Dick apprised of my illness but I hadn't expected to see Dick appear at the hospital. I walked out to the waiting area, and there he was, my big brother. At forty-six (four years older than I was that year), he was a tall man, over six feet, medium build, with high cheekbones and dark brown hair. He hadn't seen me since before I got sick weeks ago. I saw the shock dash across his face before he could hide it.

"Hi," he said, "I went to visit you at home but you weren't there. Betty told me you were here so I came a couple hours ago, while you were asleep. Wanna ride home?"

"Yeah. Thanks. What a nice surprise."

"So you've got an inner ear infection?" he asked as we walked out the emergency room doors to the parking lot. I rolled my eyes and shook my head. On the way home, we talked about inflammatory bowel disease. When I described how I felt that morning, Dick said, "Oh yeah. I know what that's like." Suddenly I felt worlds better. He got it. "Sorry you've got my disease," he said. "I brought you a book about it; it's in the back seat."

Dick dropped me off at my house. I walked up the stairs on my own with *People Not Patients: A Sourcebook about Inflammatory Bowel Disease,* tucked under one arm. I went back to bed and fell asleep immediately. I woke when Chris came into the bedroom.

As I sat up to say hello to him, my head spun. Chris kissed my forehead.

"You're hot," he said and went to get the thermometer. I thought about the body snatchers again while the thermometer rested under my tongue. Chris pulled it out and read it, "106."

"Oh. I had no idea. I guess that's why I've felt so weird all day."

"Didn't they take your temperature in the ER?"

"No. They didn't. That's kind of strange." I slid down under the sheet and shut my eyes. Cramps woke me hours later. The room was dark, and Chris was asleep beside me. I headed for the bathroom.

This time I didn't bother to turn the light on to read. I didn't feel like I could read. I sat in the dark, slipping in and out of unpleasant dreams, waiting for my body to be done.

In the morning, when Chris came in to shower, I was still sitting on the toilet.

"Up so soon?" he asked as he turned on the water and pulled the vinyl shower curtain closed.

"I've been here all night," I told him flatly. I stood up and leaned heavily on the washbasin.

Chris pushed the curtain back a few inches to look at me. "Jude, have you told Dr. Chan how much time you spend in the bathroom?"

"Yes. I think so."

"Well, have you or haven't you?"

"I'm not sure. I must have. Yes, I'm sure I have."

"Tell him again, will you?"

"OK. Sure. I will." I stumbled back to bed.

After Chris left, Jessie came in and snuggled up beside me. We watched *The Today Show* together before her father picked her up for the day. I felt almost comfortable with her on one side, smelling like Jessie, the same sweet scent her skin had emitted since infancy, and with Tim on the other, smelling like a dog. I wished every hour could be like that one.

I waited until mid-afternoon to call Dr. Chan. I wasn't sure why I kept making those calls. I never had anything new to say and neither did the doctor. I would have been tempted to skip the ritual that day if I hadn't known Chris was going to ask me about it later. So, because I promised Chris I would, I called Dr. Chan and was careful to give him every detail I could think to give him. And to my surprise he asked me questions he'd never asked me before.

"How many bowel movements are you having a day?" he asked. This almost made me laugh. What was he thinking? I didn't have bowel movements. I had waterfalls, torrents, hurricanes, not nice, orderly bowel movements.

"Umm. That's a little hard to answer," I began. "I wasn't able to leave the bathroom at all last night, the cramping never stopped, not until morning. I was in and out about twenty times during the day yesterday, I guess."

Silence on the other end of the line. Then, "Are you eating at all?"

"No. I can't."

More silence. "This doesn't sound good, Mrs. Ford. I'm going to consult with the doctor filling in for Dr. Randall. I think we may need to hospitalize you. You don't seem to be getting better, and I'm quite concerned. I'll call you right back."

I hung up. *Well,* I said to myself. *That was strange. Why is it he thinks I should be in the hospital today when just yesterday I was there and they sent me home?* In five minutes, the phone rang.

"Mrs. Ford, this is Dr. Adams, Dr. Randall's partner. I have just spoken to Dr. Chan." Dr. Adams sounded angry.

"You must get to the hospital. I want you there right away. This is totally ridiculous, leaving you home all this time. You are very, very ill. You're having twenty or more bowel movements every day?"

"Yes, more, I'd say."

"And you've taken the Lonox medicine?"

"Yes, a little more often than I should. It doesn't do anything."

The doctor was angry again. "You should never take more Lonox when it isn't working. It can make you sicker. We'll do an x-ray of your abdomen as soon as possible. It wouldn't surprise me if we found a toxic megacolon. It could be near to rupture. This is very serious."

"I think it is, yes, thank you," I said, stupidly, meaning every word even though I realized he wouldn't understand why I was thanking him for corroborating what I'd thought and been afraid to think, that my situation was in fact very serious.

"I'll meet you at the hospital. How soon can you get there?"

"Not right away . . ."

"Mrs. Ford, this is very dangerous."

"Yes. I think I know that. But no one is here except the babysitter. The baby's about to go down for a nap; the sitter can't leave him to drive me to the hospital. If I wait an hour, my daughter will be home to watch the baby."

"You'll come in one hour then, right?'

"Yes, I will. To emergency?"

"No, no. We're admitting you. We'll do an x-ray and then set you up with IV fluids. At the very least, you're dehydrated and you're starving. I'll meet you there in an hour."

Barbara was on duty at our house that day. I pulled on a robe and walked out into the kitchen where she was doing dishes. Nicolas was in his highchair, his hair drenched in SpaghettiOs. He giggled when he saw me. I told Barbara about the phone conversation.

"Thank goodness," she said. "Finally, someone's listening."

20

Something To Get Used To

It will be something to get used to,
living this way, skinless,

unwound and in the light.

—JUDITH FORD, "Rainy Day at McCreedy's"

August 15, 1990, Columbia Hospital, 5-West

MY NEW ROOM WAS blue. The last one I'd occupied just three weeks earlier had been green. But the white sheets and blankets, the hard, narrow bed in this room were identical to what I'd lain in previously. Same harsh fluorescent light emitting the same high-pitched hum. Four weeks ago, the last time I was admitted to this hospital, I'd felt abducted. This time I felt rescued. At home. Safe. Or at least safer than I'd felt in my actual home. The snatchers, I thought, would find it more difficult to suck me out of my body here. A press of a button and I could summon help. Plus, people would be coming and going all the time, bearing questions, medicines, blood pressure cuffs, ice chips, and thermometers.

I got into bed and a nurse set up my IV line. She settled the needle into a vein in my lower arm. I had to interrupt her to go to the bathroom before she could hook up the IV tube and again right after she'd attached it. The urgent signals from my colon had become more urgent and more frequent in the few hours since I was admitted to the hospital.

"Anxiety does that," said the nurse, who was patient and kind.

I was sent down to x-ray. Dr. Adams came to my room afterwards, carried the films with him. I didn't have the feared toxic megacolon.

"You still need to be here," the doctor told me, anticipating my question. "You couldn't continue the way you were at home much longer. Didn't you realize how much danger you were in with your colon not absorbing any nutrients and the bleeding continuing for so many days?"

"Sometimes I did. But I wasn't really sure."

"Be sure now. If you'd developed a megacolon it could have ruptured; you'd have gone into shock, your blood pressure would have plummeted; your kidneys might have failed. We might not have been able to save you."

Dr. Adams was trying to impress upon me the peril I'd been in. He seemed to think I'd been reckless. It wasn't recklessness; it was management. Besides the few times in the night and earlier today when, yes, I was very afraid, I'd been focusing on surviving one minute to the next. One foot after the other. No room in my mind for a serious overview, an overall assessment (except sometimes at night, briefly) that would have gotten me here in the hospital sooner. Chris, Barbara, Betty, friends who called occasionally—everyone seemed to be doing something similar, one minute, one day at a time. No panic. No what-ifs. Only in hindsight did any of us find this shared attitude strange. Dangerous.

Dr. Adams ordered Prednisone to be delivered at high dosage through my IV line. He told me that I wouldn't be eating anything solid for a while, just broth, Jell-O and apple juice. Maybe a popsicle if I'd like one. I was relieved that no one would ask me to eat anything else. But not so pleased to learn that if my symptoms didn't abate in a day or two, the doctor would order a chest tube, also known as a subclavian line, to nourish me. It might be the only way to keep me alive if my bowels continued to function as they had been.

When I was finally alone, I dozed with the reassuring feeling of being watched over by the intercom.

At six, after I'd consumed my dinner of Jell-O and chicken bouillon, a sweating, bedraggled Christopher arrived.

"I'm sorry," I told him before he had a chance to drop his suit jacket in a chair and loosen his tie.

"Shhhh," he said. "I'm glad you're here. You have no idea, do you, how hard it's been for me to have you home, so sick, and no one doing anything about it. Now I know you'll be taken care of when I have to be at work. This is good, very good."

I looked up at his face. His eyes were red. His skin was pale and shadowed with new whiskers. I hadn't noticed before how worn out he was getting. He pulled a chair over and sat beside my bed, propping his brown leather feet on the white blanket. He tipped back in the chair, his hands behind his head. "What happens now?" he asked.

And what, indeed?

Chris went home to the kids and the hospital quieted for the night. I lay in the silence looking over the damage my illness had done to my life, to my family. And no end in sight. I was fairly certain, now that I was in the hospital, I wouldn't die of this, whatever it turned out to be. The doctors told me I wouldn't. But no one could tell me when I'd be well and once I was well would I recognize myself?

Did I want to stick around long enough to see how this turned out? If this was what the program was going to be from now on, periods of minimal functioning interspersed with tectonic shifts in my immune system, rounds of fever, pain, and diarrhea, then no, I didn't think I wanted to. No. Definitely not.

I knew I didn't have to. Suicide was always an option, as long as one was alive. Some therapist had told me that when I was a depressed teenager. It was meant to buy me time, to keep me alive long enough to make my life better. It had worked, I guess.

Right now, with a high fever, constant abdominal pain, and an occluded future, suicide didn't strike me as a bad or scary solution. I'd actually given it a try when I was twenty-one, taking all ten of the Tylenol with codeine pills left over from a root canal and two or three Elavils remaining from an ineffective antidepressant prescription—ineffective in that I was even more depressed on them than off. Those, besides a couple tablespoons of cough medicine, were all the medication I'd had on hand. I washed it all down with a glass of cheap muscatel wine. I woke up ten hours later groggy and headachy but very much alive.

At first I was disappointed but after a few days of my continuing life, I regained some perspective and was glad not to have died. I never tried suicide again but I still believed it was a legitimate choice when all other choices were choked off. The one last resort that no one could deny me.

Lying in my hard narrow bed, I let the word *suicide* spread itself out in my mind. I pictured it swooping over a landscape, dropping its letters one by one, all in capitals, first a big S rolling across the hills, then all the other letters following one after another, like passing letter-shaped clouds. Cooling the air. Quieting the birds.

As so often happened when I lay in bed in a hospital room thinking, my eyes were drawn to the window. The sky out there was deep black, uninterrupted by stars. *I'm not afraid of dying,* I told myself, wondering if it was true. I'd certainly been scared earlier that day right before the ambulance came and took me to the hospital.

Sometimes when I was scared of something I found it helpful to get as close to the feared thing as possible, to immerse myself in it until I was so intimate with whatever it was that it no longer held any fear for me. I tried that now, thinking about death.

I'd been scared of death when I was a child, once I'd sort of understood what it was. I was four or five when I first noticed an occasional dead animal, a baby bird fallen from a nest, a cat who hadn't run fast enough out of the path of a car. My parents had done their best to explain death to me, in kindergarten terms, something about going to heaven with the angels. I couldn't quite get my mind around it. The idea that something or someone could be alive on earth one minute and not the next was pretty terrifying, even if they *had* gone to be with angels.

Every night before I slept I used to say a prayer to protect not just myself but my family and everybody else on the planet. I thought it was all up to me, so I added a p.s. to my nightly "Now I lay me down to sleep," prayer: something like, "Dear God, don't let anybody anywhere die tonight."

Yet deaths kept on happening. Nests fell out of trees, animals got flattened on roads. When I was seven, my Grandpa Charlie Marks died. Gone to the angels, they probably told me again.

In my seventh summer, the boy in the house behind ours abruptly stopped coming over to play. I rang his doorbell and asked his mother where he was. Her eyes filled with tears, "Peter is sick," she said and closed the door. Weeks later my mother told me Peter had died. Of cancer. I'd played softball with Peter just a few months before. How could someone I could see and hear and touch not be there anymore? I didn't like the empty Peter-shaped space that now rose up in my mind whenever I thought of my friend.

And now, the idea of my own dying was just as unimaginable. Sure, I could think about escaping my current discomfort—I wanted nothing more—but suicide? How would I manage it? When I'd made that one lame attempt when I was twenty-one, I'd used an ineffective mix of pills.

What would I do now? Put a pillow over my own face? Jump out the fifth-floor window opposite my bed? Crack open the drug safe that was near my bathroom door?

Not only did I not have the method (and most likely not the nerve, either) there was Emily standing squarely in my way. Emily, my therapist from fourteen years earlier. I pictured her now standing by my bed in her tight jeans and flowered silk shirt. The scent of her rose cologne. Emily was the other person besides Dick Olney who'd radically changed my life. Like Dick she'd been both my therapist and my teacher. It was Emily who'd taught me how to manage my emotional storms so I wouldn't be overwhelmed by them, taught me how to manage my going-numb technique, too, so it wouldn't take me over without my inviting it. And then, damn, she made me promise never ever to kill myself, looked me square in the face and made me repeat it out loud to her, "I will not harm myself by accident or on purpose no matter how I feel or what happens." No loopholes, no exceptions, no hedging.

I heard the promise in my mind now so vividly that I wasn't entirely sure I hadn't just made the promise again, out loud, to Emily standing beside my bed.

But Emily, I argued, *you knew, didn't you, that there was a sub-clause? A loophole. That I reserved the right to nullify the contract in certain extreme situations? Like terminal illness? Like now?*

I fell asleep hanging onto my loophole. Every time I woke in the night I remembered it and reminded myself of its validity. When I woke the next morning I was at first happy to remember I'd found a potential way out. By the time a nurse came to take my vitals I realized I couldn't do it. Couldn't break my promise to Emily. No loopholes, she'd said. No exceptions. I'd made a promise and I'd meant it when I said it. I prided myself on keeping my promises even when inconvenient. I couldn't undo this one without calling Emily to tell her the deal was off. Those were the terms: if you weren't going to keep the contract, you had to call to discuss it. I had no intention of calling Emily who now lived somewhere in Massachusetts. Even if I had her current phone number, which I didn't, calling a therapist to say you were breaking your no-suicide contract would unleash all kinds of unwelcome mental health interventions. I was stuck. There really was no escape.

21

Suffering's Lesson

"This is suffering's lesson: *pay attention. The*
important part might come in a form you do not
recognize. You might not know how to love it,"

—SARAH MANGUSO, *The Two Kinds of Decay*

August 18, 1990, day six in the hospital

AT SIX IN THE morning a nurse came to weigh me. She pushed a tall up-right scale on wheels into my room, helped me out of bed, and held onto one of my elbows to steady me long enough for her to get a reading. One hundred ten. I'd lost more weight in the last three weeks. I was shocked. The nurse steered me by the elbow back to bed. *Nine pounds isn't so very much,* I tried to convince myself. Yet, I hadn't weighed this little since I was in my early twenties. *I shouldn't weigh this little. 110 is too little.*

I sat on top of the rumpled blankets of my bed, staring at my pasty white legs that looked like knobby tree roots sticking out from underneath my t-shirt. *Are my legs really this scrawny?* My calves hang loose from my shinbones, as if I were already dead. These legs couldn't be the ones that ran every single day for the last five years. *How could these things belong to me?* I hid my legs under my sheet and worked on distracting myself from my shrinking body by obsessing about my rash.

The following day in the middle of a restless afternoon nap, I woke to see the long, pale face of Dr. Adams, the doctor who'd made me come to the hospital, hovering over an opened chart. Everything about Dr. Adams was pale, his wispy hair, neither blond nor gray but some nondescript color in between, his tan suit, white shirt, his tie quietly striped with shades of tan and brown. When he saw I was awake, he informed me I wasn't improving from the liquid diet and the Prednisone drip—my trips to the bathroom had, in fact, increased. I'd have guessed as much. It was time, he continued, to have an IV line inserted through my chest wall into my large subclavian vein so that nutrition could flow directly into me, bypassing my entire gastro-intestinal tract, creating total colon rest. The procedure would happen the next morning.

Barely awake, trying to grasp this information, I reverted to my therapist self. "Subclavian. I've heard of that," I told the doctor in what was probably a pedantic, albeit quiet, tone. "Some of my worst anorexics," I went on, as if he were interested, "once they're hospitalized, often need subclavian lines until they have the courage to begin to eat again on their own. In eating disorder circles, we call it hyperalimentation."

"We call it TPN," Dr. Adams, who seemed unfazed, told me, "Total Parenteral Nutrition. It should provide the rest your system needs in order to begin to heal."

"My whole system has been working way too hard; double shifts for weeks," I said, trying to be clever, still trying not to be afraid. "It does deserve a vacation."

The doctor paused, looked confused, and then offered up a patronizing smile.

"Sleep well, Mrs. Ford," he said as he left.

"I never do," I muttered to his disappearing back.

Starting with my first night of this current hospital stay, I'd set up the bathroom with everything I needed to survive my typical miserable nights. *Pilgrim at Tinker Creek*—still my favored comfort object—lay waiting on the pink floor next to the white toilet in my tiny sterile pod of a bathroom. I'd put a pillow on the other side of the toilet, planning to put it between my head and the cold tile wall as I slid into my half-asleep trance.

I was unprepared, though, for the way the pain intensified once I was in the hospital. After the first night, Dr. Adams ordered Versed for me but it hadn't even taken a splinter of an edge off the new pain. It was far more difficult to stay half-asleep when the pain got that bad.

The night before the subclavian procedure, I was anxious about that as well as worried about how bad my nighttime pain was going to be. I stayed awake as long as I could and finally fell asleep with *The Tonight Show* but only for a few minutes. I woke to an extreme abdominal cramp. It sat me up in bed and doubled me over. My colon felt as if it was twisting, clutching itself into bundles, turning itself inside out. I couldn't move. I waited until the cramping eased a little and then rushed to the bathroom. Once there, I tried to put myself into the half-asleep state; this time I couldn't do it, couldn't rise above the pain. I grabbed Annie Dillard and opened to a random page. I read the same words over and over, something about a moth. My eyes kept sliding off the page, as if it were greased. I wrapped one hand over each of my knees and held on as if on a bad rollercoaster ride. I stared down at the floor, tears running down my hot cheeks and splashing my hands. I lifted my head to wipe my eyes.

And there, on my right, at eye-level, a white cord dangled. I followed it to its connection on the wall. A small red light bulb and the words, "emergency call light" glowed right beside me. By the time I got my wits together enough to pull the cord—to realize that "emergency" applied to me, right there, right then—I'd been in the bathroom for three hours.

The nurse arrived almost instantly. She hovered over me, a dark silhouette outlined by the dim light of my room.

"Hi. Did you call? How can I help you?"

That anyone should come to me in the midst of this private and, until now solitary, suffering was to me a miracle. I had some difficulty believing she was real. She was the good witch sent to lead me out of a labyrinth, the first responder materializing at the scene of my private airplane crash.

"I've been here for hours." I gasped out the words.

"You were just admitted a couple days ago, weren't you?" The good witch misunderstood.

"No, no. I mean I've been on the toilet for hours. Happens all the time at home. I'm used to it. But it hurts now, more than before."

The good witch crouched down in front of me and took my hand.

"You were given Versed earlier, I think. Twice as much as last night."

"I'm so tired. I can't keep doing this. I'm trying. I just can't."

"You don't have to keep trying, Mrs. Ford. You're in the hospital now. It's our job to help you."

I'd forgotten I was already in the hospital. I was in the hospital and I was still dying. There was nothing left to try then. Nowhere else to go. It wasn't going to get better. *This lady is about to leave me here alone,* I told myself. *And I'm going to have to get through this on my own, like always.* I began to cry again.

"I'm sorry I pulled the cord. Sorry I bothered you," I choked the words out around my sniffles and gasps.

The nurse gave my right hand, which she was still holding in hers, a little squeeze.

"You're *supposed to* call us when you're in pain. You don't have to be alone with this anymore. I'm going to call Dr. Adams at home."

"What time is it?"

"A little past two in the morning."

"Maybe we should wait."

"Don't you be silly, Mrs. Ford. It's his job to take care of you. If you're in this much pain, he needs to do something about it. Will you be okay alone for a few minutes?"

Her question was almost funny. I'd been alone forever in this deteriorating body. Would I be okay alone for a few extra minutes? Could I handle it? What choice did I have?

Within ten minutes, my witch/first responder returned with a hypodermic needle and a smile.

"This should do the trick," she said. She unhooked the joint of the IV line, inserted the needle into it, and slowly depressed the plunger.

A cooling sensation traveled up my arm, splashed over my chest, and the pain vanished. I let out a long deep breath. I looked up at the nurse and laughed. Every muscle in my body shifted into a state I barely recognized.

"Better?" the nurse asked, still smiling.

"What was that?"

"Demerol. It did the trick?"

"Yes. Oh yes it did. I'd forgotten," I told her, "what it's like not to hurt."

The following morning the surgeon, Dr. Carlyle, arrived. He was young, thirty-five at most, slender, dark-haired, and handsome. His brown eyes were ringed by long, thick lashes. He was friendly and confident. Besides being my surgeon, he told me, it was his job to inform me of all risks associated with the subclavian procedure. The only one I really heard was the one about puncturing a lung. Seeing the fear in my eyes, Dr. Carlyle quickly assured me that he'd done hundreds of these and never

ever punctured anyone's lung. He bade me a cheery good-bye, promised to return in a few hours with a team to help him with the procedure.

I leaned back tiredly against the pillow. The pillow made a rustling sound, the sound of dry cleaning covered in plastic. The nurses had kept me supplied with Demerol all night. I was to ask for it whenever I wanted it, my night nurse told me. "And don't be brave. Ask for it," she'd added. (Back in 1990, the medical world was much less scared about drug addiction and willing to use big guns for big pain.)

Being free of pain, I could actually sleep as opposed to merely dozing. I fell asleep before lunch. When I opened my eyes, Christopher was sitting in the vinyl chair, with one of his black-shoed feet resting on the foot of my bed. It was the jiggling of that foot that woke me. The foot and the sound of pages being riffled through. Chris was reading my chart.

"Learning anything?" I asked him.

"Hi, beautiful," he smiled, a thin, tired, smile. "Not learning much, no, except that your liver panel is still abnormal, your hematocrit is lower than it was before and your white blood cell count is still very elevated. And you'll be on colon rest starting this afternoon."

"You shouldn't be reading that. Where did you get it?"

"From the rack outside your room. They often leave it there. I started reading it the last time you were here, been reading it every time I come. They wouldn't leave it there if they didn't want it read. It's legally your property anyway."

"So typical. So rude. So like a lawyer."

"I do get away with a lot."

"How was Children's Court today?"

"I lost my trial," he put the chart down and lifted his other foot up onto my bed. He began to describe the case; I tried to listen. My mind wandered off, chasing random thoughts. Like: *Why does he keep jiggling his damn foot? Makes me want to flatten that foot as if it were a big bug. I wonder if I have some kind of bug in my intestine, not colitis after all. Maybe I'll never go home again. My hair must be a mess from lying in bed all day. I wonder if I smell. Is he sick of me yet?*

I was pulled out of my meandering by Chris going suddenly silent. He sniffed, cleared his throat, put his hand over his eyes and rubbed them as if they were tired. His shoulders shook. It took me a few minutes to realize he was crying. In the three years we'd been together, I'd never seen him cry. I pulled myself out from under the weight of my blankets, put my bare feet down slowly, carefully, on the cold tile floor and walked the several steps to his chair, trailing my IV stand with its clear plastic bags of saline and Prednisone. I wrapped my arms around Chris, being careful not to jar the IV line in my left arm. He didn't seem to know I was there. He didn't lean into me the way my children would. I felt useless. I wanted him to know I saw his sadness. I wanted him to let me comfort him.

"Oh, honey, I'm so sorry that happened to you," I murmured into his ear.

He straightened up, pulled at his tie to loosen his shirt collar. "I'm just real tired, Jude," he said, patting my hand where it rested on his shoulder. I leaned over and kissed his cheek. "Get back in bed," he took my hand and pulled it in that direction.

Once I was back in bed, he chatted about the children. His sixteen-year-old niece, Kara, had flown in from Oregon to help out, he told me. Nic seemed fine. Jessie was mostly staying at her dad's house and Becky was mostly at her mom's. The dog paced sometimes and seemed to be looking for me. The swelling of compassion that had overtaken me so suddenly a few minutes before, pushing me out of bed and to Chris's side, had vanished. Without it I couldn't seem to stay tuned in.

"Mmmm, hmmm." I mumbled.

"You're tired, too," said Chris. "I think I'll head home. Good luck with the subclavian IV. I'm sure everything will be fine."

"You always are," I said.

And this time he was right. The insertion of the IV line was quick and uneventful. Another T-shaped IV bag holder was added to the machine that metered my medication and another bag of clear liquid was set up to deliver nutrition, this time through the line in my chest. On alternating days a bag containing a lipid solution would be added to the mix.

After the insertion of the subclavian line and the cessation of food-by-mouth, came a long waiting period in which my condition stayed basically the same. Because of the Prednisone, though, my fevers ceased and the remaining rash scabs disappeared entirely. The intestinal symptoms, however, continued. My days were long and boring. Beyond belief boring. I watched *The Today Show* and *Mork & Mindy*. I looked forward to my doses of Demerol and to the arrival of visitors.

22

Tedium, Despair

"Here is tedium,
despair, a painful
sense of isolation and
whimsical if pompous
self-regard . . . ."

—ROBERT CREELEY, "For Love"

August 18–25

THE SUBCLAVIAN LINE DRIPPED large nutritious molecules into my chest. The first three days of its use I lost three more pounds, one each day. My already compromised vitality diminished proportionately. I spent less time in the bathroom during the day but was still having regular attacks of cramps and bloody diarrhea at night.

Because I found it terrifying to lie in bed and do nothing to stop my slide into nonexistence, I began exercising. Once every morning and once every afternoon, I pushed myself and my IV stand around the four corridors of 5-West, and when I returned to my room I did a few leg lifts in bed. It took me twenty to thirty minutes to complete what would take the average healthy person about ten minutes. This pallid imitation of a workout was the only proactive thing I could think of to do. I wasn't even sure that exercise could have an effect on a body as malnourished as mine, but even if it couldn't it was at least more interesting than daytime TV.

Three days into this second hospital stay my ex-husband Paul called. I didn't welcome the sound of his voice. In the first five years or so after our divorce I'd trembled every time that voice came over my telephone answering machine. I hated talking to him, so many memories of his judgments, his violent temper, his impossible demands.

"Well, hello," he began. "Thought I'd call and check on you. Jessie told me you're still sick." He chuckled a little. "Gotta say, I'm really glad I'm not married to you anymore." Before I could respond with, *the feeling's mutual*, he continued. "I don't have to put up with all this drama." *Thanks for your support, Paul.*

Within a half an hour, Jim called. Jim, my colleague who believed we invite illness into our bodies in order to learn a valuable lesson. "Just checking," he said. "I'm wondering if you'd mind if we rented your therapy room to someone else. We can't keep covering your part of the rent and it doesn't seem like you're going to be able to come back to work, right?"

I was stunned. What did Jim know that I didn't? I was never getting well and going back to Therapies East again? He'd hit exactly the note of one of my worst fears. It took me a few seconds to breathe and remember that Jim wasn't a guru. In fact, he was totally insensitive and often cruel. I was able to get myself together enough to say "I have every intention of coming back to work. No, it's not okay for you to rent my room. I'll repay my back rent as soon as I have an income again." *You asshole.*

Dr. Randall returned from his vacation. Just before he was due to come to my room the first time, I pinned a button to the t-shirt I slept in: "It's been lovely but I have to scream now." Not only did Dr. Randall not comment on the button during that first visit, no one else did either, not that day or the next or the next. I kept wearing the button anyway. Somehow I felt like it connected me to my life, my old self, the people who knew my old self.

Dr. Randall checked on me twice a every day. In the afternoon of his first day back I asked him why I wasn't starting to feel better.

"You're depleted and you're anemic," he told me. "Plus, there's still a lot of inflammation going on in your body."

I sighed and looked away.

"Hey!" the doctor said. "You're still going to get well. You're going to go home to your kids and your job and you're going to be able to start forgetting about all this."

"Yeah. Right," I mumbled.

I watched too much television during the day and therefore saw a lot of commercials. Every one of them seemed to involve food. I was enraptured by two- to three-minute clips of shiny, juicy food. Hamburger Helper, Oreos, Cheetos, and pizzas from Pizza Hut. Who would have guessed that all it would take to make me want to eat would be to tell me I wasn't allowed to. Within an hour of the subclavian line beginning its slow dripping work I was lusting after junk food. Those first few days on IV feeding, they were all I wanted.

This struck me as odd, so when Barbara brought Nic in to visit me, during day three of this hospital stay, I talked to her about it. I'd been admitted this time onto 5-West, the unit Barbara worked on. She had access to everything about my treatment. She checked on the dietitian's orders and discovered that I wasn't getting the correct number of calories through my subclavian line. That's why I was so hungry. She called the necessary people and within half an hour someone came in to replace the TPN bag with a brawnier version. By the following day, my junk food craving had disappeared.

On the morning of August 25 Dr. Randall came to see me at eight. He pulled the vinyl-covered armchair close to my bed and paged through my chart. The chart, a thick manila folder, was the same one Chris had scanned when he was last here. The doctor frowned as he read.

"There are two things here that worry me," he said, raising his eyes. "One is that your weight keeps dropping. I see that you're getting more calories now so that should improve. The greater worry is that your colon isn't responding to the Prednisone. I think it's time to consider some other options."

"A different drug?" I sat up in my bed, feeling closer to better than I had for at least a month. It wasn't because the diarrhea had stopped; it hadn't. But I no longer itched or had shivering fevers, no more little red demons paid me visits in the scary nighttime, and I had Demerol to counteract the pain that had been part of my nighttime bathroom rituals. I was still weak and I knew I looked like crap to everyone else, but that morning I had the feeling that maybe, just maybe, health was slowly wending its way back to me. Now Dr. Randall's worry cast a shadow over my hope.

"Remember what I told you about the possibility of a colectomy? I think if you aren't a lot better in a few days you should consider it. I know it's radical but it's the only real cure available. I don't want you to spend the rest of your life in the hospital."

I was stunned. I couldn't form a sentence so I just stared at the doctor, my eyes filling up with yet another round of tears.

"Now hang on a second," he said and pulled his chair closer. He took one of my hands. I wanted to pull it back, but I didn't. "I'm talking about curing you. Remember? That's what we're after here. Getting you all well so you can get out of this place."

"This is kind of a shock."

"Yes, I see that. I'm sorry. Take some time to think about it. I've taken the liberty of asking Margaret Schmidt, our expert on ostomies, to come to talk to you today. She'll show you the ostomy equipment, how it all works. She can put your mind at ease."

"Somehow, I don't think ostomy equipment is going to ease my mind."

"You might be surprised. Many of my patients live complete and normal lives with ostomies."

Well, isn't that just ducky for them? a mean little voice in my head said. Out loud, I said, "That doesn't sound like a club I want to join. When you told me about the surgery before it was so remote. It sounded like a reasonable option then, but it doesn't seem at all okay to me today. I don't even think I have the strength to go through such major surgery, do I? I mean, could I survive it?"

"Yes, yes, you'd get through it. We'd make sure of that. What your body *can't* tolerate, though, is many more days of diarrhea and no food."

23

The Gift of Pain

"Nothing ever goes away until it has
taught us what we need to know."

—PEMA CHODRON

AFTER DR. RANDALL LEFT, I cried until I couldn't cry any more. Then I
turned the TV on and off, and on and off. There was nothing I wanted to
watch. There never was. I knew it was pointless to try to read. So I just sat,
reclining in my bed, wrestling with a rising panic. That's what I was doing
when Alan knocked on my hospital door.

Alan, five-foot ten, a little paunchy, balding, forty-three, walked into
my hospital room. He was one of my husband's closest friends and had
been the best man at our wedding.

"Alan. What a surprise." I tried to sound happy to see him. As fond
as I was of him I wasn't sure I was up for Alan's style of wit.

"Madam, I'm a curative for your ailment, methinks." He sat down
on a straight-backed metal chair at the foot of my bed. "You didn't know,
I suppose, that I had colitis, the same disease as you, when I was a freshman in college?"

"You did? No, I didn't know." This revelation was almost as shocking
to me as Dr. Randall's suggestion that I surrender my colon.

"Yup, one incident. One long and almost fatal incident. I thought it was the flu, kept thinking I'd get better. Lost a lot of weight and got pretty weak."

"Did you have fevers, too?"

"Yes, ma'am, the whole business. Felt like shit for a lot of weeks. Finally I had to go to the hospital. I guess I would have died if I hadn't. It got so bad that eventually I couldn't even walk. Back then there weren't a lot of options. Steroids didn't do anything but make me crazy, and I didn't have time to find out if anything else would work."

"So what happened?"

"They took my whole colon out. I suppose it could have been a hard thing for a nineteen-year-old to decide to do, but I was so sick I just went along with what the doctor said I had to do."

"You have an ostomy?" I asked him, incredulous.

"I certainly do. I've had it for over twenty years, now. It's not something I think about much."

I stared at Alan, not knowing what to say next.

"Soooo," he said, and smiled. "I am here to tell you that there is life after colitis."

I told Alan about Dr. Randall's recommendation, delivered less than an hour ago. "Did you know I might have to lose my colon, too?"

"How could I have known? No."

Alan invited me to ask him anything I wanted to about the surgery, about living with an ostomy. He described the size and shape of the ostomy opening, how the small intestine is hooked to it and how a flat bag slips over the opening, sealed with a special ointment (waterproof to protect the skin from the caustic fluids that otherwise would be irritating), and doesn't show under your clothes.

"Would you like to see it?" he asked. He tugged his shirt up from his belt.

"No, no. But thank you."

Alan re-tucked his shirt and went on talking, about how at first he'd worried about how potential lovers would react to the bag. It had made him more cautious about who he chose to go to bed with, probably a good thing. "In some ways," said Alan, "it's easier. You don't have to look for a bathroom as often when you're traveling."

He stayed and talked for almost two hours. I was exhausted before he showed any sign of getting ready to leave.

"Alan," I interrupted him to say, "I have to sleep." He leaned over my bedrail and surprised me again by kissing me lightly on the cheek. "Thank you," I said. "I'm not as scared now."

"Maybe just scared enough to make the right decision, I hope."

"Maybe just that much."

When Margaret Schmidt came later that day, the only addition she made to my knowledge about ostomies was to show me an actual ostomy bag, a small flaccid skin-colored pouch with a stretchy opening. She left several samples of bags with me, along with a catalog of ostomy equipment. I learned I could order ostomy bags in an assortment of pastel colors. I tucked the catalog into a drawer beside my bed.

I could think about the colon surgery now without tears or panic. I could even imagine myself wearing a pretty pale blue ostomy bag for the rest of my life. If that was what it took to get well, yes, I could do that.

The next morning, while I lay in bed doing sluggish leg lifts, my friend Marty strolled into the room. I'd met Marty through his wife, one of my therapist friends. He was a well-respected poet, musician, and a professor at the University of Wisconsin-Milwaukee.

So enter Marty: swinging his guitar case, dressed in blue jeans with suspenders and a pressed plaid flannel shirt. He had on a black cowboy hat and black, sharply pointed cowboy boots. His hair was shoulder-length, black streaked with gray; his beard long and wild, windblown as if he'd arrived on a Harley. Which he had. He looked like a cross between a Jewish scholar and a cattleman. The mere sight of him cheered me up.

"You look like shit," he announced as he set down his guitar case. "But I know just what you need. I brought you good medicine." He began to undo the clasps on his guitar case. Marty—like my brother Dick and, I'd just learned, Alan—also had ulcerative colitis. In the ten years I'd known Marty he'd nearly died twice. He refused hospitalization both times, although he was at least as sick as I was now. During his most recent flare-up, a year ago, he'd allowed himself to be admitted briefly to a teaching hospital in Chicago, because his doctor, a nationally known expert on IBD, was on staff there. Marty had tolerated the hospital for two days after which he'd pulled out his IV lines, gotten dressed, and left against medical advice. "They would have killed me in that place," he'd explained to me. "Leaving was my only chance."

After that he'd proceeded to live his life as if he wasn't, and had never been, sick. He went back to doing things he'd done at a younger age, namely: writing poetry and rock tunes. He organized a new back-up band and took up whiskey drinking and cigarette-smoking. This, in a forty-five-year-old man who wouldn't eat restaurant food for fear of germs and who had not touched alcohol or tobacco in twenty years. And, amazingly, over the course of a few months, he got well. Entirely well. Marty himself wasn't amazed at all. "I knew it would either cure me or kill me and either one was fine with me," he told me.

"So, give it to me, Ford. What's going on here?" Marty, with guitar in lap, said now. I updated him on my condition, including the colectomy possibility.

"Keep a close eye on those medical maniacs," Marty warned me. "They're a sneaky bunch. Don't let 'em talk you into anything. The real medicine, as you know, is poetry, music, and good whiskey. You probably aren't up to the whiskey yet, so let's get on with the music, which is poetry. I'm going to play you a tune I wrote recently." He plucked and tightened one string, checked the others, and then began to strum and sing. Loudly, Bob-Dylan-style, with a pitch range of only three or four notes, a rhythmic blend of chant and song. I was surprised that no one came to scold us about the noise.

"Nice. I like it," I told him when he finished. My powers of concentration being feeble, I hadn't picked up much of the meaning of the song. Something about selling your soul to the devil, I thought. My "Nice," was delivered in the tone you use when a kindergartener shows you a drawing and you can't figure out if it's right side up or not and you have no clue what it's a picture of. Marty scowled at me.

"Judith," he said. "I thought you would get this, but you've lost some brain cells here in the medical prison. You need me to spell out the meaning of this song."

"I guess I do."

"Remember that last time I was sick, when they almost had their way with me at that hospital in Chicago?" I nodded. "Pretty soon after I escaped, Rita and the kids and I went up to Door County. I was faking wellness, hoping to fool the demons I now knew were in charge of my insides." I raise an eyebrow at this. "Just be quiet and listen. You know I don't sleep real well."

I nodded again. His insomnia was famous. "We'd been at the resort a couple days. I was full of fever and the terrible bathroom stuff of which I will spare you the details. I'd had enough." His tone edged into anger. "I refused to tolerate this continued incursion into my body. I got out of bed at two in the morning, not sure what I wanted to do; I just knew I had to get out of there. I went down to the boat landing. I thought I might drown myself. I sat there for a long time staring out at the water, and I don't mind telling you, I fell apart. I started praying, begging my illness to leave my body alone. I got a little crazy. I started wailing like a wolf."

Now he had my total attention. This I understood.

"When I stopped wailing to catch my breath, I heard a sound coming from close by, on my right. There he was—as you would know if you'd been applying what is left of you to listen to my song—a small-sized demon, sitting right there on the landing. 'What the Hell do you want, I asked him.' 'Your soul,' was his reply. 'Can't have it. Go away,' I told him. 'Leave me alone. Can't you see I'm trying to make an important decision here?' 'That's why I came,' this little guy said.

"Then he proceeded to tell me that since I didn't seem to be interested in doing right by my soul, he'd be more than happy to take it off my hands. Ah. So. That's who he was. Now I understood. This was one of the demons who'd been making me sick. I accused him of that. And he said that he was in fact involved in my disease but not in the way I imagined. 'You are making yourself sick by not listening,' he told me. Are *you* listening to *me*, Ford? This is important stuff." Marty fixed me in a teacherly glare.

"I'm with you. Go on." And to myself I said, *Damn. Not Marty, too. More "you've chosen your illness to learn from it" bullshit.* I frowned, but Marty was too into his story to notice.

"The demon explained further. 'I'm the designer of the unique shape of your personal symptoms. I did a really fine job this time, didn't I? You have to admire my skill.' At that, I stared directly into the small red being's dark eyes. 'Let me see if I understand this,' I said. 'You're creating mayhem in my gut to show me how wrong I am?' The red guy nodded and smiled in an annoying way. I went on. 'You're saying that if I figure this out, if I change the right things, I'll be healed?' 'Now,' replied the demon, 'you're chugging down the right track. Your soul's been screaming at you but you haven't been listening. Start listening. Do what it tells you and you'll win. If you don't, then I win.'"

By now, I'd suspended disbelief. "Go on," I told him.

"I asked the demon if he meant that I should do what I'd been thinking of doing all year. 'You don't have the guts,' he said. 'But if I did change my life, you'd leave me alone?' He just narrowed his eyes—they were as deep as black granite, those eyes—and said nothing. I didn't need him to answer. His meaning was clear. I sat and stared out over the dark lake

I'd been about to throw my sorry self into and when I turned back to my companion, he was gone. Believe me about this, Judith. It's very important that you get it. That day, *the very same day,* my fever dropped and my belly stopped aching."

"What was it you needed to do?"

"Think about it. What is it I've been doing this past year? Writing poems, playing rock and roll, smoking, drinking, having myself a good old time. Not difficult now, but at the time of my talk with this little fellow, I'd only been dreaming about these things, not doing them."

"Hmmm," I said noncommittally, still expecting some New Age admonition.

"Now, do not be afraid. I won't bore you with trying to act like a therapist," Marty said, as he pulled his chair closer. "Therapists, even you, talk far too much. The story and the song that carries the story say it all. I'll send you my new CD. This song's on it, and you'll like the rest of it, too. It's the best we've done so far."

Marty then chatted on about his band, who'd been fired and who'd come on board to replace them, where they're booked to play next, the plans for the next CD.

When he picked up his guitar to leave, I thanked him. "I'll think about your story." Then I added (more to let him know I understood than because I actually was wondering), "What is it, do you suppose, that my demon wants me to do?"

"Ask him," said Marty as he went out the door.

After Marty left I mulled over his story. I knew that he really meant it when he said he'd seriously considered killing himself when he'd been so sick for so long. I knew that he'd experienced that so-called demon as if it were next to him, talking to him, just like a real person. And I'd seen for myself how suddenly his health had taken a turn in the right direction. I'd been to his concerts and his poetry readings. I also knew he'd quit his teaching job in order to do the things he loved. After he quit his job his wife, with some resentment, had gone back to full-time work to keep the family afloat.

That was Marty's story. What was mine? Assuming that some action of mine could make me entirely well, what exactly was that action? I didn't think a demon was about to come talk to me but it wouldn't hurt me to think about what I'd been longing for before I got sick. Time to write, for one thing. But what else? If the rectifying action involved getting back to writing and doing it today, I was doomed. I couldn't write a short story or a poem right now if my life depended on it. I fell asleep that night trying to remember what had been missing in my life before I got sick.

In a dream that night I was again running down a road that was turning into molten lava behind me. As it surged closer and closer, I could feel its heat on the backs of my legs. I looked around desperately for a safe island, a refuge. There was none. A few feet ahead of me, a manhole cover tilted open. A scrawny red man, naked and horned, a demon similar to the one I'd seen in that earlier dream, stood inside the open manhole and beckoned to me. "Come," he seemed to be telling me. "Come down with me. This is your only hope." I hesitated; the demon reached for me, grabbed my shoulder, and pulled me close and then down into the flaming earth. All I could see was bright orange and red fire. But, as I fell, a soft mist rose up around me and the flames died out.

I didn't understand the dream right away, but in the next few days it began to make sense. The dream contained a similar message to the one I'd given myself weeks before, during my first hospital stay, when, for some reason I'd remembered being ten and climbing that tree, how at the top I'd felt totally free of any problems—like my mother's sorrows—that I couldn't control. After revisiting that memory, I'd been able, just for that one day in the hospital, to stop mulling over how I'd gotten ill and what I was supposed to do about it.

In my dream, the demon's message was similar: I had to surrender. He was trying to save me by telling me I had to somehow give myself over to the burning heat of this weird and horrifying illness.

Will that save me, I wondered, *if I relax and stop trying to save myself?* Marty had trusted his demon; maybe I should trust mine.

I'd tried so many ways to force myself to get well. Before I'd gotten so sick that I had to go to the hospital, I'd dragged myself to work every single day for weeks. I'd tried to keep up my daily running practice. I cooked and helped the kids get ready for the next school day. I walked the dog. All the while getting sicker and sicker. In the hospital I tried to hold onto life by doing things like keeping the window in my hospital room open, doing leg lifts in bed when I was so exhausted I could barely walk two feet from my bed to the bathroom. I took my own temperature. I got surly with the nurses. I took notes, a few, so I could write this story later.

Okay, then. I had to do what my demon was urging me to do: I had to let go. I had to stop trying to make myself well when I so obviously was not well. I had to crawl down that manhole through all that heat and smoke, into the deep underworld. I remembered what my teacher Dick

Olney had taught me years ago, again and again. *Be fully where you are; don't struggle to be where you are not. Your strength lies in fully embracing this exact moment. Lean into now. Feel all of it now, keep breathing, and you will move through to whatever's next.*

Thinking of Dick and how much I trusted him, I let myself feel everything I'd been trying not to feel, the pain in my body, in my bowels, in my muscles, in my chest; I let myself feel my grief over everything I'd lost (and thought I'd lost forever): my vitality, my gracefulness, my clarity of mind, my career, my imagination, my children, my loving husband, my everyday joy and even Timmy the dog. I'd loved my life, I'd loved simply being alive, and it was all gone, everything I'd loved was gone.

I sat with all that, sat in the face of my fear of death and cried and breathed. I fell down a hole, not a fiery one, but a cold black hole that seemed to have no bottom.

But there was a bottom. This hyper-awareness was overwhelming and I couldn't sustain it longer than ten minutes. Then fatigue or self-protection or habit or whatever took over and I shut down. Or maybe I moved through it, as Dick might have said. I let it carry me to the opposite shore.

In the days that followed I had to occasionally remind myself to let go of control and to feel my feelings, as difficult as they were. I couldn't live in that place very long but I could visit. And I believed it was good for me to go there, even though it was painful. Maybe because it was painful.

I began a pattern of crying every afternoon at four o'clock. It was involuntary, like a sneeze or throwing up. I couldn't have told you at the time what all those crying spells were about, I only knew they were irresistible and that I felt a little better after each one.

One afternoon at four Dr. Randall found me crying and offered to hook me up with a psychiatrist he knew. "Maybe an antidepressant would help, too," he said.

"No," I told him. "It's good for me to cry. It's helping me get better."

He looked puzzled. "Tell me if you change your mind."

2 4

Great Winds

"Sometimes I go about pitying myself when all the
time I am carried on great wings across the sky."

—OJIBWAY SONG

THAT AFTERNOON FOLLOWING MARTY's visit, Dick Olney came to see
me. I'd asked him to do another healing hypnosis with me. This time I
intended to tape-record the session so that I could re-induce the trance
whenever I needed to. At my request, a nurse had taped a do-not-disturb
sign to my door. Dick dimmed the lights and settled himself into the
chair, picked up the microphone and flicked its "on" switch. He invited
me to stare into the blue sky and green hills of the framed print on the
wall opposite my bed.

"Whenever you're ready, your eyes will close of their own accord,"
he intoned and sure enough, my eyes closed within three seconds of his
suggestion. "Your eyelids feel heavy now, so heavy. As if little weights
were attached to them, making it impossible for you to open them." I
tried. My lids felt as if they were glued shut. I had a split-second echo of
my childhood eye infections, a thread of fear, and then I was floating in
Dick's warm, deep voice, drifting wherever he told me to drift.

The next thing I was aware of was Dick telling me my eyes would
open of their own accord as soon as I was ready. They opened without
my choosing to open them and I was back where I'd started, gazing into

the not-very-nice art print on the wall. Yet now, its colors were gleaming, as if they'd absorbed sunlight. The room was quiet in a way that I didn't remember it ever having been. A stillness beyond sound. A stillness of being. Dick had set the microphone down and was searching for the off button on the tape recorder. I had no memory of what had happened while my eyes were closed.

"Do you want to rest for a while?" Dick asked in a quiet voice.

"Yes, I guess I do. What time is it?" I was tired but not groggy and not drained-tired. Sweetly tired. Serenely tired.

"Three," he told me. "You were out for ninety minutes."

Ninety minutes?

I must have been looking confused because Dick said, "You were in deep trance."

"I was asleep."

"You were not. You showed all the signs of deep trance." (A few years from then, in a hypnosis class, he would explain to me what some of these are: a certain pattern of breathing and eye movement, a stillness in the body, an immediate response to suggestions to begin to wake up.)

Dick came to the side of my bed, lifted one of my hands and held it for a moment in both of his. Then in a low voice, almost a whisper, he chanted, "Calling all wingeds, calling all wingeds. *Haya haya ho.* Take her where she needs to go. Show her what she needs to know, *Haya haya ho.*" He was silent for what felt like a full minute, then bowed his head over the hand he held and said, "I wish you a speedy recovery, my dear." He set my hand down carefully, as if it were something fragile and cherished, an ancient artifact, or a newborn kitten. He closed my door without a sound.

The door opened a few minutes later to admit a nurse who had come to check my vital signs. They were totally normal.

Chris came late that afternoon and spent an hour with me. "Chris, do you think I'm being the best me I can be?" I asked him

"What do you mean?"

"I told you about Marty and his demon." Chris chuckled and nodded. He thought Marty was nuts. "There's something I need to do differently in my life. I don't know that I've got it figured out quite but something to do with being more myself. Or being more present. I don't know. Something about that."

"I'm not real sure what you're talking about and I think you need to get some rest," Chris said.

I shook my head in frustration. "It was clear to me a minute ago. I hate this damn fog that takes over my brain!"

"You're just worn out."

"I suppose. See you tomorrow."

As the nurses made their final, bedtime rounds, I watched *Northern Exposure* and *The Tonight Show*. At midnight, someone brought me a sleeping pill. I drifted off to sleep remembering the words Dick had sung: *O mitakuye oyasin. Haya haya ho.* I expected to wake in a few hours despite the sleeping pill.

But I woke to sunlight. I woke to pain that was significant in its absence.

"I slept," I told the nurse when she came in, realizing this only as I voiced it. *I'd slept.* From midnight until six thirty. I hadn't woken up once. I hadn't had cramps. I hadn't spent even a minute on the toilet. I'd slept all night long and even now, I felt no urge to go to the bathroom.

"Oh my God," I whispered. "I'm okay." I called Chris and told him the news. He was less impressed than I wanted him to be. I didn't care.

I spent my morning expecting a return of the intestinal symptoms— maybe even a worsening, to make up for what I'd missed out on yesterday and last night. I'd have been quite willing to cope with it if it had happened. It wouldn't have diminished the significance of having had nearly twenty-four hours of freedom from the bathroom.

On August 22, the morning after my second good night of sleep, the day I was supposed to meet with a surgeon to schedule my colectomy, Dr. Randall came to me at seven, as usual.

"Guess what?" I said when he walked into the room. "I slept all night again and I've had no attacks of diarrhea for more than forty-eight hours."

"So I heard," he replied, smiling. "That's great!"

"What do you think it means?"

"Well, your colon seems to be recovering. I'm not at all sure why this happened so suddenly but I can't argue with success."

"What about the surgery?" I asked him.

"I think you're going to have forego that particular pleasure. I'll cancel the surgeon. This is really quite amazing, Mrs. Ford."

"My hypnotist friend was here yesterday. He told me I was going to recover completely."

Dr. Randall gave me the kind of look I'd give one of my kids if they told me they'd just been speaking with a unicorn in the backyard. "I'd put my money on the combination of medications and the subclavian line," he said.

Later that morning, I finally played the tape of my last session with Dick. I half-expected it to be blank after the "close your eyes" business, but it wasn't. Dick talked beyond that point in his droning induction voice. And soon, against my will again and counter to my intention to stay alert and listen, my eyes sagged and shut. The whole rest of the tape played without my hearing another word. I rewound and pressed "play" again. I stretched my eyes overly open. I even got out of bed and stood while I listened. I changed my gaze from window to wall to floor and back. I dug my fingernails into the palms of my hands. The tape was poor quality, full of static whisperings and rustlings. I caught a phrase here and there, and then, towards the end, these words, clearly : "Your colon will return to its natural pale pink color, to full healthy function, so rapidly that you will be amazed. You will amaze your doctors. They will not understand how this is possible, but it is possible. You will continue to recover at a rapid rate until you are fully recovered in every way."

Amazed. You will be amazed. Your doctors will be amazed.

Well, well. This was it then: I was getting well.

25

Alleluia!

"I return from one walk knowing where the killdeer
nests are in the field by the creek and the hour the
laurel blooms. I return from the same walk a day later
scarcely knowing my own name. Litanies hum in my
ears; my tongue flaps in my mouth Ailinon, alleluia!"

—ANNIE DILLARD, *Pilgrim at Tinker Creek*

THINGS STEADILY IMPROVED OVER the week. I was still being fed via the
subclavian line and I still felt like last week's garbage, but I hadn't had a
fever in over a week and although I still had some diarrhea, the agonizing
cramping had stopped.

And I was enjoying music again. I couldn't remember what it was I'd
found so annoying about it just a few days ago. Now I kept a tape playing
constantly on the boom box next to my bed. I did leg lifts and stretches
to the rhythms of folk tunes, concertos, and rock. I napped to New Age
melodies that repeated the same few musical phrases over and over and
to popular ballads as sweet and ordinary as a pack of puppies. Between
my morning exercise and my nap, I could now concentrate well enough
to read a chapter in *Busman's Holiday* by Dorothy Sayers or a few articles
in *Time Magazine*.

On Thursday, I went for a walk. I waited until the afternoon to ask a nurse to disconnect the clear plastic tube, the subclavian line, my umbilical cord. She flattened the entry port against my chest and fixed it there with broad white tape. And there I was, cut loose, on my own, for the first time in two weeks. I felt the way I imagined a skydiver would feel, cut loose from a parachute, falling free. The ground rushing up to meet me.

In the hospital lobby I passed the gift shop that smelled of scented candles and chocolate bars, turned the corner, and there they were: the doors to *Outside*. They were made of gray glass but I could see it was a fiercely sunny day out there. I hesitated. A young man in a suit, carrying a drug sample case and smelling of expensive cologne, strode past me and shoved open the door with the heel of his hand. I followed him out.

I stood motionless on the sidewalk outside the doors. If light were sound, there would have been a rock concert going on out there. The noises, the smells, the silken breeze against my skin, sunlight spraying all over everything. So much, so all at once. I steadied myself and took a big, breath, inhaling it all, suddenly euphoric: the sounds and the sunlight; the heat rising in transparent ripples from the street; the humid air, the exhalations of green leaves and blades of grass; all this humming, swirling life. I stood still, taking it all in while people walked around me, in and out the doors behind me. Cars pulled up to the curb and stopped. The hospital valet came out and opened doors, held shaky elbows, eased people into wheelchairs or walked them to the doors.

Eventually I took the first steps that would carry me across the parking lot, to the corner of Hartford and Maryland and onto the University campus. I walked slowly, still overwhelmed, not trusting that it was okay for me to be doing this. Not sure it was safe. Talking to myself. *I can do this. I can do this. Nothing bad will happen. I can do this.*

I traveled one slow block, turned into a service drive, walked another block to a long quad edged in layers of brick and shining glass: the math building, the School of Architecture, the daycare center. Parking meters, sunlight sparking off red and blue and silver cars, black tar oozing from cracks in the surface of the parking lot; small, square plots of young maple trees and impatiens. The sun beamed down on the top of my head. My legs felt insubstantial, hesitant and shaky, in spite of their many laps around 5-West. Walking in the real world required a different kind of motion. There were cracks and pebbles and inclines. I concentrated on the pragmatic concerns of balance and rhythm. Although my initial rapture had thinned, there was still a strong, steady beat of an unfamiliar happiness somewhere in the back of my mind.

Walking back to the hospital took a very long time. I was extremely tired. The focus required to keep me moving forward banished any hint of happiness. By the time I got back to the nurses' station on 5-West, an hour and a half had passed, an hour and a half to travel less than twelve blocks. When I walked off the elevator, I was no longer thinking about my exhaustion. I was thinking, *Well, that wasn't so bad. Tomorrow I'll do this again and go further.*

The next day as soon as Dr. Randall made his morning visit and the nurse unhooked my IV, I pulled on a pair of white athletic socks and my Nikes, which Chris had brought me the night before. I'd decided to walk all the way to the lake.

No hesitation at the hospital's doors this time; I walked right out into the blazing sun, as if it were nothing, and was instantly swept up in the heat and the light and the wondrous shapes and colors of ordinary, spectacular maple trees and cars and grass and wild chicory and dust and the sleek skin of the melting street, a cardinal singing loud above my head, a squirrel dashing up a tree, a young woman walking a golden retriever whose ears bounced with each step he took. My eyes darted from shadow to light to color to sparkle to shine. I was crying. This time not for fear. Not for pain. Or loss. I was crying because I was filled up with happiness beyond my capacity to contain.

I stopped crying by the time I reached the stoplight at the corner of Lake and Kenwood where I stood and waited for the walk sign to give me permission to cross. I knew I couldn't run across the street as I would done before I got sick, but when the light changed I walked across as quickly as I dared. I was winded when I reached the curb. I bent over and put my hands against my thighs, waiting for my heart rate to slow back to normal. A whole family of sparrows was singing in the leaves of a nearby mock-orange bush.

I walked a half-block further and reached the top of the bluff. Lake Michigan spread out to the horizon, sunlight caught in its waves, spar-kling up at me like a million winking eyes. As I began the trek down the steep hill to the beach I realized for the first time how far away I'd been all those weeks, how deeply buried.

I walked. I walked without filters, nearly skinless, murmuring out loud, not caring, *thank you, thank you, thank you.* Thanking God, I guess, and Dr. Randall, and Dick Olney, and myself. And more, thanking something enormous, something unnamable. For all of this, this simple act of walking down a hill on a sunlit morning.

Haya haya ho.

Six days later I would be sent home.

26

I Take My Waking Slow

"I wake to sleep and take my waking slow.
I learn by going where I have to go."
—THEODORE ROETHKE, "The Waking"

CHRIS CARRIED MY BOOKS and tapes, the boom box, the small duffel into which I'd tossed my few clothes, toiletries and prescriptions. Jessie pushed me in my required wheelchair and a nurse brought along a wheeled cart for the many plants and vases of flowers. We travelled down to the lobby and out the doors, into the parking lot where a nurse held my elbow as I got into the car and buckled myself in. And then, finally, I was home.

And back in bed.

It had been two months since my first hospitalization, about nine months since the earliest symptoms of my disease hit. Most of the time during the last two months, I'd been sick enough to believe I was dying. It would be another month before I could stay awake more than three hours at a time. Not only had I lost muscle mass and weight (about fifteen pounds from a starting weight of 124), I also was anemic, partly because of my formerly bleeding colon but mostly because of a proliferation of white cells and not enough red. This imbalance—called hemophagocytosis, or macrophage activation syndrome—I learned many years later (via an episode of *Grey's Anatomy*, Season 16, Episode 14) was particular to Still's disease but not ulcerative colitis. Every day I tried a few more of my formerly normal activities. Things like feeding the dog, reading to Nic, making myself a sandwich, taking a bath without help.

I read book after book about how other people integrate serious illness and injury into their sense of who they are. I read Sontag's *Illness as Metaphor,* Anatole Broyard's *Intoxicated by My Illness,* May Sarton's *After the Stroke,* Alice Sebold's *Lucky,* Lucy Grealy's *About a Face,* to name just a few. One of my favorites was *A Whole New Life* by Reynolds Price. In it Mr. Price describes, without a shred of self-aggrandizement or pity, his adjustment to living with a paralyzing and painful spinal tumor. "Come back to life, whoever you'll be," he wrote. "Only you can do it. How you'll manage that huge transformation is your problem, though, and nobody else's."[1]

I was coming back to life. I found my way back into my work life slowly. I went back to work in October when I'd been out of the hospital for about six weeks, but I limited my load to just five clients a week. (My usual schedule before the illness was twenty to twenty-five clients a week.) Every afternoon I lay down on the floor of my office, plugged headphones into my Walkman, and listened to as much of the Olney tape as I was able to stay awake for, usually only a few minutes. When I got home I napped for two or three hours. Every day. For weeks.

I stayed on high doses (60 milligrams a day) of Prednisone until January. It's dangerous to stop Prednisone all at once because the drug shuts down your adrenal glands. When you take away the Prednisone the adrenals need days, sometimes weeks, to reboot. In the interim, you feel like crap and also your symptoms are apt to recur. Dr. Randall tried to reduce my dosage by five milligrams sometime in mid-November and again a month later but both times my colon cramped and bled, indicating that my adrenals weren't up and running and that the drug was still essential for my healing. I had to go back up to the usual 60 milligrams. Finally, in early December, I made it through a whole week on a slightly lowered dose without any problems and then at the end of January I was drug-free at last. By then I'd also built my client load back up to full-time level.

As I picked up more and more of the threads of my life, I tried not to duplicate the pattern of overwork and self-denial that had contributed, I thought, to my immune system malfunctioning.

The daily naps helped and so did the long walks I took. I walked and listened to music. I walked and listened to my breath. I walked and smelled the changes in the air as September's ripe tomatoes and chrysanthemums

1. Price, *A Whole New Life,* 184.

leaned into October's falling leaves, as November soaked and baked the dead leaves and the scent of snow filtered into the cold mornings. I was walking when I met a red fox in the middle of an urban park on a bluff above Lake Michigan. I was walking when a flock of migrating hawks flew over my head, their calls bringing tears to my eyes.

Those walks brought things into my life that I badly needed and wasn't getting anywhere else, things more important than being jazzed up on running or overwork. But when I was back to working full-time again, I didn't have time for *both* naps and walking. I dropped the naps as soon as I was able to make it through a whole day without one. I dropped the walks because I could get more benefit from a thirty-minute run, I thought, than from a walk that took an hour or two. Running was more efficient and I loved it, loved the way it woke my every muscle and joint and flushed out the debris in my head.

I went for my first run since July in early November, two months post-discharge and still on Prednisone. My first run since that hot, humid day in July when I couldn't complete my planned distance and had to be rescued. I ran slowly but well enough in November and returned home exultant. The run was the proof I needed that I was getting my life back, all of it; I was getting myself back. I continued to regain the weight and the stamina that I'd lost while I was ill, and by January you wouldn't have been able to tell by looking at me that anything unusual had happened to me six months before.

Once in a while, usually in the middle of a run, I experienced an abrupt shift of consciousness, as if I hadn't been occupying my body and then suddenly I'd slipped back into it and opened my eyes. Saw how everything around me was haloed in light, made of light maybe, every smell and every sound heightened. And I'd be running along Lake Drive or Lincoln Memorial in a state of joy as intense as those first walks outdoors when I was in the hospital. And I'd remember how close it always was, this rapture, this wide-awakeness.

I imagined I would never take one second of my life for granted again. I would be wrong about that.

Even as I slowly accelerated back into my habit of packing every day until its seams gaped, I never forgot that at any moment my immune system could over-activate and slam me to the floor. This awareness made me want to get everything done even more quickly, have everything in even better order, because I might not have another shot at it. I must not, I thought, let a moment go to waste. Thinking of my life in this way, as if I'd been placed on the endangered list, also made me want to be wide-awake and completely alive every minute. I wrote the word *meditate* on my to-do list every week, but I never seemed to get around to it. The other items, like client phone calls and paperwork, grocery shopping and bill paying, raking leaves and carrying out garbage, always came first.

I thought I was managing my life fairly well even though I was back to being very, very busy. I considered my busyness to be simply what I had to do to be a good full-time therapist and a good mother. And an athlete. And a writer. And a supportive, fun-loving wife. In order to keep everything running I kept detailed daily schedules. As long as nothing interfered with these, I felt pretty good. I was doing just fine.

But life being what it is, there were always interferences. Every time the stressors mounted I expected to end up in the hospital. I calmed myself by remembering that yesterday and last week and the week before I had lots of stress too and I didn't get sick. I always found a way to pry open just enough space to accommodate whatever last-minute thing needed accommodating. Days and weeks and months of this and still I didn't get sick.

Once in a while late at night, when I was alone with Chris, I'd lose my equanimity. I ranted about my life, tearfully telling him that I didn't have long to live, that it was tragic for me to have survived the summer of 1990 only to find myself trapped now in a schedule that was killing me. Chris listened with a pained expression, not saying much, waiting it out. The next morning I'd go back to thinking I was fine and feeling embarrassed about what I said the night before. I'd get ready for work and go on as usual, promising myself I'd take more breaks. Promising myself that once I'd finished the major tasks of the day and everyone in my sphere—my clients, my family—was okay, I'd go for a long walk or take a nap or read a novel or write. Or meditate. Sometimes I'd even block out time on my calendar to do one or more of those things, but all too often something spilled over into that reserved time and washed it away, every minute of it.

If I had to put a number on it, I'd say that about 75 percent of the time I was okay, even happy. I felt very fortunate to be alive. To be alive and living with the love of my life, and to have come back from the near dead so recently. I liked my work, mostly, and was happy that my body worked well most days. I had lots of books and music, three healthy children, a parrot named Bill, and a bouncy golden retriever (Timmy). Not to mention food and shelter, all the basic survival needs covered.

On my refrigerator, I pasted a line from Dylan Thomas' poem "Fern Hill": "Time held me green and dying/ Though I sang/ in my chains like the sea."[2]

I sang in my chains like the sea.

And then, two years after recovering from my illness, as I was preparing to apply to a graduate writing program, my mother had a massive stroke.

2. Thomas, *Fern Hill*, 178–80.

27

Close to the Beasts

"You are still yourself, but you are no longer yourself:
from a near-angel like Ariel you have become a dull mass
which, like Caliban, is close to the beasts. As I said, in
human language, this is quite simply
called an apoplexy or stroke."

—ALEXANDRE DUMAS

November 8, 1992, 10:00 a.m.

THE PHONE RANG. I heard it. I ignored it. I expected it would be my father Bert. Again. He might be calling to ask me to run an errand or fix something for him. Not later. Now. No, it couldn't wait. The six- by eight-foot patio behind my parents' condo needed sweeping maybe. Or a loose screw in a bookshelf bracket needed tightening. Could I help him write out his checks? Buy a plant for Mom?

Could I come over?

I always had a hard time saying no to my father. He never whined or pleaded, but the desperation and fear folded into the tone of his voice, his choice of words, could always hook me. If I talked to him in the morning I ran the risk of giving away my whole day.

"No," I said to myself now, "not today. Today belongs to Jessie." Jessie already had her coat on; we were almost out the door.

143

As I picked up my purse and dug out my car keys I heard my father's hoarse breathless voice rise up like smoke from the answering machine. He was speaking slowly and carefully, leaving long gaps between his phrases. This was not unusual; he didn't have a lot of air or energy to spend on talking.

"Having a little . . . problem . . . with your mother this . . . morning," the voice wheezed. I stood in the hallway, my arm halfway into my jacket sleeve, weighing whether or not to pick up.

I knew that in a few hours my father wouldn't remember that he'd called me. He would call again. And then again an hour later. He had emphysema and was always short of breath. Whether due to his brain never getting enough oxygen or the effects of aging, his short-term memory had a tendency to erase parts of itself at random. He might be aware of what day of the week it was but he wouldn't have thought about whether or not it was a workday for me. On the days he did remember he generally failed to take into account that I was a psychotherapist, that people depended on me to show up for their sessions. I couldn't drop everything to come help him, I reminded him many times a week.

Whenever I succeeded in not talking to my father for a whole day—because I was at work or being particularly resolute—my answering machine would fill to its limit with his messages, each one more panicked and insistent. Almost every day when I came home from work my answering machine's red light would be flashing its message: too full, too full.

This particular day, November 5, 1992, was a teacher's convention holiday. No school for my fourteen-year-old daughter Jessie; I'd rescheduled my Thursday clients; Jessie's little brother Nic (age four) was in daycare; her stepsister Becky (fourteen like Jessie) was spending the day with her own mother. Jessie and I were planning to drive to Madison, ninety miles away, shop the boutiques on State Street and have lunch in this little French restaurant that had the best croissants in Wisconsin.

We rarely had time alone together anymore. When I left Jessie's father back in 1979 she was only eighteen months old. It was just the two of us until I remarried eight years later. She'd acquired a stepfather, a stepsister, and then a baby brother all within the span of a year. It was a lot to get used to. She didn't complain much but I could see that she sometimes felt overlooked.

For Jessie's sake as well as my own I decided I would call my father back when I got home in the evening.

I was halfway into my coat, one hand on the back-door knob, when my father said, "The paramedics . . . are here now. I think it might . . . be a stroke." I reached for the receiver. "I could use a ride . . . to the hospital." I picked up the phone.

"I'm here. What happened?"

"I was upstairs shaving," he said, haltingly but calmly, as if he were reporting on an article he'd read in the morning paper. "Your mother was eating her toast and reading a book in the living room like she does every morning. She screamed and I heard her fall. I got there as fast as I could. She was on the floor. Coffee and toast spilled all over. She was crying. It was hard for me to understand her."

"She was able to talk?" I asked. Jessie was standing in the hallway beside me leaning against a doorjamb, her body tense with listening. She loved her grandfather.

"Yeah, but real softly. I called 911. I had to. I tried to sit her up but I couldn't do it." Of course he couldn't do it, I thought. My mother probably weighed 160 pounds. He got worn out just walking across his tiny living room.

"Joojy? I think it's pretty bad."

Now I could hear the voices of the EMTs in the background. I pictured the black gurney filling my parents' narrow living room. The broad-shouldered young men leaning over my mother on the floor. The front door would be left open, cold November air challenging the furnace. The thermostat would have clicked on and the heat registers would be pushing hot air into an already stifling room.

"Do you suppose you could come get me?" His voice trembled slightly. "I don't think I should drive."

My parents lived in a community called Cherrywood Village, in a two-story, two-bedroom condominium, about ten miles from my house. The drive there usually took twenty minutes. Today it took ten. I drove as fast as I dared. And as I drove I pictured my father waiting, sitting in his chair, the one with the loose arms and the pilled, brown upholstery, the flattened cushions. He would be leaning his elbows on his knees, his chin in his hands, his face clouded with worry.

As I turned into Cherrywood Village I thought about how we all—Chris, Jessie, Becky, Nic, our golden retriever Timmy, and I—had dinner at my parents' house last weekend. My mother served spaghetti, my grandmother's recipe, the version I'd loved as a child. After dinner the girls cleared the dishes while my father told them a couple of bad jokes.

They laughed, their affection for him eclipsing their usual middle-school contempt. My mother told him he was a not-funny old fart and a silly old man. He pretended not to hear. He went to the sink to start the dishes, turned on the water, and grumbled something that I couldn't hear. As I turned onto the Cherrywood Village Road I realized we might never again share an evening like that with my parents.

I spotted my father standing outside the gray-and-white clapboard building (one of twelve identical gray and white buildings) that contained his condo unit. He waved a veiny hand at me as I slid the car up against the curb to save him steps. Six feet tall and 125 pounds (down from 190), wispy gray hair, cadaverous face. He was 74 years old but looked more like he was 90. As he bent to get into the car his portable oxygen tank, hanging by a strap over his shoulder, swung forward and clunked against the door. He eased himself into the passenger seat with a grunt, setting the tank down on the floor between his worn brown leather shoes.

"How is she doing?" I asked him.

"Doesn't look good," he said.

❧

As I brought the car to a stop outside the emergency room entrance, my father lapsed into guilty what-ifs. "Maybe if I hadn't had our Abby put to sleep this wouldn't have happened."

Abby, an elderly collie, my parents' favorite dog out of a series of five, had been more than just a pet: she'd been their only shared mission since my brother and I had grown up and built our own lives, our own families. A few months earlier, the morning my mother was in the hospital having her arthritic right knee replaced, Abby had collapsed, lain on the carpet breathing hard, and peed on the floor. My father was unable to lift or drag her outside to the doggy-bathroom of the lawn. Nor could he wrestle her into the people-bathroom or the kitchen to wash her matted soiled fur. She'd turned away from her last three bowls of kibble without even sniffing them. After much anxiety and deliberation, my father decided there was no choice but to drag her into the car and drive her to the vet and have her put to sleep.

It wasn't surprising that later he would second-guess this decision. It's always hard to let go of a beloved animal and my parents both loved Abby as much as (maybe more than) any of their own children. What made this situation even harder was that my father wasn't used to making decisions of this magnitude on his own. For decades he'd been the moon to my mother's planet. She was, in his opinion, emotionally fragile, easily overwhelmed and not nearly as bright as he was. He did his best to avoid upsetting her, but this time, he couldn't wait for her make the decision. She was in surgery, for one thing, but more importantly, he couldn't stand seeing anyone, human or animal, suffer. He was a kind man and when called upon, was a skilled healer. He'd nursed my brother and me through all our childhood illnesses and minor accidents. He'd never entirely let go of thinking of himself as a potential doctor. When Abby was failing, he had to take action; he had to end her suffering.

While my mother's knee was still being operated on my father had called me, choking back tears. He'd just said his final good-bye to Abby at the vet clinic. "How am I going to be able to break this news to your mother?" he'd asked me.

We went together to her hospital room the day after her surgery. "Abby's kidneys failed. She's gone," my father told her and both of us started crying. Surprisingly, my mother just said, "Oh no" and shed a few tears. We'd expected much worse: rage at my dad, the deepest grieving, full-out emotional collapse. None of that happened.

However, when the nurses brought her a bouquet of yellow daisies and a sympathy card the next day, the loss hit her harder. She called me right after that to complain about how stupid my father was and to ask me, "How could he kill our poor Abby?" I reminded her that there had been no other choice. She stopped crying. "Oh," she said. "That's right. I forgot she was so old." She was quiet for a minute and then said, "I know what I'll do. I'll sneak some of the grocery money out and save it every week so we can get a new dog in a few months. Don't tell your father."

Now as my father and I arrived at the hospital again, just three months after my mother's knee operation, I tried to reassure him that his decision to euthanize Abby hadn't caused my mother's stroke. "She would have died anyway, Dad. The vet told you her kidneys had shut down, remember? And Mom would have had this stroke even if Abby was still alive."

I glanced over at my father. His thin face was ashen and sad. His oxygen tank made soft, rhythmic click-clicks as he breathed. The transparent oxygen tube ran up beside his leg and across his lap, splitting into two tubes at the level of his throat and running behind each ear and to his nose.

"I suppose you're right," he mumbled.

As we approached the ER intake desk, a nurse hurried to get my father a wheelchair; I could see she thought he was the patient. Not surprising. His ten-year struggle with COPD (aka, emphysema; aka, a lifetime of smoking four packs of cigarettes a day) had so weakened him that by this point he could barely walk and couldn't do stairs at all, not even the short flight up to his second-floor bedroom. A few months ago Chris had installed a secondhand electric chairlift in my parents' condo.

My father had never been a paragon of physical or mental health. He was introverted, bookish and awkward, what psychotherapists call "emotionally constricted." Of course, he *had* feelings. I could remember seeing tears in his eyes on at least three occasions. But it was his inclination, his reflex, to diminish any feeling that struggled to rise up inside him. He would tamp it down, drench it with whatever it took to scatter the embers, and turn away. The accumulated residue had transformed into perpetual anxiety. A layer of depression had settled on top of that like the soot that covers everything in a burned-out building. The overall result was quiet gloom. In truth, way before emphysema narrowed his world his depression and anxiety had already done such a number on him that he felt comfortable only at home and to a lesser degree at work (when he had work). His few friendships had died of neglect.

The person the ER admissions nurse saw shuffling toward the reception desk was a wraith, a bedraggled, shriveled, frightened man hunched over from years of struggling to breathe and by the weight of his relatively light (light to me) portable oxygen tank.

As soon as I made it clear why we had come, the nurse led us back to an ER cubicle where my mother lay under a white sheet, another nurse holding her right hand. "Here's your family, I'll bet," that nurse said as my father and I entered. My mother's face lit up with recognition. The nurse let go of her hand and it fluttered up through the air above her body like a frightened bird.

"Somebody hold my hand!" she cried softly. Her voice was tense, as if straining with the effort of escaping through her constricted throat. Her eyes were half-shut and her face was tight with pain. My father shuffled to her bedside and captured her right hand in both of his. I reached for her left hand. It was limp and didn't hold on in return. My mother had never been much for holding hands with anyone other than small children but this wasn't reticence; it was paralysis.

Once we'd corralled both of my mother's hands my father and I stood, silent, at opposite sides of her bed, not knowing what to do next.

"I'm here," I told my mother. "I'm holding your hand. Can you feel it?"

"Yes," she said. "Oh, thank God you're here. I'm so scared."

"I'm sure you are," my therapist-self responded. My daughter-self didn't know what to say. I couldn't remember the last time I'd held my mother's hand. Was I ten or eleven? Younger?

"What happened?" she asked, opening her right eye wider to look at me. "Oh, I remember now. I fell down. It took your stupid father such a long time to find me. I yelled and yelled."

"You've probably had a stroke, Mom. That's what the doctor thinks. That's why you fell down."

"I ran down the stairs. It couldn't have been more than a minute before I got to you," my father said. "The paramedics brought you here and I called Judy."

As I watched my mother's face to see how she was taking this information, I was struck by how different the left side was from the right. On the left, her mouth drooped and her left eyelid was halfway closed over an unfocused sleepy-looking eye. The lines on that side of her face had vanished; she looked years younger.

She closed her right eye and whispered in a small, squashed voice, "A stroke. Just like my mother. I never wanted this to happen to me. My poor mother." Then, with more force, she moaned, "Oh! I'm in such pain!"

I looked down at her left hand and my eyes filled with tears. My mother had always taken good care of her hands. Her nails were shaped and polished, her fingers were long and smooth. The hand I was holding could have belonged to someone half my mother's age.

"Hold my hand," she moaned as if she didn't know I was already holding it. "I'm in so much pain. This is awful. I need Ativan. Get Dr. Amundson! I want Ativan. Why won't they give me my Ativan?"

"I don't think they can do that yet," I told her in the gentle voice I used with small children. "They're still running some tests."

"Hold my hand," she said again. My father and I were still holding her hands; I had the left one, he had the right one. He was sitting on a round stool a nurse had brought for him a few minutes ago and I was standing close beside the bed.

"We're both holding your hands," I said.

"Oh," she murmured. Then, gasping, "I'm in so much pain!"

"Where is the pain, Mom?"

She freed her right hand from my father's and fluttered it over her body, up and down. "Where is the soul located?" she said. "I don't know where it is."

For a moment I didn't realize she was answering my question. "You mean that's where the bad pain is? In your soul? Your soul is in pain?"

Her hand slowed and sought my father's hand again. "Yes," she whispered, sounding relieved that I had understood. "That's right. So much pain."

My mother held my father's hand, as if this weren't the same man she'd maligned every day of my childhood, as if this man was someone to trust and treasure. I had an inappropriate urge to laugh. I looked up and caught my father's eye. A little smile hovered over his mouth as he returned my glance. I imagined that he too had been touched by her saying her soul was in pain.

What am I supposed to say or do now? I wondered. In my professional life, I had confidence in my ability to guess what people needed and to provide comfort. I didn't guess right every time, of course. Jessie, for example, when she was a kindergartener, had insisted that my kisses didn't do a darn thing to make owies feel better. Kisses would certainly do no good here.

All my life I'd tried to come up with ways to make my mother feel better. She'd always been the one person whose skin I could never inhabit, whose white slip-on Keds I could never walk a mile in.

By the time I was in first grade I knew she wasn't happy. I thought it was at least partly my fault, as young children always do. But I couldn't figure out how to be a better kid and I didn't understand what else was the source of her pain.

One day while searching for dress-up options in the back of my mother's closet I found a tailored black suit and a black hat with a veil. I asked if I could have it, but no, my mother said; that suit and hat were what she'd worn for her wedding to my father. I was shocked. Where was the long white lacey dress and the puffy white veil, like my bride doll had? Poor Mommy. I felt so sorry for her. No wonder she was unhappy! But no, my mother explained. It wasn't the black suit that made her unhappy; what made her unhappy was having married my father.

So that was one thing: my father, this man I loved and relied upon, was somehow making her sad. Over time I also realized, from short snippets of stories about my mother's childhood, that her parents hadn't been as nice as mine. I felt sorry for her about that, too. I thought my parents were pretty cool. And in hindsight, yeah, they kind of were, from a grade school perspective. They noticed me and bought me nice things, took me nice places; they gave Dick and me a lot of freedom even before we reached our teen years, to ride our bikes with our friends around our small suburb and to hang out with just our friends, no parents, at the local movie theater on Saturday afternoons. All things that mattered a lot to me at the time.

Once I even told my mother I wished I could shrink her down to my age and have her share my childhood with me. She'd be my best friend and I'd share with her every cool thing I owned, like Toodles, my walking doll, or my vast collection of stuffed animals. I told her I'd invite her to sleep over at my house and how at night, after the grownups turned off the lights, we'd get in my bed and make each other laugh till our tummies hurt. We'd kick our feet between the white cotton sheets and make sparks. In the morning we'd have French toast with puddles of maple syrup.

When I was a grade school kid I didn't understand about depression or alcoholism and didn't recognize either condition, both of which existed in my otherwise good parents. I was aware of course that my mom and dad were shaky sometimes, said mean things to each other, or got very quiet for hours or even days. But I didn't dwell on any of that. Looking back, though, I realize I didn't entirely trust them to keep me safe, not from Gary the bully who lived two doors away or from the monsters that lived under my bed and in my nightmares.

If my mom had had parents like the ones I thought I had when I was in second grade, could that have lightened her darkness? Help her not be depressed? Would she have been able to avoid drinking?

As I stood by my mother's bed I was sad for her again and felt as helpless as I had when I was a child.

I resisted the urge to chew on my lip the way I used to when I was seven.

"Why doesn't God love me? What did I do to deserve this?" my mother moaned. A quick glance at her face told me that these words were no joke to her. She was deadly serious. Her eyes were closed and the muscles of the mobile side of her face were clenched in a grimace. She tried to roll over onto her inert left side and fell back onto the mattress. She lifted her head slightly and dropped it again, obviously unable to get comfortable. "I know why I'm being punished," she said in a whisper, opening her eyes, directing this comment to me.

"Why, Mom?" I leaned closer to her so I could hear her answer.

"It's because of how mean I've been to your father."

Surprised by this admission I looked over at my father, hoping he would answer her. Hoping, I suppose, that he would exonerate her. He was studying the hand he was holding, or maybe focusing on the floor. I couldn't tell if he'd heard her or not.

After a few minutes of silence I offered, "God wouldn't hurt you like this." Which was easy for me to say since on most days I didn't believe in God or any other kind of anthropomorphized or punitive life force. I wanted to reassure my mother that she hadn't been so very mean to my father. But of course all three of us knew that she had been.

My father had begun his habit of being my mother's personal attendant and footstool in the early years of their marriage when my mother was probably at her healthiest. It didn't seem to matter to him that over time her criticisms of him grew more and more barbed. "I suppose you're going to sit there and look stupid all day," she would toss at him on her way out the door on an errand. "Hey, useless," she'd say when she returned. "Why don't you get off your big duff and help me with these groceries?" When my father finally traded his cigarettes for supplemental oxygen, she started calling him the dope on a rope.

My father had wanted nothing more for his precarious peace of mind than to make his wife happy. This goal had proven, despite his 180+ IQ, to be unreachable. The longer she was married to him the less she seemed to notice my father's better qualities, like his commitment to our family, his loyalty to her, his patience, his predictability. Maybe that was in part because she was only nineteen when they married and she probably thought that marriage would fix her whole life, make her feel attractive and important and keep her entertained and of course no spouse on the planet could have lived up to that. Or maybe it was more about her having grown up with a philandering alcoholic father and a disappointed judgmental mother.

Although my father tried to please his wife, he wasn't good at reading her. He was sometimes clumsy. Sometimes he decided that something he'd promised my mother he'd do was really not so important. He would do it differently. Or later. Or not at all. I imagined that once in a while it must have felt good to him to screw up. It allowed him to take up a little more space in their joint lives. Most of the time, though, he ministered to my mother without complaint.

Suddenly she cried out again in her thin childlike voice, "It hurts, it hurts!" She pulled her right hand free from my father's hand and grabbed the left side rail on her narrow bed. She pulled hard, lifting her right shoulder then flopping back against the mattress with a gasp.

"Oh, this awful feeling!"

For some reason, right then I realized that the room we were in was familiar. Even before I could nail down the memory, my heart began to race with fear. I'd lain in this very same room two and a half years ago, maybe on the same bed my mother now occupied. My joints were aching, my head was on fire with fever, my skin prickled with rash. I had no idea how sick I was that first night, or how many months it was going to take before I'd be well again. I still didn't totally trust that my health would last.

I'd thought I was in complete charge of my life before I ended up in this ER. I knew who I was, where I was headed, and how it should all work. There was no room for illness in that picture. By the time I got sick in 1990, I'd also done a pretty good job of untangling the stuff I needed to untangle from my childhood. I'd found ways to hold onto the good things my parents had taught me and to drop the stuff that wasn't helpful. I'd identified areas I needed to fix and fixed what was fixable. Freud defined mental health as success in love and work. I had all that. I'd finally found the right man, the right career. What I didn't have was an ability to set everything down and rest; what I didn't know how to do was to stop running everything and let someone else take over. What I didn't know— what the illness had shown me and I was still trying to accept—was that illness is inevitable, as inevitable as death.

It would do me no good to linger on all that now, I thought. The fear, the vulnerability, the denial that had made me resist the help I'd so badly needed.

I made myself refocus on my mother, on her hand in mine, on whatever was going to happen next for her. I tried to imagine what that might be but my brain refused to move away from the present where we—my parents and I—waited, encircled by a pastel blue curtain that hung from the ceiling.

28

Rabbits

"We'll have a cow," said George. "An' we'll have
maybe a pig an' chickens . . . an' down the
flat we'll have a . . . little piece alfalfa—"
"For the rabbits," Lennie shouted.
"For the rabbits," George repeated.
"An' I get to tend the rabbits."
"An' you get to tend the rabbits."

—JOHN STEINBECK, *Of Mice and Men*

WE'D BEEN WAITING AT my mother's bedside for around half an hour when we heard approaching footsteps and the curtain was pushed back. A tall brown-haired man in khaki pants and a short-sleeved yellow shirt entered our circle. He introduced himself as Dr. Amundson. I offered him my chair. He sat down and took my mother's hand.

"I'm so sorry this happened to you," he said to her. "The blood thinners were supposed to prevent it. This should never have happened." He sounded sad, not just sad like a doctor who wants you to be well but sad like a brother or a cousin or a friend. Sad like someone who'd wanted to protect you and had failed.

Although I'd never met Dr. Amundson I knew my mother had been seeing him for the past several years and that she'd confided in him about her unhappy marriage. According to my mother, the doctor had advised her to get a divorce, assuring her she didn't have to put up with her husband's mistreatment. She'd clearly been pleased to have this guy on her side. I guessed she'd told him the same kinds of things she'd told me over the years, that Bert was vicious and stupid and dense as a stone. That if it weren't for him she'd be happy. Obviously she hadn't told Dr. Amundson about my father's loyalty and kindness or the many ways she demeaned him.

I wished Dr. Amundson had had the opportunity to observe these two in their natural habitat, their overheated living room with its smoke-yellowed wallpaper. Then maybe he would have revised his opinion about who'd done what to whom.

Now it occurred to me to wonder what my mother might have told this man about me. That I'd been a lovely little girl until I hit college and turned into a wanton, rebellious, pot-smoking hippie who was totally beyond her understanding? That I'd abandoned her by moving out on my own at nineteen? Refused to visit her in any of her many alcohol rehab stays? Or that I was a loving mom, a successful career woman, and a delight in every way?

The doctor patted my mother's mobile right arm, said, "I'll be right back, Mary," and asked me to join him in the corridor. There, he opened a manila folder and showed me an image of her brain. "This area here," he pointed to an irregularly shaped cloud that covered about a quarter of the right side of her brain, "indicates that your mother has had a massive stroke. I'm not sure whether we should hope for recovery."

"She might die, then?" I asked this bravely enough. As if I could stand to hear the answer.

I'd expected my mother to die at any given moment during my entire childhood. I'd never been sure what was wrong with her but I knew, even as young as six, that she wasn't well. She had asthma; that much was obvious because from time to time she was taken to the ER in an ambulance to receive life-giving IV epinephrine. This was back before the day of the rescue inhaler. My mother also napped every afternoon for at least half an hour. She had agoraphobia that prevented her from attending many of my school events. I knew these things weren't just normal mom things; my friends' mothers weren't as frail as mine.

My efforts to be perfect began as early as first grade when I won the PTA early reader award. I liked the attention but even more I liked seeing my mother smile. I did my best from then on (or maybe this started even earlier?) to never upset her, to be helpful and obedient. I loved her ferociously and I didn't want her to come apart.

I learned to watch her like a meteorologist watches the sky. I always knew before my father did when she was going into one of her dark depressions but I never knew what to do about it. Of course not, I was a child and her unhappiness wasn't about me. I didn't begin to see that until I was in my teens.

When I was in high school my mother told me about her periods of depression, her bouts with less than effective outpatient psychiatric treatments including taking Thorazine which had made her feel crazy. She confided in me about her many anxiety attacks which she blamed on my father. When I was in school at the University of Wisconsin in Madison I took advantage of the University library's medical section to try to diagnose my mother. Looking through the heavy books for answers, I discovered the word "neurasthenia," an old-fashioned word for "fatigue, weakness, anxiety, and localized pain without physical cause" (we now might call it chronic fatigue syndrome) and thought maybe that was her diagnosis. Or was it her immaturity and her inexperience with life beyond the walls of her own house?

That her drinking was a factor for many years—as cause or coping mechanism or both—is indisputable. One drink would make her face redden. Two sharpened her voice to a glittering edge. At that point anyone, including my brother or me, could become the focus of her nasty biting wit. Three drinks or more and she'd slur her words and walk with a loose and precarious gait. By the time I was seventeen I'd learned to stay in my bedroom after five. And later, when I was on my own, I never phoned my mother in the evenings.

Eventually one of my mother's many doctors speculated that she might have the autoimmune disorder lupus, although her blood work didn't have any of the earmarks of lupus. When, years after my mother's stroke, I finally got a definitive diagnosis of my own illness, I wondered if maybe my mother had actually had a mild version of the same disease, adult-onset Still's, AOSD. It's a notoriously difficult disease to diagnose and during my mother's time they probably didn't even know it existed.

In her mid-thirties, when I was in grade school, my mother decided her drinking was out of control. For the next fifteen years she careened in and out of sobriety, attending AA meetings sporadically, changing sponsors often. It took six stints in inpatient alcohol rehab centers before she was able to give up her Manhattans. In the early seventies, when I was in college, her roommate hanged herself in their shared bathroom at the Dewey Center, a Milwaukee inpatient alcoholism treatment center. During a family session the next day my mother announced that this woman's death had woken her up. She was never going to drink again. And she didn't.

My mother changed so much in the years following that I still sometimes had trouble reconciling the person she'd become with the one I remembered from my childhood. At the time of her stroke, she hadn't had a Manhattan—or any other form of alcohol—since that last rehab nearly twenty years ago. Wouldn't even eat a rum ball or use mouthwash or a cough suppressant that had an alcohol base. She'd earned her real estate license, started taking yoga classes and begun keeping a journal. She never slurred her speech and the only person at whom she still aimed poisonous words these days was my father.

Despite her sobriety, my mother had continued to have health problems. In 1989, the year before I got so seriously sick, my mother needed the mitral valve in her heart replaced. She'd slid through the surgery without any complications. Five days later they sent her home with a prescription for Coumadin, the blood-thinning medication she'd still been on when she had her stroke.

In 1990, just before I went to DC for that family therapy conference, she'd been diagnosed with lymphoma but one course of chemo and several radiation treatments had pushed it into remission. The lymphoma had barely had time to become a memory when my mother found she needed a knee replacement. That had happened just a few months ago.

"Do you think she'll die?" I asked Dr. Amundson again.

"Yes. She might," the doctor said. "And if she lives, she is going to have significant disability."

Behind me I heard the soft hiss of the automatic doors of the ambulance bay sliding open, the sound of footsteps, indistinct voices, the roll of the wheels of a gurney. I felt the chill of a November breeze against my back and my hair blew forward and into my eyes. The automatic doors closed and I pushed the hair off my face. The light in the corridor where we stood seemed to have dimmed slightly, the edges of the doorways softened and blurred. As if a fog had rolled in.

"Is her left side paralyzed?"

"Yes. There will be some cognitive impairment too. We won't really know how much for a while. Her brain is swelling now. She'll probably be sleepy and confused for the next twenty-four to forty-eight hours."

I nodded and swallowed hard.

This was so damn unfair, I thought. My mother had been doing so well. She'd recently finished the PT for her new knee, was still walking with a cane but walking well. She'd given up her habit of eating a large Hershey's milk chocolate bar every afternoon and had been losing weight. She was an active member of the Milwaukee Spinners' Guild and had been looking forward to the day when her new knee would be strong enough for her to return to the monthly meetings. She owned two spinning wheels and over many months had spun enough yarn to knit sweaters and mittens for her children and grandchildren; she'd hoped to be done by Christmas.

"You should consider a do-not-resuscitate order," Dr. Amundson continued. "I don't think she would want to be stuck on a ventilator that she'd probably never get off of." I looked into his tense face; his eyes still fixed on the CT scan results. I was surprised again to see that this man seemed to care so much about my mother.

I knew his statement was logical and that it fit the situation. But I couldn't think about a do-not-resuscitate order. I mean that literally. I was shocked at my inability to think or speak. I knew I had to do something to protect my mother from spending her final days on a ventilator or from having white-coated medical people shock her with electric paddles and pound on her chest, but I didn't think I had the authority to make this kind of decision. It should be my dad, shouldn't it? He was the medical brain of our family and her closest kin; Maybe Dr. Amundson didn't consider my dad competent after the way my mother had described him to the doctor?

"This isn't my decision to make alone," I managed to say. "I'll need to discuss it with my father and brother." I looked away from Dr. Amundson, away from the nearby room where my mother lay, looked down the hazy hallway towards the waiting room. Three people sat there with the nearly empty coffeepot. A silent television was mounted high on the wall above their heads.

I used the pay phone to try to reach my brother Dick, left him a message at his home and at work. I called Jessie, too, to tell her I wouldn't be home any time soon.

I walked back into the curtained area where my mother lay. She was still groaning and pulling herself upright, falling back against the mattress, over and over again. My father was still holding her right hand. He looked across her restless body at me and nodded a greeting. I took my place next to the bed and picked up her other hand, the one that couldn't move.

It felt warm and still, reminding me of the feel of Jessie's little hamster, Herman, when he'd curl up and sleep in the palm of my hand. I stroked my mother's long thin fingers, noticing her narrow gold wedding band and the tiny diamond engagement ring that matched it. There wasn't much point in doing anything other than this, this sitting and being-with. It didn't matter anymore that I couldn't figure out some right thing to say. There was no right thing to say.

The fog that had cushioned the impact of Dr. Amundson's words had dissipated. Now my chest ached with a peculiar sensation of heaviness and void. The low hum of voices, footsteps, fluorescent lights, and machines spread out over and around my parents and me like water flowing over stones. My mother's new voice, a little less desperate now, broke the silence. "This is too much."

"You're damn right it is," I responded with more force than I intended.

"Be sweet. Say sweet things to me," my mother whispered.

A nurse walked in. "Dr. Amundson said you could have some Ativan now, Mary." She unhooked part of the IV tube and squeezed the contents of a clear syringe into it.

"Call me Honey," my mother said. This, like the handholding, was uncharacteristic. She was not in the habit of calling anyone Honey or Dearest or Sweetie.

The nurse smiled down at her. "Sure. You should start to feel a little less uncomfortable now, Honey."

My mother smiled back with half her mouth and closed her eyes. Her imperfectly dyed hair straggled limply against a bright white pillow. Her body looked small under the equally white hospital blanket, as if she were a ten-year-old.

"George," she said, her eyes still closed. She seemed to be addressing my father. Whose name was not George. "Tell me, George . . ."

I looked at my father, questioningly. His glance met mine; his eyes were red.

The skin around them was soft and puffy, ringed in blue gray, a paler shade than his stubbled chin and upper lip.

"About the rabbits . . . tell me about the rabbits, George."

My father's face flushed. "Okay." he said, "I'll tell you about the rabbits. Only for us it's dogs. We'll have another dog. You just get well and we can get another dog."

"A collie." she said. "Make sure it's a collie."

"Yes." he said. "A collie." He nodded. His eyes were closed, a wry smile on his face. His lower lashes were damp with tears.

And then, my mother opened her eyes and looked directly at me for the first time since I'd arrived. She no longer looked like a child; she'd re-inhabited her treacherous body for what would turn out to be only a minute or so, and for this short time she was entirely herself. The woman she'd been until this morning, the one who had the use of all four of her limbs as well as her mind, the one who could crack jokes, slide a steely remark in between your ribs so fast you'd never see it coming, who every morning would sit on her couch with a Hollywood biography and eat toast and drink coffee—*my mother*—was there in those eyes. The only clue that something unusual had happened to her was that she had to turn her head at a coy angle so that the right side of her field of vision could find me.

"Well," she said with incongruous clarity and cheerfulness. "Now you'll have something worthwhile to write about."

29

An Infant in a Woman's Body

"On the morning of the hemorrhage, I could not
walk, talk, read, write or recall any of my life. I
essentially became an infant in a woman's body."

—JILL BOLTE TAYLOR

November 8, 1992, 4:00 p.m.

WHEN I THINK BACK to the day my mother had her stroke, I remember
it as two distinct parts: the first part, six hours in the emergency room,
bathed in bright fluorescent light, shock and urgency; the second, a quiet
room on the hospital's third floor, my father and I sitting, waiting, listening to the sound of his oxygen tank and my mother's quiet breathing. The
Ativan, delivered through her IV line, coupled with the swelling of her
injured brain, had dampened her pain and restlessness. She floated now
in a light coma, from which, the doctor had predicted, she would begin to
emerge in a day or two. Then, he'd said, we would know more.

"How long do you want to stay, Dad?" I asked. My father sat in a
flesh-colored armchair, bent over with exhaustion, resting his head in
his hands. A few strands of thinning, gray hair wilted over his forehead.

"She needs us here," he answered, not looking up.

"Okay. You tell me when you think it's time to go."

"I will," he said. A few seconds passed. Then he added, almost to himself, "She doesn't know we're here, does she? I guess it's me that needs us to stay."

"That's fine, Dad. We'll stay." My father nodded. Then, sighed loudly down at his lap.

I sat near him on the wide sill of the room's one window. I reached over and laid my hand on his back. I could feel his shoulder blades, unprotected by any body fat, moving with the hard work of his breathing. His portable tank had long ago run out of oxygen. The hospital had provided him with a loaner, a green metal, bullet-shaped thing that stood upright beside his left leg. The hiss of the new tank, my parents' breathing, the heating system fan that pushed hot air into the room, all blended together into a lulling hum.

In the relative quiet of that room, I remembered my mother words in the ER: "Tell me about the rabbits, George."

"Dad," I asked, "that thing Mom said, about the rabbits? Who's George and why rabbits?"

My father smiled, chuckled almost silently. "It's a line from the ending of the movie *Of Mice and Men*. We watched it on TV last week."

"Really?" I was amazed. I knew *Of Mice and Men* well, both the book and the film; it hadn't occurred to me that that was what my mother was referencing. I remembered the ending scene as clearly as if I were in my parent's condo right that minute watching their old color TV with them. You never forget that ending once you've read the book or seen the movie. Lennie, a mentally disabled young man, has accidentally killed a woman. He and his brother George, who has sworn to take care of Lennie forever, are hiding from a lynch mob. George has a gun; the reader or the viewer is pretty sure this isn't going to be a happy ending. Many times in the story when Lennie's upset about something, he asks George to tell him about the rabbits. George describes the farm and the animals he and Lennie will own someday. Lennie will get to be in charge of the rabbits, George reminds him every time. Lennie loves soft things like rabbits.

In the final scene of the film, with sounds of the posse approaching, George tells Lennie to turn away from him, supposedly so the images he's describing—their future home with its cows and sheep and rabbits—will be more vivid. "An' I still get to tend the rabbits, George?" Lennie asks in a cheerful childlike voice. Then George shoots him in the back of the head just before the posse appears.

It occurred to me, sitting there beside my father that my mother loved soft things, too. Dogs calmed her the way soft things calmed Lennie. For years she'd slept with a series of dogs while my father had slept alone in his own room.

"So, Dad," I said. "Did Mom mean she wanted you to calm her or reassure her like George did with Lennie? Or did she mean she knew she was doomed, like Lennie? No way out."

"I don't know," my father shook his tired head. "Maybe both. I took it that she wanted me to somehow save her. And she wanted me to promise we'd get another dog."

I nodded, thinking but not saying, *Like Lennie; no one will be able to save her either.*

We sat quietly after that, until my brother Dick arrived.

"I came as soon as I got your message," he said, as he walked into the room. "I was out in the truck, and no one was home. I'm sorry."

"I'm glad to see you," I told him. I filled him in about what the doctor had said and that the next twenty-four hours would determine whether our mother would survive or not. Dick nodded, his eyes on her.

He leaned over the railing of her bed and spoke softly into her ear. "Hi, Mom. It's Dick." She gave no sign of having heard him. He straightened up and came to sit beside me on the windowsill, his long legs filling the space between the window and her bed. "Maybe she'd rest better if we dimmed the lights," he suggested, his eyes never leaving her face.

My mother looked peaceful to me, compared with how she'd thrashed and moaned in the ER before they'd given her the Ativan. But if my brother thought a dark room would help, that was fine with me. I'd been with her since nine in the morning; it was now close to four. I had learned through these hours that nothing any of us could do was going to help, or even reach her, but I understood the need to try. I found the switch near the doorway and turned off the bright ceiling light.

The next to arrive was Chris. Chris was forty that year, about the same height as Dick, a little thinner. Although he was the youngest person in the room, he had more gray hair than any of us, a gift of genetics. His graying hair plus his thick, wire-rimmed glasses, his lankiness, and his prominent nose, gave him an Abe Lincoln kind of look. People tended to trust Chris even before they knew him. The sight of him as he walked, backlit by the bright hospital hallway, into my mother's dim room, was enough to make me believe, for the first time that day and against all evidence, that somehow everything was going to turn out okay.

Chris hugged me and kissed my cheek. I took his hand and walked him out into the corridor so we could talk. He immediately started asking questions, like the lawyer he was, listening for what was said and what was left out, listening for inconsistencies. "They're sure it's a stroke?" *Yes, absolutely.* "Is she paralyzed?" *Looks like it.* "What are they doing for her?" *Waiting. For now. Just waiting.*

"Is she going to make it?" he asked at last. I shrugged and looked away, the tears I'd resisted all day welling up again in my eyes and throat. Later I would be able to get the words out, to tell him that even though the doctor gave her a fifty/fifty chance of survival, I knew my mother was gone. She would never again be the complex woman who'd known me all my life, taken me to ballet classes, held me on her lap, read stories in funny voices, had been desperately sad, obscenely angry, this woman, who in my childhood had created the best and the worst of times, was lost.

When I was a little girl, worrying about my mother's survival, I couldn't imagine that I would continue to live if she died. Even after I was old enough to be aware that we were separate people, not one unit, I believed that if she died, it would be the end of me, too. I thought I'd follow her the way a train car is pulled by the one in front of it. Right off the tracks and sideways onto the ground. Or if not that, I'd simply blink out. And the world with me. I couldn't imagine a world existing without her in it. Now, at the age of forty-four, I knew I wouldn't die when my mother did. I also knew that her death would be no small thing for me. I loved her, with less ambivalence than I'd realized, and I would miss her.

I couldn't say any of this then. Chris wrapped his arms around me and the rest of my composure dissolved. People walked by us in the hospital corridor. The sight of someone weeping in someone else's arms was, I knew, as common here as the intercoms that called for Dr. So-and-so to answer line, a gurney's wheels whispering against the linoleum, the exhalation of an elevator door closing.

30

Side Effects

"Is the runway icy?
Was the gun loaded?
Could this cause side effects?
(...)
Will it get any worse?"

—JEANNE MARIE BEAUMONT, "Afraid So"

November 9, 1992

IT WAS 9:00 P.M.; twelve hours after my mother's stroke. Exhausted and numb from sitting so long at her bedside, I finally went home. As I drove I compiled a lengthy to-do-before-bed list. Which immediately began to make me feel better. My heart rate slowed, my shoulders dropped down from around my ears and my brain cleared. By the time I walked into our flat, I remembered the things I'd been concerned with before my father had called me that morning, before I'd heard those words, "having a little problem with your mother."

I could hardly wait to get back into my own life, back to my house, my husband, and my kids.

After saying hello to everyone and answering "How's Grandma?" with as few words as possible, I went straight to the kitchen. Never in my life had I so welcomed housework, emptying and reloading the dishwasher and wiping off the countertops, picking up toys. Next, I checked Jessie's homework in spite of the fact she'd been doing homework all on her own for years. Then I not only read Nic a bedtime story, I also made up another episode in the ongoing tale of Mumford, the moon man.

Mumford was a family creation, a soothing story made up in nightly sequels tailored to help Nic deal with normal kindergarten fears like monsters under the bed, thunderstorms, burglars, or classroom meanies. The night of my mother's stroke, my version of the Mumford tale involved our hero curing a miniature planet of red creatures with terrible headaches. After the story, Nic and I arranged his dream team, the twenty-three stuffed animals, dogs, bears, birds, and dragons in their correct order (Nic remembered the order; I never did) to protect the bed's perimeters. Their steadfastness and implied immortality gave my four-year-old son the courage he needed to close his eyes and trust he'd come out whole in the morning.

By the time I went to sleep that night, I'd built my own magic circle out of washing dishes, packing lunches, and kissing children goodnight.

The next morning, I went to work and, for eight hours, dealt with problems that were mostly solvable, talked to people who could respond in complete and cogent sentences, and didn't dwell on my newly paralyzed mother. Of course, I thought of her, but only here and there for a minute or two. My mind needed to be occupied (and wanted to be occupied) with my clients' concerns, not my own.

At noon, I called my mother's primary nurse. There was no change in her condition; she was still asleep or unconscious most of the time. At around five I drove back to the hospital.

As I rode up to the third floor on the elevator, I reminded myself not to expect my mother to look like herself. When I'd last seen her she'd been in a light coma, pale and limp, lying on her back, mouth gaping slightly open. The bed had been adjusted so that its head was elevated, to reduce the possibility of her choking on her saliva and the metal side rails on both sides were raised. She'd looked as if she were sleeping in an oversized crib.

I walked into her room. All the lights were off. The window directly across from the doorway caught my eye: rows of small yellow rectangles, the fluorescently lit classrooms of the university building across the street, the same building I'd watched from my own hospital bed two summers ago. I still remembered the daycare children sitting in three red wagons being pulled by three young women. All of them, adults and children alike, wearing bright yellow and red and blue in the glaring July sunlight. Nighttime out there now, and cold.

Enough fading autumn light spilled in from the window and from the fluorescent lights in the corridor behind me to illuminate the shape of my mother's body in the bed although the bed itself and chair beside it were furred with shadows. Her face was turned away from the door, towards the wall. I walked around the bed, and the "hello" I'd been planning to deliver stopped in my throat. Even in the dim light, I could see the right side of her face was swollen, her right eye surrounded with a red and purple bruise, her right cheekbone scuffed. There was a scab on her lower lip.

"Mom?" I put my hand on her shoulder and squeezed it to wake her. Her eyes fluttered open.

"Hullo," she mumbled, not very clearly.

"What happened?" I asked, trying to keep my voice casual and steady. My heart was racing.

"Ah had a shtroke," she slurred the words. Her voice was a whisper. "M'in the hospital. Sh'at right?" she looked up into my face, as if she could read the correct answer there. "Sh'at's wha a nursh toll me."

"That's right. Yes, you had a stroke yesterday. But, Mom, something happened since I left you last night. Your face is all bruised."

"Ih hurtsh," she told me, as if she'd just noticed. She raised a trembling right hand to her forehead, flinched when her fingers brushed against the angry bruise surrounding her eyebrow.

"How did that happen, Mom?"

"Dunn no," she looked frightened and confused. "Don remembah." She paused. "They say fell out ma bed."

"You fell out of bed?" I repeated. "How?" My voice was getting louder; I wanted to pace, which is what I always did (still do) when anxious, but instead, I grasped her bedrail and held on to it tight. My mother was able to tell me, in her crippled speech, that she'd tried to get up to go to the bathroom. Much to her surprise, she'd landed on the floor. She remembered that someone had come and helped her back to bed.

"But you've got bedrails on your bed. How did you get out?"

"Dunno," my mother answered. Her forehead furrowed as she tried to remember.

"Your bedrail must have been down. How in the world could that happen?" I jiggled the rail. It stayed right where it should. I walked to the other side and gave the other rail an irritated jerk. It was fine, too. As I pulled at it, I noticed the clear plastic bag hooked to the bed, slowly filling with yellow fluid.

"You have a catheter now, Mom. You won't have to get up to go to the bathroom."

"No caffetah!" she protested. "Don't wann a caffetah!"

"It's for the best, Mom," I told her. "Here. Give me your right hand." I placed the control for her call light in her right palm. Her fingers closed around it. "Whenever you need anything, you push that button, the big one. Can you do that, use the call light?"

"Ah couldn't fine ih," she explained, apologetically, as if she was to blame for her fall.

In my outrage, I'd forgotten that her brain was still in child-mode. I softened my tone and volume.

"Well, now you have it, right? I need to go talk to someone about this, Mom. I'll be right back."

"Give 'em hell," she tried to say, with some vigor. But with her half-paralyzed mouth, it was a breathy "Give a mell," instead. She could see I was angry. She seemed to understand it had something to do with the fact that her face hurt, but I doubted she had any of the details straight.

I strode down the hallway to the nurse's station, my eyes pinpointed with rage. Every feeling I'd felt in the last thirty-six hours was flash flooding my body. I understood this and even told myself to control my temper, reminded myself I was *converting* my fear and sadness into rage. I located the charge nurse and, my voice quavering with anger, told her very slowly and carefully that it was obvious someone's negligence had led to my mother being injured. She misunderstood, whether by accident or as a ploy, I couldn't tell.

"Your mother had a massive stroke. These things happen. It's not anyone's fault."

"I'm not talking about the stroke. Some idiot left her bedrail down, and she fell out of bed. It is not okay to leave bedrails down when someone has just had a stroke and has brain swelling and is paralyzed!"

Now that she got my meaning, the nurse turned crafty. "I don't know how your mother fell," she told me.

"Well, you damn well better find out!"

"Please calm down, ma'am. People are trying to rest."

"I am not going to calm down," I shouted at her. *Because this feels so good*, I wanted to say, *to just stand here and yell at you with all that's in me. You are a complete, blithering moron with no clue how to handle me and I get to yell at you all I like*. But I didn't say any of that. Instead, I said: "Has a doctor looked at my mother since she fell?"

"Not to my knowledge."

"You pick up that phone and get a doctor in here to examine her!"

"It's after office hours."

"Then you call whoever is covering for this floor. Right now!" I stood with my hands on my hips, leaning towards her. "I need to know that my mother will be safe after I leave here tonight," I added. "What are you going to do to be sure that's the case?"

Through clenched teeth, the nurse, pale from restraining her own anger, was making no move to pick up the phone. "I can't be sure," she told me, "that she'll be safe. Accidents happen everywhere. You could even get hit by a car on your way home. Who knows?" She was, I imagined, hoping I *would* get hit by a car on my way home.

"I can't believe you said that to me," I said as I turned and strode down the hall back to my mother's room. I was about to cry and didn't want to lose my edge in front of this stupid nurse. "I'm going to file a complaint in the morning," I shouted back over my shoulder, "and the hospital will hear from my mother's lawyer. You have been no help at all!" By the time I got to my mother's room, I was choking back sobs. Had to stand in the hall, cry some, and calm myself down before I could go back in.

There was a doctor, a resident, in my mother's room within ten minutes. He handled us, both my mother and me, perfectly. He asked questions and listened patiently to my mother's distorted words. He also let me tell him what I guessed had happened, and replied, "This was pure carelessness on somebody's part." He ordered a head scan and moved my mother up to the ICU for observation.

"Why bein' moved?" my mother complained as the doctor himself pushed her gurney towards the elevator.

"You're being moved so you'll be safe." I told her.

"Wha?! Uh liked mah room!"

"I hear you liked it, Mom, but the nurses here didn't take good care of you."

The following day, after the doctor was certain that nothing serious had occurred as a result of her fall, my mother was moved back to a regular hospital room on a different unit. My father sued the hospital for negligence and, many months later, won. The award was only $600 because there had been no significant or lasting injuries. Still, the lawsuit was important. There was so little else any of us could do to help.

31

Fate Is What Befalls Us

"People who invite leukemia patients to take responsibility for their disease by getting in touch with their anger can't say they didn't ask for it when they get punched in the nose. (. . .)To intimate that the soul [has] made a choice [seems] almost a form of cruelty."

—CHIP BROWN, *Afterwards You're a Genius*

November 1992

I VISITED MY MOTHER every day the first week after her stroke. As her brain swelling subsided, she slept less and, day by day, was more alert. She understood and could keep track of the fact that she'd had a stroke. At times, she'd be overcome with grief—there were days when she'd cry whenever she was awake—but she seemed to believe that, like a cold, the discomfort and pain of the stroke damage would pass in time.

"Would you call Jan at the Spinning Guild?" my mother whispered to me one morning a week after the stroke. She could speak more distinctly by then, but not with any volume. "Tell her I'll have to skip this month's meeting. I'll see her in December." The day after that she said, "Do you think you could bring the car and leave it in the parking lot here? I'd like to know I can leave when I want to." I answered her with things like "I'll check on that for you." Or "It'll be good when you can spin again, won't it?" Avoiding saying what I was thinking, that she wasn't going to be spinning any time soon, nor driving, nor walking a dog, ever again probably.

One afternoon I watched her struggle to keep hold of a section of *The Milwaukee Journal-Sentinel*. No matter where she pinched the paper with the fingers of her good, right hand, some other part of the paper would always fold over and obstruct her view. She finally got it to hold still but couldn't focus on the words and hold the paper at the same time. The fingers of her right hand forgot what they were doing and the newspaper slid onto her lap and off the bed. When I bent to retrieve it, she shook her head and waved me away. She didn't want to try again. She closed her eyes and fell asleep. Her whole face relaxed, instead of just the paralyzed left side. The sides almost matched when she slept, the sagging of her left cheek perceptible only if you knew to look for it. Her left hand lay inert against the blanket. The fingers were beginning to bend and twist inward in a hardening spiral.

Last night when I was visiting she'd complained that her hand hurt. A nurse had come to massage it, carefully unbending one finger at a time, stroking it with lotion before letting it curl back into the palm.

I'd watched, touched by the nurse's gentleness and by my memories of my mother's hands.

I thought of how, when I was little, something like a current used to pass between us every time I took her hand to cross a street when we were taking one of our morning constitutionals; I remembered the haven of those warm, thin fingers. How she would handle strands of fleece while her left foot pumped the pedal of her spinning wheel and her fingers and thumbs worked together to pull the strands with the right amount of tension, twisting them together into a perfect cable of yarn. She'd tried to teach me once, showed me how to hold a strand of between my thumbs and forefingers while pumping the pedal with my right foot. In seconds I'd produced a twisted knotted mess on the bobbin. I tried a few more times with her clear and patient instructions; I just couldn't do it. "Try again another time," she'd kindly offered. I never did. My hands weren't clever in the ways hers were. With her instructions, I tried knitting and needlepoint, too, but I wasn't talented with those either.

She was also quick with whatever lighter she was using for her cigarettes: the polished chrome Zippo she kept in her purse; the lightweight Bic of the last years of her tobacco habit. I remember the bright red arrows of her painted nails as she flicked a lighter's wheel with her right hand and lit a Salem held in her left. She'd started smoking when she was sixteen and didn't quit until she was in her fifties when my father was diagnosed with emphysema.

I was already missing those talented hands.

While my mother napped I folded up the sheets of fallen newspaper and pushed them down deep into her wastebasket. Then I went to the visitors' lounge to call my father from the pay phone to give him an update on the current physical therapy plan and the latest blood test results.

"Thank you," he said in a leaden voice. Then added, "Do you suppose there was any way this could have been avoided? I keep thinking about it. Maybe she shouldn't have had that knee replacement."

"I think this stroke was in the cards way before her knee replacement," I said. "The same thing happened to her mother and her grandmother."

"Seems unfair when she worked so hard at being well. After all those Manhattans, all those stints in rehab, she hadn't had a drink or a cigarette in years; she and Abby walked every day. Did you know they did that, every day, even in the rain? She was making both of us eat healthier. She did all the right things," my father continued. "It didn't make a goddamn bit of difference." He sounded angry.

"Maybe it helped somehow."

"Hah! I don't see how."

I walked back down the hospital corridor past rooms occupied by people with all manner of sicknesses and injuries and wondered if they'd all been doing the right things, too.

I'd been doing lots of right things myself and had still gotten sick a few years ago. My first or second day in the hospital one of my colleagues called me and said, "How could this happen? You seemed so healthy and happy." And, yes, I had been happy and healthy. Newly married to my second husband, two middle-school daughters and a toddler between us. I loved my work and had a very successful private practice.

I'd been even more careful since that summer. I made sure my food was mostly organic; I researched the best vitamins to decrease inflammation and I took them daily, I ran—as I had been doing for ten years when I got sick—every day for three or four miles. I did my best to sleep well every night although my kids interrupted sometimes with nightmares or sick tummies. I practiced meditation and did yoga three times a week or more. I had been doing everything I knew to do to stay healthy. And so had my mother.

Nobody's exempt from unexpected illness, no matter what protective magic they call upon. I'd have said I accepted that after my first bad flare-up in 1990. And yet there I was, dealing with my mother's stroke and wondering how this could have happened to her. She'd been doing so much better. So why now? Why her?

Why me?

When I got back to my mother's room, I found a pretty, young nurse whose nametag read "Carolyn" standing beside the bed. She was giving my mother a mini lesson in mindfulness meditation. "When your mind wanders," Carolyn suggested, "just bring it back to the sound of your breath." My mother was watching her with intense concentration. I suspected that, rather than hanging onto Carolyn's every word, my mother was working hard to organize the woman's features into a coherent face. My mother's eyes still didn't work well together.

At this point, less than a week post-stroke, my mother couldn't keep her mind on a conversation long enough to participate in any relevant ways. She couldn't follow the plot of the simplest TV program; by the time they brought her dinner tray in the late afternoon, she'd have no memory of breakfast or lunch, didn't remember her visitors or her speech therapy sessions. She'd often forget her left arm didn't work and would think she was using it, to wave hello, to scratch an itch, while sitting motionless in her bed.

I contained my impulse to laugh as I sat beside the room's noisy heating unit and watched Carolyn's performance.

"We are trying to wake up your inside healer," Carolyn explained. My mother fell asleep right after the word healer.

Mindfulness meditation is one of those all-purpose life skills that I believed everyone should know how to do. I used it for myself (and still use it) and taught it to my clients. To reduce stress, to center, to learn to wake up instead of sleepwalking through life. To stay calm for dental procedures. But for a stroke patient? I was hoping that my mother's return to mobility didn't depend upon her organizing herself to meditate.

I wondered, as Carolyn droned on and my mother's head nodded, if a more traditional form of prayer might suit my mother better. Could she remember how to pray? Would she even consider her God a potential source of help or comfort?

My mother's history with religion was checkered. She'd been raised Christian Scientist and, as a child, had suffered a resultant lack of good medical care. I remembered her telling me when I was in grade school how misguided her parents had been and how abandoned by them she'd felt when she was ill. During most of my childhood, we'd attended a liberal Lutheran Church. It surprised me when my mother went back to Christian Science when I was in college, reading the Christian Science Monitor and attending services. When I'd returned for a visit home from Madison, dressed in bell-bottom jeans, wire-rimmed glasses, and a large black felt hat with an orange feather in it, my mother was alarmed. She surmised from my appearance that I'd not only embraced the antiwar movement (I had) but that I'd also sunken into depths of depravity (I hadn't). She wanted me to go to church with her. I declined. She accused me of not believing in God. I agreed; I didn't believe in God anymore.

"How do you know right from wrong?" she'd asked, appalled.

"I know because you taught me," I'd replied.

My mother had said in the ER, right after her stroke, that she thought God was punishing her. I wondered now, whether she believed, as many of my New Age friends probably would, that her stroke had been "sent" as a teaching device? Or did she think it was it more primitive? An unforgiving and vengeful God, with no mercy in his imagined heart, had made her have this stroke?

I was still a nonbeliever but not so vehement as I had been in my twenties. These days when I thought about my position on God or no-God, I thought of the phrase Julian Barnes used in the opening of his book, *Nothing to be Frightened Of:* "I don't believe in God, but I miss him."[1]

I'd developed some respect for believers of all kinds and didn't insist even to myself that I had the right answer, the no-God answer, the everything-is-random answer. I'd experienced my own unexpected miracle, hadn't I? I'd rapidly gotten well right when my doctors had thought I wouldn't. I'd given up and surrendered to the plan to have my colon removed. And then I didn't need that surgery. I gave a lot of credit for my recovery to the IV Prednisone and the anti-inflammatory enemas but couldn't dismiss the role Dick Olney had played. It was immediately after his visit that I started to heal. Who was I to doubt the existence of unseen and powerful forces?

I did, however, find the idea repugnant, that a supernatural being, aka: God, was punishing my mother for her very human flaws or, just as bad, was trying to teach my beleaguered mother one more very hard lesson. He'd already provided her with so many. She'd paid attention; she'd

1. Barnes, *Nothing to be Frightened Of,* 1.

changed her whole life. She'd stopped drinking, lost weight, done yoga, and created fiber art of all kinds. Wasn't that enough?

Setting aside both my doubts and my annoyance with what I was guessing was my mother's concept of God, I decided to suggest she try praying. Maybe prayer could do what nothing else could. As soon as the mindfulness meditation failure ended, I asked if she'd like me to arrange for the hospital chaplain to pray with her.

"Why?" she asked. "Do you think I'm going to die?"

"No, Mom. I thought it might make you feel better."

"Being able to walk would make me feel better. Can the chaplain do that for me?"

How sensible that response seemed to me. She didn't want to beg for mercy; she didn't want to pray, accept, or call on her inner healer. She wanted her legs and her wits back. She wanted to get up and walk out to her car in the parking structure and drive home.

I admired her practicality.

32

This Need to Be Safely Held

"(...) they think they're dying
from this same disease
this need to be safely held."

—CARROLL TERRY, "Poem"

BY THE END OF the second week following the stroke, I'd reduced my hospital visits from every day to three times a week. I couldn't keep spending so much time away from my children and my clients. And I had decreasing tolerance for watching my mother not try to do what her occupational therapist instructed her to do, like button her own shirt with one hand, lay out the toothpaste first and then brush and floss, in that order, so that she wouldn't end up squirting toothpaste in the sink, brushing with a bare brush, and throwing the floss in the trash. The rehab doctor had recommended that she tear a page off the Page-A-Day calendar (that I'd provided) every morning, to help orient herself and feel less anxious. She never did it. I'd visit on a Thursday and the calendar would still be announcing it was Sunday. I'd rip off Monday through Wednesday with an anger my mother neither deserved nor noticed.

I was all over the place back then in regard to what my mother should and shouldn't be expected to do post-stroke. On the one hand, I was impressed at times by how willful and stubborn she was. On the other hand, I was also impressed, negatively, by her helplessness. As much as she longed to return to normal, she didn't seem to have any backbone when it came to applying herself to the things that could help, like practicing motor skills or writing notes to herself to prop up her fractured memory. One day I'd accept that she really couldn't do what was being suggested to her and the next day I'd feel irritated by her passivity.

I'd always been irritated by what I thought was my mother's passivity. When I was a kid, it didn't seem to me that she did anything beyond making meals, cleaning the house, and reading biographies of movie stars. I don't think she was drinking a lot when I was in grade school but I wouldn't have noticed if she was. I also wouldn't have known or understood that she was clinically depressed, disappointed in her marriage and bored. She also was fearful. I knew that because she'd told me how hard it was for her leave the house, how hard it was for her to show up at my school events because being in a crowd made her too nervous.

Poor mommy. I was sad for her but I also was confused about why she didn't do things differently. At six, things are simple: you don't like something; you don't do it. Something hurts you; you yell at it and walk away.

By the time I was a senior in high school I was sick of limiting myself in order not to burden my mother. Sick of her telling me I was selfish and rude when I was doing my damnedest to be perfect. I knew I had to let my mother go, stop caring what she said or did. Stop expecting her to be the kind of mother I, as a young woman, longed for. The kind of mother I'd thought she was when I was six. But it wasn't easy to let go of her. Her unhappiness was a burden that was difficult to put down, no matter how much it irritated me. I loved her and knew she wasn't okay. How could I turn away from someone so sad? I couldn't.

Until the second time (that I knew of) she threatened to kill herself. The first time was when I was in fifth grade, sitting in the kitchen doing homework while my mother paced back and forth, talking to herself about how hard she worked and how no one appreciated her. No one would care if she stuck her head in the oven and turned on the gas. I ran upstairs to where my father and brother were working on building a miniature model car. "Mom's going to kill herself with gas," I told them. At first, neither of them believed me. *Okay,* I thought. *It's up to me, then.* As I turned to go back downstairs to save my mother (I had no idea how I was going to do that) my father stopped me, told me to stay with my brother; he would take care of it. By dinnertime everything seemed back to normal.

I was twenty when my mother threatened suicide again. Maybe in the intervening ten years, there were other incidents but if there were, I never heard about them. I'd dropped out of school at the University of Wisconsin in Madison and was living with my parents, working a dismal secretarial job until I'd finally saved enough money to rent my own apartment. My father had helped me find a pleasant flat near the university's Milwaukee campus. He'd helped me buy inexpensive kitchenware and towels. He'd rented a trailer for me and helped me load it with two twin beds, a card table and chairs and an old black-and-white TV salvaged from my parents' basement.

The night before I was to move out, I came home from work and found my mother sitting in the living room, a Manhattan in her hand and a slippery smile on her face. She was very drunk and told me that since no one in her family gave a damn about her, she was going to kill herself. Everyone was leaving her anyway, she said. She'd hidden pills all over the house and was going to take them all. "You'll never be able to find them!" She giggled.

My father, who was unemployed at that time, was in the kitchen staring out the window at the dog playing in the backyard. "I don't know what to do anymore," he told me. "She won't listen to me."

The whole situation made me angry. My father's paralysis and my mother's apparent manipulation. I thought she was staging this to stop me from leaving her. (I learned many years later, from my mother, that losing me was only one small part of her desperation that night.) I wanted to turn around and walk right out the front door and leave these two to deal with this mess without me. But my father obviously wasn't going to intervene and I knew I couldn't move out the next day, couldn't take this giant step towards independence, if it came on the heels of my mother's death. So, I did the one thing I could think to do; I called Karen, my mother's AA sponsor.

"I'll be there in ten minutes," Karen said. "Thank you for calling me but you have to step aside now. I've got this."

I opened the door to Karen. She gave me a hug and whispered in my ear, "Move out tomorrow like you planned." When she sat down beside my mother and took her hand, the weight of my mother's sorrows lifted up and off my shoulders.

That night my mother began her first month of rehab at the Dewey Center. It would take ten years and six more month-long stays in various treatment centers (including one more stay at Dewey) before she'd be able to maintain her sobriety.

My father helped me move the next day. His support meant everything to me. It was confirmation of my decision to take charge of my own life no matter what was going on with Mom. That first night all by myself in my new small apartment was heaven. I hadn't been that relaxed and happy in years. It would, however, take years of therapy for me to completely believe it was okay for me to be happy and successful when my mother was not, years for me to unplug that thing in my brain that was tuned into my mother's pain, tuned into everyone's pain. That thing that made schizophrenics talk to me on crowded buses, in busy shopping malls. Took me years to learn that I could choose who to help and how much. I built a career that involved helping, but on my terms. My efforts were appreciated, valued, and time limited. These were responsibilities I could carry lightly and well.

It turned out that the best way for me to limit my sense of responsibility for my mother was to cut her out of my life. I got a low-wage job to support myself in a series of low-rent apartments and didn't speak to my mother for a full year. And, then slowly, after she got sober and stayed sober, we forged a different, easier and less intimate, relationship. We were careful with each other, skirting potentially loaded issues, like her history with alcohol or the serial monogamy of my twenties. We'd shop together, discuss things like *The Mary Tyler Moore Show* or Nic's brainy-boy accomplishments, Jessie's semester abroad in New Zealand. We loved each other at arm's length.

❖

I think the hardest part for me about my mother's stroke and the disability it left her with was that she was once again in trouble and there was no sponsor or family member or friend who could step in to fill her enormous, legitimate needs. No one with money enough or time enough. No one with the skills. Knowing it was impossible for anyone, including me, to do much to help her, did little to reduce my guilt and my resentment at being plunked back into this old familiar discomfort: my mother in danger; my instinct to fix things for her; knowing I couldn't; feeling I must; wanting to run away.

One afternoon on my way to visit my mother, while pulling into a space in the hospital parking pavilion, I caught myself shaking my head over my mother's unwillingness to do what her therapists' were telling her to do. At this rate, I thought, she was never going to walk again. If only she would take charge of herself. Damn her!

The thought startled me. Did I really believe my mother could walk again if she'd apply more willpower and a good attitude? Yes, in fact, that seemed to be exactly what I'd been thinking as I plucked the ticket out of the parking lot machine and set it on my dashboard: if she'd just take charge of herself, she could save herself. I realized I was thinking like a child, wanting my mommy to be okay and angry that she wasn't. I hate to admit that. It doesn't sound very compassionate. The truth is I simply couldn't abide the idea that she wasn't going to get better. I felt trapped again and this time, there was no way to move out, no way to cut the ties.

As I walked through the hospital lobby I reminded myself I wasn't a little girl anymore and my mother wasn't the sickly depressed woman she'd once been. In the twenty years before this stroke my mother had demonstrated all the strength and courage I'd have liked to have seen in her when I was growing up. But all that strength and courage wasn't going to be enough to pull her through this latest event. It wasn't her fault.

Eventually I would understand and accept that the stroke had pretty much wiped out the part of her that had accomplished sobriety, had learned to spin yarn from fleece, had reconstructed herself in the previous two decades. The skill set she needed, what the doctors and physical therapists called "executive functioning," was mostly gone. Offline. Disconnected.

I never gave up trying to reach those inaccessible skills.

There were a couple things I was sure would help her because I thought they would help me if I was in her spot. I was conveniently forgetting that when I was sick myself, I was pretty helpless, too. I wasn't able to focus on anything more complicated than *Mork & Mindy* and *Reader's Digest Condensed Book*s. I hadn't been able to will myself well. I was also forgetting how different we were, my mother and I. Always had been. Where I was a bit of a control freak, my mother was more into letting everything go. I believed that if I wanted or needed something it was up to me to make it happen. Until my mother's final stint in rehab, she had been giving up, accepting—miserably—that she was stuck in a bad marriage, a failed life, and would never really be happy. When I realized my own first marriage was making me feel dead inside, I moved out with my infant daughter and began repairing my broken spirit.

I brought my mother soothing taped music and a boom box to play it on. She never used it. I suggested that perhaps it would help her brain recover if she spent time picturing the fingers of her left hand doing some of the things they used to do. It seemed logical to me that picturing herself knitting, for example, might light up the broken places in her brain, maybe generate some new circuits. I also urged her to read some of the hospital pamphlets that were piling up on—and falling off of—her bedside table. *Coming Back to Life,* was the title of one glossy brochure; on its cover, a gray-haired woman in a loose, blue cardigan, leaned on her walker, head tilted, smiling at the camera.

My mother listened to all my suggestions, said, "Hmmm, yes, sounds like that might help," and forgot every word I said. When I repeated my suggestions, she looked away from me and changed the subject.

One day when I found my mother asleep in her hospital bed, rather than being irritated by her limpness, I actually let myself see it. That particular day, for some reason, I could look at her and accept that she was how she was. Nothing to fix or blame or tolerate. In fact, I found myself touched by her frailty.

She was sleeping against the bedrail on the left side of her bed, as she often did. I thought the metal might be cold and hard against her back so I wrapped an arm behind her shoulders, carefully so as not to wake her, and straightened her onto her pillow. Her shoulder blades were bony, her body thinned from several weeks of not being able to eat solid food.

I pulled the blanket up to her chest and rested my hand on the top of her head, as if I were putting one of my kids to bed in their crib. The same wish to shelter. Good night. Sleep tight.

I didn't want to leave my mother quite yet, so I sat down in a chair near her bed and began to tidy up her bedside table, tossing used tissues in the waste basket, squaring the pamphlets and papers, and lining a pen vertically beside the stack.

The intercom out in the hallway began to beep and a bodiless voice called the code team to someone's room, "Code blue, code blue to room 517. Code blue, code blue." The voice was deceptively calm. As if someone wasn't dying right that second.

"Things fall apart; the centre cannot hold."[1] a line from the Yeats poem I'd reread recently, came to mind. One day both my mother and I would die. That was another truth I was having a hard time getting comfortable with.

things fall apart

1. Yeats, "The Second Coming," 506–7.

Mid-day sunlight was streaming in through the hospital window, stopping just short of the bed where my mother slept. The fluorescent lights were off; the room was warm and quiet. Nothing scary or bad was happening right now in this room. A person could catch their breath here.

My mother whimpered in her sleep. A trickle of drool ran from the left corner of her open mouth. The left side of her face was creased with pillowcase wrinkles. I leaned forward, took a tissue from the box on her bedside cabinet and wiped her chin. The tissue was scratchy as burlap. Even though I barely touched her with it, she bent her still sleeping head away from me in weak, sleeping protest.

My body tensed; my jaw tightened with an old familiar irritation. What was there to be irritated about, I wondered. Then I realized that the way she looked was familiar, the semi-consciousness, the sagging face, the damp, red lines on her forehead and cheeks. I was unconsciously connecting this face with the way she'd looked during one of the daily afternoon naps she took when I was a young child. Missing her, I would sometimes open her door and peek in; her mouth would be slightly open and damp, her face flushed. Not from drinking, she never drank before 5:00 p.m., but probably she was sick or fatigued. Whatever was the issue and no matter how much I disliked her naps, I believed she needed them. In fact, I believed that without them she wouldn't survive.

In her room that day, I reminded myself of where I was and why and, instead of averting my eyes, I looked down at her face and stroked her oily, uncombed hair.

"I'll check on you tomorrow morning, Mom," I whispered in her ear.

3 3

Letting Go

"I also know that if we are to live ourselves there
comes a point at which we must relinquish
the dead, let them go, keep them dead."

—JOAN DIDION

Early December 1992

NEARLY A MONTH HAD passed since my mother's stroke. Even though her
left side remained inert, she could sit up now, after a fashion, in bed and
in her wheelchair. After about ten minutes she'd start to tip to the left, like
a car with two flat tires on one side. She wouldn't notice until someone
put an arm around her shoulders and straightened her. She still couldn't
walk or stand, was frequently anxious, cried easily, and couldn't keep
track of time. Because her swallowing reflex hadn't fully recovered, she
sometimes drooled. She also couldn't remember sequences. Like which
one should come first, putting on the shoe or the sock? Do you put the
toothbrush in your mouth before or after you put toothpaste on it?

You would think I'd have adjusted by now, made accommodations
so that my life would feel more possible. I hadn't; Chris kept telling me
I needed to let something go, stop trying so hard to cover all the bases.
I didn't see any part that was expendable, except my writing time, but
when I'd sacrifice that, even for a few days, I'd veer into an almost suicidal

183

sadness. As rational as it might have been to postpone writing for the duration, I couldn't bear the loss of it. It was precisely *because* things were so difficult and confusing that I needed the writing, now more than ever. So, when I couldn't manage longer blocks, I tried to feel satisfied with whatever time I could get.

I started scavenging spare minutes for my writing the way my mother had scavenged grocery money to buy another dog after Abby died. I'd use thirty minutes in the early morning before the kids woke up or, I'd skip my lunchtime run now and then and use that hour. Occasionally, one of my clients would cancel at the last minute. I'd shut my office door and pull out my notebook. I resigned myself to only doing quick, writing practices, picking a topic and for ten minutes letting my mind wander wherever it was inclined to. Easy stuff. No revisions. No final products.

One morning in December, three weeks into my mother's hospitalization, I'd rescheduled all my clients for a day and thought I'd succeeded in taking care of enough other details that I could afford to spend two full hours writing, before lunch. I'd set my oven timer for thirty minutes and given myself the starting phrase of "I don't want to remember . . ." When my mother called I was ten minutes into my free-write, lost in memories of my 1990 illness, the pain, the worry, the bad body smells, the empty hours in the hospital, the countless blood draws. These memories were never far from my mind. I sometimes woke at night thinking there was an IV in the back of my hand, or that a sore muscle was a sign of the return of inflammation.

My mother's voice rose out of my answering machine. I paused to listen. I had to at least make sure it wasn't an emergency. "This is your mother. Are you *ever* coming to see me?" The machine clicked off, its LED flashing "1." The phone rang again within five minutes. And then in ten more. Each time, my mother said "hello" to the machine as if she were calling for the first time. Each time a similar message, "When are you coming to see me? I'm lonely." When my oven timer chimed to tell me my thirty minutes were up, the LED on my answering machine read "9." There were seven calls from my mother and two, also not emergency, from my father.

I wished this were one of the days when my mother had hours in a row of occupational, physical and speech therapy and that my father was there, too, staring up at her TV or watching Mary practice breathing, eating, putting toothpaste on a brush. Sometimes I got lucky like that. Not this day.

At eleven, an hour into my available time, I'd written only a page and a half, I shut the computer down, laid my head on my desk and cried. Not for long, though.

At 11:02, the phone rang. My mother, calling to ask me to bring her a Hershey chocolate bar.

"You can't eat a Hershey bar, Mom," I reminded her, hoping she wouldn't be able to tell I'd been crying. Before her stroke I'd never have been able to hide it from her.

"Why not?" she asked.

"Because you're still not able to swallow well. Remember? They've been giving you those thick liquid meals? I'd love to bring you chocolate. As soon as it's safe, I will."

"Bring Timmy then."

"I don't think dogs are allowed, Mom."

"I can't have anything I want!" she said with petulance. "When can I get out of here?"

"I'll be there in a little while, Mom. Let's talk about it then."

"You don't want to talk to me. Okay." And, abruptly, she hung up.

There were days, and this was one of them, when I fantasized about getting in my car, driving it to the airport, leaving it there forever, getting on a plane, maybe going somewhere out West, and never checking in again with anyone who knew me in my current life. But then I would think about Chris and the kids. No matter how badly I wanted to disappear, I couldn't figure out what to do about them. If they came with me, then the rest of my family would track me down for sure. If they didn't, I would die from missing them.

At 11:40, I dashed cold water on my face to reduce the swelling that my crying had created around my eyes. Not that my mother was likely to notice. She was about five years old these days and didn't notice anyone but herself. Was I worried about the nurses knowing I'd been crying? If not them, then who? Who would care? I would care. I needed my face to look normal. My face should be the one normal thing in this whole abnormal situation.

At 11:55, I walked into my mother's hospital room. Walked slam up against a wall of hot air and the smell of urine and Lysol. Her portable toilet, a plastic contraption they called a commode, was pushed over to the far side of the room and obviously needed cleaning. My mother wasn't there. In one of her therapy sessions, I assumed.

I sat down on the chair next to her bed. The downtime would be good for me, I thought, give me a chance to close my eyes and relax for a few minutes. But I didn't close my eyes. Instead, I tucked my legs up under me in the chair and looked around the room.

With everything I'd experienced in 1990 and in the two years since, you'd think I'd have learned that downtime was what I most needed, time to check in with myself, to listen to what my soul was telling me it needed. I forgot I even had a soul during the weeks following my mother's stroke. While my head had sort of learned Marty's lesson about the cost of ignoring your heart's desire, my body had not. When I was stressed, when there were multiple untouched to-do lists yammering in my head, as there were most of the time these days—I got anxious. Instead of resting, I fidgeted. I organized and tidied up.

The picture on the wall opposite my mother's bed was crooked. I walked over to it, a grocery-store-art print of several stout ladies in aprons and kerchiefs picking flowers; I straightened it. Wiped some dust off the top of it with my thumb. Then I tidied up the bedside tray-table, lined up the six little sponges on sticks that were used to moisten my mother's mouth because she couldn't drink water without choking. I squared her Kleenex box beside the swabs, lined up her *TV Guide* beside the Kleenex box. While I arranged her things, I thought about her.

She'd been more alert this week than last, and, thanks to the speech therapy, able to articulate her words more clearly. Whenever I arrived for a visit, she'd greet me with something like "You here again?" or "Look what the cat dragged in," or, frequently, "They're trying to kill me in this place." I could almost believe she was turning back into her old self.

Except she didn't look much like her old self. Without her makeup, her face looked washed out, weathered as old barn wood. Her hair was always uncombed unless a nurse had had extra time to comb it for her. Someone had removed her bridge (it held two false molars) from her mouth in the ER and although it sat in a cup on her sink, she'd never bothered to put it back in. Its absence made her right cheek appear more hollow than the left. And she'd lost so much weight in the past three weeks that her bathrobe kept slipping off her shoulders. The more skills she reclaimed, like feeding herself or operating her TV controls, the more her dishevelment stood out. She looked like a person caught halfway between life and decay, still undecided about which way she was heading.

Having finished organizing the few items on the bed tray, I perused the rest of the room in search of something else with which to occupy myself.

I could make her bed.

This didn't take long. I pulled the blankets up, smoothed out a few wrinkles, folded down the top edge of the sheet neatly, invitingly, I hoped. A suggestion of comfort. As I leaned over the bed, I saw that her call light control was tied—again—to the bedrail on the left side. *I cannot count,* I muttered to myself, *how often I've reminded the nurses NOT to put the call button thing on the left.* They probably didn't realize, some of them, that she couldn't see anything to the left of the centerline of her body. Irritated, I unknotted the call light control, moved it to the right side of the bed and twisted its cord around the rail so that it would stay where she could find it.

I picked up the newspaper pages that sprawled all over the cabinet next to her bed. She asked for a paper every morning, even though she couldn't read it. The first time I'd found her holding a book, I'd been excited. "Mom, you're reading. That's wonderful," I'd exclaimed. Then I'd noticed that the book was upside down. I'd pointed this out to her.

"It is not," she'd insisted.

When there was nothing left in my mother's room to tidy up (I drew the line at cleaning the commode) I sat down to wait for her. I picked up the newspaper, read the headlines on the front page, my horoscope, and a review of the new John Irving novel. I wondered how many books the man had written and published. Ten? Fifteen? I was sure he had a wife who cooked, did his laundry, cleaned his house, and kept the kids out of his hair so that he could write. Would I ever see my own work in print? Was I wasting my time?

Then I remembered that the night before I'd given Chris some pages from the chapters I'd been working on and asked him to read them and tell me what he thought. He hadn't said anything before he went to sleep. He'd left for work that morning in a rush. Had he even read the chapters? Maybe he had and he didn't know how to tell me he hated them. Maybe he hadn't even bothered. Maybe he didn't realize how much it mattered to me. I rarely showed him any of my writing and the anxiety that was now gnawing at my stomach was the reason why.

Better to get this over with, I thought. I picked up the telephone that was on the bedside cabinet and called Chris at work.

He picked up after two rings, "ChrisFord." He always answered the phone that way, even at home. I pictured him sitting in a wooden desk chair, reclining back in it with his feet on his cluttered desk, a pen in his hand, legal folders in stacks on the desk and on the floor. He worked in the County Courthouse. Offices there were simple, utilitarian. Gray metal-topped desks, gray metal wastebaskets, gray metal file cabinets, tall and wide. The office was always dusty, the windows grimy with downtown dirt. There'd be a big wall calendar beside his desk on which he'd have written a month's worth of court appearances.

"Hi, Chrisford. Did you have a chance to read those pages I gave you?"

"Read them this morning at my desk, while I drank my coffee."

"Well?"

A silence. I heard him breathing.

"Well, what did you think?"

"Oh, Judith," he said with an aggravated sigh.

"What? Were they that bad?" I knew it, I knew he'd hate my writing. He was wrong to hate it, but I knew he would.

"No, not bad. That's not what I meant. It just scares me so much to remember that summer."

He didn't hate it. This meant he didn't hate it.

"I suppose," he continued. I heard his desk chair squeak as he shifted his position. "I suppose the fact that reading what you wrote got me worked up means that you did a good job. I probably should read it again. The first time through I couldn't get beyond remembering how much I hate it that you drive yourself the way you do. Like you did that day you wrote about, when you ran when you were so sick."

"Oh, come on, Chris. I didn't know I was so sick. I wouldn't have tried to run those seven miles to Ellison Bay and back that summer if I'd known."

"But you still push yourself way too hard."

"Not like that, Chris. You know I don't do that anymore."

"You still do way too much."

"Only because I'm unwilling to give up things I love, like my writing. Maybe if you did more of the housework, I could do less."

"I suppose . . ." He didn't want to argue with me. He stopped talking. I pictured him looking over at his wall calendar, thinking about what he had to do to prepare for tomorrow morning's cases. He'd forgotten what he was talking to me about. He'd maybe even forgotten that he was talking to me.

In the resultant space, I found myself remembering the relief I'd felt that hot morning when I'd been sitting on that rock, worrying, and had seen Chris coming to pick me up in the old black car. It was then it occurred to me.

"Wait a minute," I mumbled to myself, but into the phone.

"What? Oh, I'm sorry, I was distracted by something here on my desk." I heard his chair squeak, more loudly this time, and the sound of his feet hitting the floor as he made himself sit up and pay better attention.

"I just realized something. This is really strange. Do you know, all this time, when I thought about how you rescued me that day, I've pictured you coming in an old black taxi? That didn't happen, did it?"

There was a longish silence at the other end of the phone. Then Chris said, "I did come to get you but I don't remember any black car."

"It had to have been our old red Toyota, right? And *you* were driving, not someone else?"

"Yes, of course, I was driving. I don't remember it exactly, but I can't think of any reason for me to have used someone else's car."

"I don't know why I remembered a black taxi, then."

"It definitely wasn't a black taxi."

I hung up and sat in the quiet of my mother's hospital room letting this realization sink in. I could have sworn that everything about that hot summer day was indelibly recorded in my brain. I remembered seeing the red Toyota coming toward me on Mink River Road, but I also remembered that after the car turned around and pulled up beside me, it was an old fashioned 1930s English taxi. Of course it wasn't! How could it have been? That meant it was an illusion, a hallucination maybe. Was I really that out of it that afternoon? I remembered so many details from that day: the unrelenting sunshine; the salt of my sweat dripping off my eyebrows and down my cheeks onto my lips; the way the grass in the fields beside the road rippled, like a green sea. Was that even true? A green sea?

I remembered the mental chatter going on in my head as I pushed and pushed myself, trying to do what had always been joyful for me, running. I loved running. That day running wasn't joyful. It was hot and empty and terrifying on a level I was unwilling to acknowledge until I finally had to sit down. My brain must have been as out of order as my mother's brain was now.

Why did the air feel so wrong that day? Full of danger, full of threat. Was it the intense heat or something in me? I thought it would all get better if I just kept going. That's what would normally happen if a run wasn't going well; the key was to run through the bad bits and then everything would ease up and be okay. I thought it would actually be dangerous to sit down and rest. Was I in trouble? Or just tired? Was this a real emergency? Or an overreaction?

I think I sensed that day that if I stopped running, I'd have to notice the danger I was in and I'd have to stop everything, stop working and mothering and writing and talking and everything else, and then what?

Still alone in my mother's room, remembering that hot July day, I felt sweat break out across my forehead. I needed air. I walked over to the window and cracked it open a few inches. The November sky was gray; the pale sun cast dim shadows of bare tree limbs across the sidewalks three stories down. I cooled off quickly breathing the cold air that wafted through the small opening.

The day of the black taxi, the day of that failed run, I'd been so hot—it was ninety degrees—hot from the keeping-on, from the voice inside that kept saying, keep going, keep going. That hot sweaty thirsty day, when I sat down on that rock, when I finally stopped, I had a moment of realizing how sick I was, of sensing the tsunami that was coming, that was going to take me down. And then the car came and it wasn't the real car because I couldn't tolerate seeing what was real.

So what about now? My mother's devastation, my father's illness, wasn't all this intolerable too? I was barely aware at this point of how much all of what was happening to them was going to push me back into my instinctive self-preservation mode. The pushing forward through exhaustion. Doing what I did when Jessie was a new and colicky baby and I went back to work when she was only a month old because I had to. We needed the money and I needed the connection with my at-work self, my smart self, my successful self, rather than drowning in the relentlessness of feeding, burping, rocking, jiggling, a screaming, beautiful, incredible child whose existence was going to hollow me out if I didn't resist.

My parents' needs, I sensed even at this early stage, were going to hollow me out, too. It had only been a couple years since I'd gotten well, only four years since Nic, my last (not colicky) baby had demanded the things that normal babies demand. Was I about to lose myself again? I didn't know on this day that this time of doing what was impossible would pull me back in different ways but really, at the core, similar. I was going to go numb, dead inside, as if one of those body snatcher pods had landed in my bedroom and a wind-up woman had taken my place.

This day in my mother's room I was determined to hold onto myself. I would do more for myself, I thought. Not give anything up. I would fit in whatever I had to fit in to take care of what no one else could take care of for my mom, for my dad; but I would also set limits and do no more than what I could do. I didn't realize at this early stage that trying to keep hold of everything was going to make my heart turn to stone, was going to make all the juice in me stop flowing, was going to shut down all my appetites. Except on the rare days when everything would fall apart and I would collapse into my bed and cry.

34

The Dying of Bert's Light

"And you, my father, there on the sad height
(. . .)
Do not go gentle into that good night.
Rage, rage against the dying of the light."

—DYLAN THOMAS, "Do Not Go
Gentle into That Good Night"

December 1992

"POOR OLD GIRL," MY father said, as we drove to the appointment with Dr. Mary Alice. The poor old girl he was referring to was my mother. "She doesn't deserve this. She's always been a child. How can she deal with this? Poor old girl."

"How are *you* doing, Dad?" I asked as I turned onto the short road that would take us to valet parking at the hospital entrance.

"Oh, I'm okay. Just a little tired, worried about your mom."

We were driving to my father's once-a-month appointment with the psychiatrist, Dr. Mary Alice. Usually, he went alone, not for therapy, but for what they called a routine med check, a brief discussion about how my father's latest antidepressant was affecting him. If he reported no side effects and there were no other changes in his health, the session took no more than fifteen minutes.

My father had decided, however, that today's appointment should be different: he had scheduled a full hour and invited me to come. "Because of your mom," he'd said. I'd welcomed the opportunity. Maybe Dr. Mary Alice would know of some resource we didn't. I thought we could use all the help we could get.

⊸⬦⊸

Many years ago my father had tried talk-type psychotherapy at my mother's insistence. She claimed he was the source of all her unhappiness and needed to get some help. He was gloomy, she said. He was always negative; no wonder he had no friends. He hadn't liked the psychiatrist. "He diagnosed me with depression," my father told me once when I asked what he hadn't liked. "Didn't take a genius to see I was depressed. He prescribed pills. I took the damn things. Better that than trying to talk to the man."

My father had every right to be depressed. When I was sixteen and he was forty-three, he was fired from his job in a Milwaukee electronics lab where he'd worked for over twenty years. He found a new job in Los Angeles and moved us, my mother and me, to Whittier, California where I managed to earn straight As while attending only half the days at my new high school. I was miserable there, lonely and bored, and so was not upset when my dad lost the California job after just one year. He tried for months to get rehired in Milwaukee but failed. So, he took the only job offered to him at the time, a product development position in Erie, Pennsylvania. My mother and I moved back to Wisconsin without him and I re-enrolled in my old high school. My father assured us that he'd find something in Milwaukee and come back to live with us within the year. In the meantime, he would commute home (twelve hours) every other weekend.

On those long drives home, my father would listen to news talk shows and baseball games and think about driving his car into a tree. He felt, he told me later, bleak and alone. He missed us terribly. What was the meaning of anything for a man without his family? What was the worth of a man without a career he could point to with pride? My father at that point had had three different jobs in two years.

Every time my father came home for a weekend, he looked thinner. His pants bunched a little more under his narrowing belt. Whisker stubble on his chin, circles under his eyes, his face paler and paler. He was fading out. Then, at the end of this dismal year, he had a painful gall bladder attack, drove himself home to Milwaukee and had surgery the next day. He never went back to Erie.

He got a new job quickly this time, again as a product developer, with a start-up company only thirty miles outside of Milwaukee. By this time, my brother was married and I was in school in Madison. For the first time in twenty-four years my parents were alone together, with no one but Cal, the collie dog they'd bought to try to make me happy when we'd lived in Whittier.

At first, my father's new job seemed to buoy him up. But it wasn't more than a few months before the depression returned. He'd never taken up much space and couldn't expand to fill up the holes left by his departing children. Instead, he compressed himself down, did less and less other than work and got quieter and quieter until he'd gone nearly silent.

His conversations were short and efficient back then—this would have been in the late sixties and the seventies. He would, my mother reported to me during one of our weekly phone calls, talk about errands mostly, who was going to stop at the store to buy milk, what vegetable they should have for dinner, when he planned to mow the lawn, but that was about it.

"It takes a crowbar to get anything else out of him. He doesn't say much about his job. That's a bad sign. What's he doing there all day long? I'll tell you what *I* think. I think he's screwing up again," my mother told me.

My first visit home, during October of my freshman year in college in Madison, my father picked me up at the Badger Bus station downtown. I remember looking through the bus window, searching for him, as we turned into the Badger Bus parking lot. I located him as he stepped out of his ten- year-old Comet and was struck by the resemblance between them, the old Comet and my dad. Both of them were faded, a little rusty, with pieces hanging loose here and there. Both were still useful, to be sure, but neither was in their prime. My father was still six feet tall, but he seemed shorter than I remembered him being. He crossed the parking lot, smiling and quickening his pace when he spotted me stepping off the bus. I noticed that his hair looked thinner and then, that his face did. His eyes, in spite of his smile, were red-ringed and weary. He wore a nondescript navy-blue cotton jacket with a knit collar rather like the top of a sock. There were white streaks here and there on the sleeves and the front of the jacket, as if he'd brushed against the dirty car as he'd gotten out. Which he had. He wore black rubbers over his brown oxfords. When he hugged me he smelled of cigarettes and day-old sweat barely masked by Old Spice after-shave lotion.

Then, in the car on the way home, he seemed okay. He was animated and cheerful, obviously glad to see me. He even cracked a few of his *groaner* dad jokes. But as the weekend progressed, the animation drained out of him. He deflated and folded in on himself like a tire with a leaky rim. He looked strained, as if his mere existence required immense effort. He sighed every ten minutes or so. He'd become less adept at camouflage than he'd been when I was younger. It was obvious to me that he wasn't simply being reticent or self-contained. He was deeply depressed.

The patience with which he'd taught me the Krebs citric acid cycle when I was drowning in Honors Biology and helped Dick build a radio from scratch when he was in middle school, had dried up. He responded to all kinds of minor frustrations with loud angry tirades and a litany of epithets which included "Goddamn jackass" and "For the love of Mike!" and "Damn it all to Hell!" His anger was triggered by things that refused to bend to his will: an unexpected snowfall that he had to shovel, a lamp that refused to light after he'd rewired it; a liberal politician quoted on the six o'clock news. He was especially short-fused with other drivers ("Get off the road! You're a death trap!") and salespeople who made mistakes ("Do you think you could be any stupider than you currently are?").

IN 1969, three years after getting his latest job, my father was fired again. From that point on, until 1985 when he stopped working altogether, he worked at a series of short-term jobs, the longest one lasting about two years. As he aged, the jobs became shorter, more like projects than actual jobs.

During this same time his "smoker's cough" worsened. He was diagnosed first with chronic bronchitis, then with emphysema. In 1975, when I was in my first year of grad school, he was not only unable to get or keep a good job, he was also losing the ability to do a lot of the other things he expected himself to do, like paint a room, fix the car, carry bags of groceries in from the garage. His illness was slowly robbing him of the energy he needed for even the simple acts of eating and walking. He spent hours, sometimes whole days, sitting motionless in his favorite padded rocker, watching television. He was still the self-effacing, generous man I was used to, on his good days. On the ever more frequent bad days, his eyes never left the ground and his frown turned downward so severely it looked as if he'd painted it on with clown make-up. He shuffled. He muttered and grumbled, the eternal cigarette wilting between his lips.

In 1977, when he was fifty-nine and I was twenty-nine, my father called me and asked me for the name of a therapist who might help him quit smoking. I was by then in my second clinical job, an alternative, no fee, counseling service called The Counseling Center of Milwaukee. Through my referral, he joined a therapy group. During the two years he was in the group, he began to—there's no other word for it—*blossom*. He quit smoking. It was the hardest thing he'd ever undertaken, he told me; he was very proud of having done it. And he started calling me more often, just to talk, and actually *talked*. I mean, he talked about things that mattered to him. After one year of therapy, he told me, he was happier than he'd ever been in his life. He was enjoying simple things like playing Frisbee with the dog or baby games with one-year old Jessie. He was making friends with the neighbors. He'd bought himself a model airplane kit and was building the *Spirit of St. Louis* out of balsa wood. He was having fun, he said, in a way he hadn't even done when he was a kid.

He also told me what those years of job changes had done to him, how he'd felt like he was being eroded away like a riverbank. He paused mid-sentence more than once, to keep the tears out of his voice (I heard them anyway) as he explained to me that my brother and I were the best parts of a lifetime of often desperate unhappiness. He'd grown up feeling like a displaced Martian and believing himself to be worthless. Being a husband and a father had made him feel human. He also told me how much he'd loved my mother, from the day he met her, but that his life with her hadn't turned out to be what he'd hoped. He was careful not to blame her for this. "She's had a lot to deal with," he said.

My mother called me to tell me how sappy he'd gotten, how she didn't trust the therapist he was seeing, how he wanted to touch her all the time. It gave her the creeps. What was with these therapy people that they needed to be hugging everybody? My father was getting, she said, "out of hand."

These changes lasted only a year. One cold January morning my father's car was t-boned while he was making a left-hand turn across a busy road. He was knocked unconscious. When I saw him in the ER soon after the ambulance delivered him there, he asked me to call his boss (he was still working part-time, mostly from home, for a firm in Chicago) and tell him he'd be a couple of hours late. He slid into a coma soon after that. He had a concussion, a ruptured eardrum and crushed auditory nerve on the left side, a broken wrist, and double vision. The only visitor he wanted was my daughter Jessie, who was one year old at the that time. I brought her to his room. From her perch in my arms she was fascinated by the tubes and the bright lights, the rippling white line of his heartbeat on the screen. My father smiled, reached out a bruised hand to touch her head, and said, "Better take her home now," before he slipped back into unconsciousness.

After ten days he was discharged. The Chicago company, who obviously valued him, sent a private plane to take him from Milwaukee to their headquarters a few times a week. After about three months, though, they laid him off. Over time his broken wrist mended, his vision cleared, and he bought a hearing aid for his damaged left ear.

As soon as he could go out and buy cigarettes, he started smoking again. He never went back to his therapy group or to the therapist who'd led it. He never had a real job again.

About six months after the accident, I asked him why he'd gone back to smoking. He told me that although he knew the thought was irrational, it felt to him like the car accident had been punishment for his having stepped out of line, for having dared to want things, for having asserted himself with my mother, and, especially, for having fun.

Three years later, while talking on the phone with him, I noticed he sounded breathless. He was, I knew, back to smoking his habitual four packs a day. For as long as I could remember, my father had always had a lit cigarette between two fingers, except when he was asleep. And except for that one year before his car accident.

"Dad," I began, "your breathing is terrible. Can't you feel how your smoking is making it worse?"

"Don't you worry about me," he assured me. "It's just a little asthma." He was, I was certain, smiling reassuringly into the phone. The way he used to smile when I was a little girl and scared of something trivial, like a June bug beating against my bedroom window.

I was speechless. I held the phone receiver away from my ear and stared at it as if the phone itself had just said something preposterous. I was remembering how, a few weeks earlier, I was right there in his doctor's office while the doctor gave him the facts in a voice like chilled steel: his emphysema—also known as chronic obstructive pulmonary disease (COPD)—was advanced; his alveoli were becoming rigid; his lung capacity was terribly diminished; he'd have to use a nebulizer daily to loosen the phlegm in his lungs. Emphysema is progressive. If he quit smoking again, its advance would be slower but it would still advance. He'd been smoking since he was thirteen. That was about half a century ago. It was way past time to quit. He'd be needing supplemental oxygen soon. And if he continued to smoke, the doctor said, he'd eventually end up in a nursing home dependent on a ventilator.

I put the phone back up against my ear. "It's *not*," I said, slowly, emphasizing the "not," "asthma, Dad. You know it isn't."

"Sooo, you and Chris and the kids coming over for dinner on Sunday?"

I put down the phone. I couldn't believe what I'd heard. I walked around my house and ranted at the walls. How could anyone be so entirely in denial? I knew denial; I'd done my own denial when I was sick; I'd witnessed denial in lots of my therapy clients. None of that was as extreme as my father's denial. This was the stupidest thing I'd ever heard. How could he do this to himself? I called my friend Alice and ranted some more.

"The question really is," she said, "how can he do this to *you*?" I stopped being angry. I hung up the phone and cried.

My father had closed back up. He was not the person he'd been during the year he hadn't smoked. His skin tone had gone back to pale gray. He shaved badly. His shoulders sagged again. The shuffle was back. He stopped doing anything other than the intermittent technical writing jobs assigned to him by the temp agency and whatever my mother directed him to do around the house. I imagined all these little lights inside him flickering and blinking out. I felt like I was watching him die, in excruciating slow motion.

"He's his old self again," my mother told me. "And I don't particularly like this one either."

My father kept smoking his three or four packs a day until 1987, when he was sixty-nine. That fall he caught a cold that dug in and wouldn't quit. It turned into pneumonia. When his lips started turning blue, he was finally scared enough to go to the hospital. He stayed for two weeks, antibiotics streaming into his veins through an IV, oxygen into his lungs through a nasal tube. I visited him every day and every day he begged me to buy him cigarettes. I refused. He got angry. I don't think he'd expressed anger at me since I was about seven, and even then it was only once, that I remembered. His anger now was almost enough to make me do what he asked. "I wouldn't be able to sleep at night if I brought you cigarettes," I told him. I already felt guilty about not having tried harder to make him stop.

His sister, Jeanne, a smoker herself, was the one who finally brought the Salems to him. The nurses were irate. Not only was he slowing his own recovery, he also was jeopardizing the whole hospital wing. "You can't smoke while you're on oxygen," his primary nurse scolded. "You'll blow us all up." Every time she came in, she'd find him holding a lit cigarette, tapping the ashes into a wastebasket next to his bed.

When my father was finally discharged, he was given a portable oxygen tank and a prescription for a larger tank to use at home. He would need to receive supplemental oxygen, awake or asleep, through a nasal cannula for the rest of his life. That was the day he finally quit smoking for good. It was far too late to make any difference.

My father dwindled further. He lost weight. He walked with the posture of an emphysema victim: stooped over, head thrust forward, chest caved in. It was hard for him to walk up or down stairs. His muscles were wasting. Everything in his head had dimmed, he told me, as if his thoughts were on a rheostat and someone had turned down the intensity.

When he was seventy-one he began to have full-fledged anxiety attacks: hours of his heart pounding, his head spinning, his stomach knotted with fear. He also had mornings when he couldn't figure out why he should get out of bed. On one such morning he called me to ask for my help again. "I've been kind of down in the dumps," he said. (As if I hadn't noticed.) "Just can't seem to shake this blue feeling." I suggested he call Mary Alice, a geriatric psychiatrist I'd recently met at a professional party. She could prescribe an antidepressant for him. He and I both knew that he needed more than drugs. He could have used a cure for his whole situation, a palliative for the constant wash of disappointments. A way to reverse his increasing resignation. He was sliding, a bit more quickly every day, towards oblivion. He didn't seem to mind. I suggested that perhaps some more therapy would be in order. He declined, saying, "I just want to be more comfortable."

So we made an appointment with Dr. Mary Alice.

And indeed, the Paxil that Dr. Mary Alice prescribed blew some of the cobwebs out of his head, filed down the sharp edge of the anxiety, and pumped up his energy so that he was willing to get out of bed in the morning. It had no impact at all on his malfunctioning short-term memory or on his apparent acceptance of defeat, what looked to me like a decision to collapse in the middle of the highway and wait to be run over.

My father was managing surprisingly well in the aftermath of my mother's stroke—better than I would have predicted. He was sleeping soundly at night and didn't call me any more often than before. In fact, this crisis seemed to have worked even better than Paxil. He was more himself than I'd seen him be since he'd started carrying that oxygen tank around with him. I supposed that the situation had called up the best parts of him. He was sad, of course, but he was responding as he always had when an emergency arose: he was mobilizing.

Very different from the way I was feeling and nothing like the devastation I knew I'd experience if I were in my dad's shoes and it was Chris brought down by a stroke. I hoped I'd be able to regroup, like my father was doing, but I had my doubts. I remembered how I felt the day of my mother's stroke, walking out of the hospital at night after spending all those hours with my mother in the ER. The sky was gray, pocked with clouds. It took me a few minutes to remember where I'd parked my car. I drove home feeling dulled and sad. Emptied, like you do after a bad case of food poisoning. The next day I'd been able to think a bit better. There were a lot of concrete details that needed attention, having to do with money and doctors and visiting hours. Working on them was a relief. But then, as my mother began to get better, slowly and incompletely, I sank down again, into what was becoming a chronic state of emotional anesthesia.

Every day in the ensuing weeks, I'd gone to work (late, tired), concentrated on my clients' worries (easier to think about than my own). I ran four or five miles (not well or fast) every day at lunchtime, and I visited my mother in the hospital, three or four times a week. I made sure the kids ate, slept, and got to school on time. I couldn't seem to locate the pieces that would allow *me* to eat, sleep and get places on time. My appetite vanished and my weight plummeted even lower than it had two years before when I'd spent all those weeks in the hospital with my own illness. The demands on me were unceasing and impossible to meet and yet I tried. I always tried. I was running not exactly on empty, but worse, on constantly high levels of adrenaline. I expected that at any moment I was going to be struck down by a terrible flare-up of my Still's disease. That didn't happen.

I wouldn't realize until many years later that stress wasn't the trigger for flare-ups of my Still's. The worst flare-ups had more to do with hormonal shifts: the very first one, the one that was mild and undiagnosed and lasted two years, came a year after Jessie was born; the next one, the one that landed me in the hospital for so many weeks, occurred eighteen months after Nic's birth; and the last bad one would come six months after my hysterectomy in 1997, seven years after the worst one. These events, birth and hysterectomy, both cause big hormonal shifts. Over the years I've noticed that the milder flares, consisting of mostly fatigue and mind fog, seem to run on their own schedule, not triggered by any one factor. They're infrequent but powerful enough to require a couple days of bed rest—and never seem connected to stress. Or poor nutrition or weight loss. Or emotional shutdown.

35

Aging, Everybody Knows It

"To grow old is to lose everything.
Aging, everybody knows it."

—DONALD HALL, "Affirmation"

MARY ALICE'S OFFICE WAS on the ground floor of the same hospital my mother was in. My father and I planned to go upstairs to visit her when the appointment was over. He'd driven his old blue Datsun to my house to pick me up. Because he didn't see well and because he had always been a careful person, he had driven to my house very slowly. I mean, *very, very* slowly. It took him forty-five minutes to travel the ten miles that separated our houses. To my vast relief, he asked me to drive the rest of the way to the hospital.

When we pulled up to the valet parking entrance, a white-haired volunteer (his name tag identified him as "Hal") hurried to the car to help my dad get out. This was not our first experience with Hal. Hal knew that my father's legs were unreliable, so before I'd even brought the old Datsun to a full stop, Hal had set a wheelchair in place beside the car. He opened the passenger side door, braced it with his right hip, clasped my dad's right elbow and shoulder, and supported him up the curb and into the chair. My father could walk, of course, after a fashion, but Mary Alice's office was three long corridors away, a great distance for someone who could barely breathe. And if I held his arm all that way, we would move so slowly we'd miss the entire appointment. Thus, the wheelchair.

We sat for a short time in Mary Alice's small, overly clean waiting room. Like everything in this hospital, it smelled of disinfectant. Plastic chairs in shades of dull yellow and fogged-over orange. Industrial-strength, brown, tweed carpeting. Side tables with two or three battered copies of *Milwaukee Magazine* and *Ladies Home Journal*. Displays of pamphlets that advertised drugs for bladder control, described how to call the Medicare hotline. A pamphlet on how to know if your loved one's habit of leaving her keys in the freezer and mixing up the dog's name with yours is Alzheimer's or simple ditziness. I reached for an Alzheimer's pamphlet.

A nurse in street clothes greeted my father warmly and helped him up and out of the wheelchair. "I'll take that for you," she told my dad as she tucked his oxygen tank under her left arm. As Hal had done, she held my dad's elbow to steady him as he lifted his bony butt up out of the chair and slowly, painfully straightened his legs. The nurse continued to cradle my dad's arm as she led him away to weigh him before guiding him to the doctor's consultation room.

"How does she manage that?" I wondered to myself, impressed with how cheerful she seemed, as if there were nothing she'd rather be doing than this, this creeping alongside the tottering wreck who was my father.

"Good afternoon."

I looked up from my *Is It Alzheimer's?* pamphlet to see Dr. Mary Alice coming toward me. She was a little older than I was, not much, about my height and slender, her dark hair pulled back into a ponytail and held loosely at the base of her neck. It was wrapped with a scrunchy, one of those elasticized fabric bands that were currently popular with schoolgirls. She wore a blue plaid kilt, fastened at its fringed open edge with an oversized gold safety pin. Her matching blue knee socks didn't quite hide her knees. She sat down in the faded plastic yellow chair beside me.

"I hear your mother's had a bad stroke," she said. "How are you doing?"

I was startled by the question. Here we were in a public waiting area and, granted, no one else was there, but no way was I about to start talking in this open arena about how my chest ached, how little interest I had in food, or how often these days, in a therapy session, I'd missed whole paragraphs of what a client had been telling me.

"It's been hard," I told her. "But Dad is coping okay."

"Yes," the doctor answered. "He does seem to be holding up rather well, doesn't he?" Was it my imagination or did she suspect that, unlike my father, I wasn't holding up particularly well? She was looking into my eyes, I thought, in that studying way that therapists do.

"I'm glad to have this chance to talk to you without him," the doctor went on. I braced myself. I wouldn't admit anything, I told myself. I'd tell her I was just fine.

"We all know, of course, that your father is in end-stage emphysema."

In the first millisecond following Mary Alice's statement, I felt relief that I wasn't going to be the subject of this conversation. And then her words, chilling in their irrefutable finality, sank in. Still in the sway of my decision to appear unflappable, I put on what I hoped was a calm demeanor, the look of someone who had heard the term "end-stage" applied to my father before. Which I hadn't. I'd known for years that my father was shortening his life by smoking. And, of course I knew he'd spent more time in the hospital lately—I'd visited him there—but I hadn't realized he was so close to his end.

My stomach hurt. It seemed to have curled itself into a hard lump and pressed itself tight up against my spine.

"Does your father have a living will?" Dr. Mary Alice asked.

I shook my head, no.

"Has he told you his wishes about life support?" She was looking down at what I now noticed was a packet of white papers. Her thumb rifled the top few pages.

"I think I know what he'd want," I told her, "But we haven't actually talked about it."

"This is hard stuff to talk about." Mary Alice tilted her head and seemed to be studying me again, so warmly that my unflappable-ness began to unravel at its edges. I stared at the spray of fine lines at the corners of her eyes while a lump rose in my throat. Then, I shifted my gaze quickly to the floor so that if I did start to cry, I'd be able to hide it.

The doctor went on. "It would be a good idea to make some plans now. Before your father gets sicker. You won't want to have to think about all this in the middle of a crisis, with him unconscious and unable to say what he wants. It would all be up to you, then. You don't want that."

For a few seconds, I was back there, three weeks ago, standing in the corridor beside Dr. Amundson, while the doors to the ER opened and closed and the cold wind swirled around us, my thoughts swirling, too. That was when I'd first heard the words, "no code," "do-not-resuscitate."

I'd hated being asked to make that decision, hadn't known how to weigh the value of my mother's life against the cost of her suffering. I hadn't been able to explain to Dr. Amundson why I stood there silent for so long. Like a grade school kid who's been called on and doesn't know the answer. No, I didn't want to do a replay of all of that in the event of my father's total incapacitation. Which incapacitation was more imminent than I'd realized.

The sound of shuffling footsteps brought me back to the waiting room and Dr. Mary Alice. I looked up from the spot on the carpet that I'd been staring at. An old woman, bent over a cane, wobbled to a plastic chair. "Good morning," she chirped as she swayed herself down onto it.

"Good morning, Louise," said Dr. Mary Alice. "Dr. Severance will be right with you." She turned back to me.

This time I met the doctor's glance. "You're right," I told her. "I was asked to make a decision about my mother's DNR when she had her stroke. I don't want to be the one making that decision for anybody ever again."

"When my father was dying, we knew exactly what his final directives were." Mary Alice leaned forward and rested her elbows on her knees. "He'd had a near-death experience a few months before, during heart surgery. Saw the tunnel, the white light, the whole deal. And when he came back, he wasn't afraid anymore. He told us that when the next time came, he didn't want to be called back. No paddles, no breathing machines. He was ready."

She looked over at me again. Her eyes, I was surprised to see, were wet with tears.

"It's never easy to say good-bye," she said in a quiet voice. "I loved my father. When he had his next heart attack, we did what he'd requested. We did nothing other than spend time with him while he died. We were all there together when the moment came, the whole family. We didn't have to struggle—and maybe argue with each other—about whether or not to do the extraordinary measures. That part was clear."

I pictured Dr. Mary Alice sitting in her father's hospital room with her mother, a brother, a few sisters maybe. I envied them what I imagined had been their way of being together. No tension, not a lot of words left to say, the right ones having already been spoken. An atmosphere of mutual respect and support. There was no way, I told myself, *my* family could pull off something like that. My mother, if she was able to be there, wouldn't demonstrate any respect or affection for my father. My brother and I were basically fond of each other, but we hadn't spent much time together since he'd moved out of our parents' house twenty-five years ago, and if we were at my father's deathbed together we'd have to invent brand new ways of talking to each other. It would probably help some if we could reduce the number of painful decisions we were going to have to make together. I liked the idea of my father deciding for himself whether or not to put his poor old, tired body through those extraordinary measures.

"If your father develops pneumonia, they'll probably want to put him on a ventilator," Dr. Mary Alice continued.

"He wouldn't want that. I know he wouldn't want that."

"He'd never get off," she answered. "He'd live the rest of his days hooked up to a machine, unable to speak. Unless you have a document telling the hospital that your father doesn't want things like that done to him, they have to do everything they can to preserve his life."

I pictured my father lying inert in a bed, a tube taped to his mouth, his eyes closed, his chest forced to fill and empty, moving up and down. His used-up body an appendage of a monstrous machine. I shuddered and shook my head.

"I'd better talk to him."

"Yes. I think that would be wise."

❦

Later on that afternoon, after my father and I spent a short time visiting my mother in her hospital room four floors above Dr. Mary Alice's office, my father dropped me off at my house and then drove himself home in his rattling blue car. About thirty minutes later, my mother called me. On most days she called me three or four times before dinner. She called Bert closer to twenty times. She'd made it clear to anyone who would listen to her that she didn't call Bert because she liked him. He was an "old coot" and she was furious with him for having smoked for so long and gotten so ill.

"I told him to quit smoking eighteen years ago, when I did. Why didn't he ever listen to me?" she complained angrily and often. She kept forgetting that she'd said this to the same nurse or aide or to me just ten minutes before—and at least twice the previous day.

But this time she hadn't called to complain about his smoking. She was scared. "Your father hasn't called to let me know he got home okay. He should have called by now. And he isn't answering the phone. You have to go to our house and be sure he's not dead."

I struggled to keep my irritation in check. I took a deep breath while a mental photograph of my to-do list for today popped into my head. Only a few items had been crossed off. It was a very long list. My neck and the base of my skull ached with anxiety. I rolled my head and tried to ease my shoulders down from around my ears. *First things first,* I told myself. *I can't do everything at once.*

My parents' condo was a twenty-minute drive away. I had dinner to make, client phone calls to return, and four-year-old Nic to take care of. In fact, right that moment, I noticed that Nic's agitated voice, blowing in from the front yard, was rising steadily in pitch and volume. I carried the phone into the living room and looked out the window while my mother described, in more detail than anyone needs, all the ways she'd tried over the years to get my father to take better care of himself. "Uh huh," I muttered.

There was Nic, standing with his hands on his hips, head thrust forward, shouting at Andy and Paul, the two seven-year-olds who lived next door and around the corner respectively. In a few minutes Nic would break down and start to cry. That would be my cue to make him come inside. He would resist my rescue. He wouldn't want to give up. He wouldn't realize that this battle, like every other battle he had with these boys, was utterly unwinnable. Andy and Paul didn't for one second care about the subject of the argument. All they cared about was inflaming Nic. So several times a week Nic worked himself into a red-faced fury of impassioned logic while Andy and Paul mocked his tone, his stance, and the polysyllabic words he used. Andy and Paul probably thought Nic was talking down to them, the little punk. And that, no doubt, made them mad. But Nic wasn't being condescending. That was just how he talked. He liked big words and he remembered every one he'd ever heard. As a result, his vocabulary had become a social handicap, not just with Andy and Paul, but also on the playground and in his kindergarten classroom. Just the other day at school he'd described the caging of the class guinea pig as "incarceration" and told a playmate who had cheated at *Candyland* that his behavior was "unethical." Teachers loved Nic. Kids his own age mostly avoided him.

Nic's brilliance, both a gift and a burden, had not escaped my father's notice. "He's just like I was at that age," my father told me. "And no one knew how to handle me. You're doing a great job with Nic. He's learning about love." I wasn't so sure when Nic was in kindergarten, and even less sure as he progressed through public school, that we were doing such a great job. That anyone could. Like my dad when he was a child, Nic was a unique little boy, and like my father he was destined to grow up very aware of his differentness and, through grade school and high school, very lonely.

I held the phone to my ear. I wasn't sure how many minutes had passed since my mother had stopped talking. She was waiting, I assumed, for me to tell her I was going to drop everything and rush to my father's aid.

"Mom," I said into the phone. "Nic's outside crying. I'm going to have to go out there and help him. I'm sure Dad's fine." (*Why*, I wondered, *was I sure Dad was fine? He hadn't been fine for the last fifteen years.*) "Let's wait another half hour. Then I'll drive to your house if Dad hasn't called. Chris will be home from work by then and I won't have to take Nic with me. Okay?"

My mother reluctantly accepted my putting her off. I spent the next half hour reading to Nic and then, while I worked on dinner, scaring myself with mental pictures of my father's emaciated body lying crumpled at the foot of the basement stairs. My mother spent the time calling my brother and my aunt, trying to get someone to respond more satisfactorily than I had.

Before Chris got home, I called my father myself. He answered on the second ring.

"Guess I had the ringer turned off for a while there," he said. "I called your mother a few minutes ago and she told me she'd been trying to reach me. She was pretty mad at me. The ringer's turned on now."

He wasn't sprawled on the basement floor. He wasn't dead. There was no additional crisis for me to respond to. Even as I let myself relax, though, I knew that sometime soon, maybe very soon, we weren't going to be so lucky.

3 6

There Is No Ship for You

"There is no ship for you, there is no road.
As you have destroyed your life here
In this little corner, you have ruined
it in the entire world."

—C. P. CAVAFY, "The City"

December 1992, four and a half weeks post-stroke

ONE DAY IN EARLY December, I was in my office working with a client
when Doris, our office manager, interrupted me to let me know that my
mother's primary nurse, Linda, had called and wanted me to call back
right away.

Expecting bad news—another fall, perhaps—I apologized to my client and went to Doris's office to talk to Linda.

"Your mother's going to be discharged tomorrow," Linda told me. "I
wasn't sure anyone had let you know yet."

"Discharged? To where?"

"Well, that's up to you. That's why I'm calling. So that you'd have
some time to get ready. There is someone at home who can care for her?"

"No. There isn't."

"Oh. We were under the impression that family would be caring for
her in the home." Linda, who usually spoke in a friendly, casual manner,

now sounded like a brochure for care of the elderly. *The Family. In the Home.* She went on to inform me that my mother had used up all the time Medicare allowed for stroke rehab in a hospital and that Medicare wanted her discharged that very day. Her doctor had had to fight to get one more night approved. To give us a little more time.

"You can pick Mary up after ten tomorrow morning,"

I was stunned. I should have realized my mother might be discharged at any time. I should have learned from my own experience, two years earlier in that same hospital, that a patient doesn't have to be well to be sent home. I should have been ready.

My father, my brother, and I hadn't spent much—well, not any— time planning for Mary's recovery. No one had ever asked us to participate in any of the treatment decisions. We vaguely assumed that when it was time, someone at the hospital would call us and offer us access to publicly funded nursing care. An attendant to keep my mother company at home or a charming room at a modern rehab center with a state-of-the-art physical therapy room, potted plants in the lobby and great food.

Surprising that I, the one who always wanted to know not just the next step, but also the next ten steps, would have tolerated this lack of planning. I'd avoided thinking about the next steps because I sensed there might not be a good solution. It was clear that my mother wasn't going to recover much of what she'd lost.

There was no one in my family with time on their hands to devote to my mother's full-time care. My father probably could puree her meals and supervise her eating, but he'd never have been able to lift her on and off a toilet or keep track of her medications. My aunt Jeanne was both unwilling and too frail herself to take a shift. My brother and I both worked full-time and had kids at home. And no one in our small family had any extra money stashed anywhere. Jeanne had called me once and suggested that Dick and I start looking at nursing homes. I had no idea how we could afford a nursing home so I'd procrastinated. We'd all procrastinated.

"I can't pick her up tomorrow," I said to Linda. "I'm scheduled to work all day. "This was not the bigger issue, of course. As upset as some of my clients would be at being rescheduled at the last minute, the more pressing issue was what to do with my mother. It wasn't as if we could plop her down in her customary cushion on the loveseat in her condo and go on with our lives.

"I'm sorry," Linda continued, "but someone will have to come get her."

"What happens if no one does?" I asked.

There was silence on the other end of the line. It occurred to me that maybe no one had ever asked Linda this question before.

"You wouldn't want to treat your mother like that, would you?" Linda finally said.

"What would the hospital do, Linda?" I persisted.

"Well, we wouldn't wheel her out to the street and leave her, if that's what you're getting at."

"Good. Because we don't have anything set up for her yet. We don't even know what she needs or how to find it. Or how to pay for it." My voice had begun to rise in pitch.

"We'll be expecting someone to come get her tomorrow."

"Expect all you like. It won't happen."

I hung up the phone and struggled to collect myself before returning to my client. I was shocked by the abruptness of the decision to discharge my mother. I was also overwhelmed again with that familiar sense of helplessness and guilt. Years before my mother's stroke I'd promised her I'd take care of her when she got old. Now I was being called upon to make good on that promise. And I couldn't do it.

We'd had the conversation five years ago while I was driving my mother on some errand. My parents, who'd been living on a small social security check and an even smaller pension, had recently declared bankruptcy and they were still having trouble covering the basics. My mother was worried. Her parents had gone bankrupt and lost their house when she was a teenager. She still remembered the impact of that loss—and the family's reduced circumstances afterwards. She told me she thought the stress had caused her mother's stroke. With tears in her voice, she told me she was afraid that when she got old she'd "end up on the street," a bag lady living in some cold alley.

"Don't be silly," I assured her. "I'd never let that happen to you. I'll help you when you're old." I didn't say those words lightly. I really thought about them as they came out of my mouth. Could I keep a promise like that? I'd thought I could. I could make sure she had food and shelter, drive her to doctors' appointments, help her write the checks to pay her bills. Clean her bathroom and her kitchen. Even make her bed, walk her dog. No problem.

I couldn't possibly have imagined the enormity of what she would end up needing. Even if I gave up my job (and lost my own house, thereby) and spent all my time with her, I wouldn't be able to cover everything. Or, the opposite scenario, if I worked twice as many hours the money would still fall short of the care she needed. And it would never have occurred to me to ask anyone else in the family to step up, to include them in the promise. *We* will take care of you. No. I was the one. Good little child of an alcoholic that I was (am), I assumed it had to be me.

Linda called me back later that same day to tell me they had somehow wangled another couple of days from Medicare. The following morning my father and I went to see the hospital social worker. Even though I wasn't going to go to my office afterwards, I dressed in work clothes, a mid-calf soft skirt and a matching sweater, and I carried my black briefcase. Holding on for dear life to the fact of my career: busy me, too busy to be take over my mother's care. I knew that if I sank down into the remnants of my little girl self there was a risk I'd sell myself out and offer to do way more than I could.

I parked my father, seated in a hospital loaner wheelchair, in front of the social worker's desk. His narrow hands, knobby and freckled, were folded together on top of the oxygen tank in his lap. He had done a poor job shaving that morning. His eyes were rheumy and sad.

I sat in the straight-backed wooden chair beside him. My own hands, narrow and long fingered like his, played with the edge of the black briefcase in my lap.

Cheryl, the social worker, introduced herself and, ignoring my father, asked me sweetly how she might help. As if my father was a child, or worse, a brain-addled adult who couldn't answer for himself. I hated it when medical people did that to my parents. I didn't answer Cheryl. Instead, I met her eyes and turned toward my father, hoping she would follow my gaze. She did.

My father summarized, efficiently, like the engineer he would always be. He described the stroke and the long, sad weeks that had followed. Cheryl asked about what my mother could and couldn't do and Bert's accuracy flew out the window. An unwarranted optimism took its place.

"Those therapists are going to have her up and walking real soon," he said, "but she'll have to use a cane."

"Sounds like you might need to have a visiting nurse come every day for a while," Cheryl said.

Oh my God, I thought. *A visiting nurse?* Not only was walking pretty much out of the question forever, but my mother also still couldn't even sit up straight without being belted into her wheelchair. She couldn't work the TV remote. The stroke had affected every part of her.

It strikes me now how vulnerable my father was that day. What if I hadn't been there to set the record straight? Would he have driven Mary home, somehow wrestled her out of the car and into her chair without dropping her on the concrete garage floor? Could he have tilted the wheelchair back just enough to clear the threshold, without unbalancing both the chair and himself? And what then? How in the world would he have gotten her upstairs to her bed? This kind of thing must happen all the time to old people who have no one to speak for them.

"They're going to need a lot more than just an occasional visiting nurse," I interjected. "My mother can't do much of anything for herself yet. She can't walk at all."

"Well, not right now she can't," my father grumbled to the gauge on his oxygen tank.

"She can't walk at all yet?" asked Cheryl.

"Not one step," I answered before my father had a chance. I filled Cheryl in on the facts as I saw them, adding, "On top of her physical limitations, her judgment pretty much sucks right now. I don't think she'd be safe alone at all."

Cheryl raised her eyebrows in surprise. "You could learn how to help her with those things," she said to my father. "It's not difficult."

"Sure," he answered, to my horror. "I could do it. She needs to come home."

"Dad," I began, not wanting to embarrass him in front of this stranger, "Dad. Think about it. How would you get her upstairs?"

"Oh," said the social worker. "You have two floors. I didn't realize that. Is there a bedroom downstairs?"

No. There wasn't.

And so it went. After a little while the social worker addressed all her questions to me and I let her. I ended up contradicting just about everything my father had said. He went silent, his jaw slack as he stared out the window behind Cheryl.

The picture got clearer and clearer. There was only one thing to do. My mother would have to go to a nursing home. My father would have to apply for Title 19 as soon as possible. The social worker thought she could squeeze another week out of Medicare while we visited nursing homes and the welfare office.

"I don't want her in one of those places," Bert said as I pushed his wheelchair out into the parking garage. His shoulders, bony and narrow under his navy-blue parka, were hunched against a cold breeze that blew through the open sides of the garage. A few snowflakes danced between the parked cars and swirled up around the wheels of the wheelchair. I looked down at the top of my father's head. His hair lay flat and greasy in thin streaks against his pink scalp. A faint sour smell emanated from his head or his body, maybe both.

"There has to be something else we can do," he moaned.

"I don't think there is. It stinks but I don't see another solution."

❧◇❧

During the next few days Dick and I visited nursing homes. There weren't a lot of choices. Not every nursing home accepted Title 19 patients. Not any of the charming ones with potted plants and great food. We picked The Shores because it smelled better than the others, wasn't too long a drive for any of us, and had a room immediately available.

The morning I went to my mother's hospital room to tell her about her new home, I found her talking to Cheryl, the social worker.

"We're doing the alcohol assessment," Cheryl informed me.

"Hi," said my mother. "This lady thinks I have a drinking problem." She grinned her lopsided grin at me. Her eyes were more alert and her face less pale than when I'd last seen her. Her hair had been washed and combed. It retained its two-toned dusty color and had no particular style or shape but still, it was obvious that attention had been paid. And, I noticed, someone had helped her dress in real clothes, a pair of elastic waist pants, red ones, and a yellow t-shirt. The clothes hung on her body. She'd dropped forty pounds from her five-foot, seven-inch frame, going from 165 to 125, during her hospital stay. The overall effect of her clean hair and her street clothes was to make her seem more alive and at the same time more diminished.

"Did you tell this nice lady that you haven't had any alcohol for almost two decades, Mom?"

"No. She didn't ask me that." Mary seemed to be very pleased with the conversation she'd been having with the social worker.

"She doesn't drink anymore?" Cheryl interjected.

"No. Not for a very long time. She was in rehab a bunch of times. She's been to nearly a thousand AA meetings. No slips in over fifteen years. Why did you think she needed this assessment?"

"It was ordered." The social worker looked embarrassed. She slid her pen into the pocket of her navy-blue jacket, picked up her papers, and stood up.

"Sorry," she said to me. I looked toward my mother, indicating that the apology was owed to her, not to me. Cheryl missed the cue and continued to talk to me.

"I just assumed, since it was ordered . . ."

"Wrong assumption."

My mother looked puzzled as the woman, with another "Sorry," left the room.

"Why did she leave all of a sudden? We were having such a good talk."

"You don't need an alcohol assessment, Mom."

"That's what she was doing? I don't drink, do I?"

37

Not a Happy Life

"I believe you did not have a happy life.
I believe you were cheated.
I believe your best friends were loneliness and misery"

—MARY OLIVER, "A Bitterness"

DRIVING HOME FROM THAT visit with my mother, I wondered if she really didn't remember her alcohol addiction or if she'd been joking. *I* remembered her drinking, of course. Her drinking was at its worst when I was a senior in high school. Maybe it was because my father was still working in Pennsylvania that year and my mother and I were living without him in Wisconsin. Or maybe she'd just reached that point in her alcoholism trajectory. She'd been going to AA meetings for years by then and she was still going in 1966 but the meetings didn't seem to be helping much. The fact that my mother drank, and drank a *lot*, that year meant that I was never very certain about anything, least of all my mother's ability to make it alive from morning to evening, and, more so, from cocktail hour to the following day. She'd attempted suicide only once, that I knew of, but had threatened a number of other times. I didn't ever quite trust her to be okay. It wasn't that big drunken scenes occurred every night in our house. It was more that I never knew when one would.

It was obvious to me that year that my mother was in trouble. And because she was in trouble, everywhere I went—to a friend's house, to school, even at home—I felt off-balance and a little lost. I didn't know why. I thought there was something wrong with *me* but I couldn't figure out what it was or how to fix it.

One Friday night I walked downstairs intending to put my coat on and leave for my ushering job for the Bay Players' performance of *The Importance of Being Earnest.* I was a member of the High School Drama Club, the Bay Teen Players, and was taking a theater arts class in school. Ushering for the Bay Players was one more way I could roll around in the entertainment world. We ushers got to hang out in the theater before and after the shows and in between our ushering duties we could watch the plays for free. The more time I spent in the school theater, the more I felt I belonged there. I was grateful to have an alternative "home," even one which was only available during rehearsals and from six to ten on weekends.

As I pulled my olive green Loden coat from its hanger and slid my arm into a sleeve, my mother's voice caught me.

"Going out again?" she purred, but not nicely, not cozily. This purr was chilling, a spider's voice. I steeled myself as I slipped my other arm through the other sleeve and shrugged the rest of the way into the coat. I turned to face her.

"I already told you," I said, and stopped. Her cheeks were red. A Manhattan in a large tumbler sat on a metal coaster on the end table beside her. A cigarette swooped to her lips and away, like a needle stitching a puffy red wound. My whole body tensed. I could tell from her mean smile, the narrowing of her eyes, and the way her cigarette shimmied as it moved to the ashtray, that she was already very drunk. This wasn't going to be easy.

"I told you I was going to usher tonight, with Alice and Jackie." I pulled a green-striped knit hat on my head and wrapped a matching scarf around my neck. I held my mittens in one hand, hoping that I looked the picture of a person in a hurry to get outside.

"Well . . ." she inhaled deeply, blew out a cloud of smoke, and chuckled. Like the purr of her voice, her chuckle was not friendly. "You just be on your merry way then. Have fun with your little friends. Don't worry about me, young lady. When you get home, I'll be dead."

I turned to stone, as if I'd just seen Medusa-like snakes surrounding my mother's head. I couldn't move. I stood a few feet from the front door, my mittened hands hanging limp at my sides. I half-expected her to get up, go to the kitchen, and stick her head in the oven like she'd done back when I was ten and she was deeply depressed and angry at my father, my brother and me. Except this time, my father was in Pennsylvania and my brother lived thirty miles away. This time there was only me. While I stood, petrified, my mother pressed her advantage.

"I suppose all your little friends are going to be there, too. You know what? One of these days, you're going to get into real trouble, hanging out with those supposed *friends*." She rolled the word "friends," out of her mouth as it were an insect she'd accidentally sucked in. "Don't think I don't know what you and Alice are doing with those boys. When you get into big time trouble, and you will, don't come crying to me, Missy!"

Now I was confused. My friends and I were all good students who did our homework on time and never skipped class. We never got detentions. We were into community service; we put on plays for little kids and went to the school recreation center every Friday night.

"Mom, what are you talking about? You're crazy!" As soon as I heard my words, I regretted them.

"You know damn well what I'm talking about! You gutter tramp! Now you just take your cheap self right out that door and have a fun night. Don't you worry about me here all alone. I told you: I won't be around when you get home."

I should have run right out the door and to the theater, where my friends were waiting for me. Instead, I turned and ran up the stairs to my bedroom. I sat on my bed and cried, blotting inky mascara off my cheeks with a Kleenex. When I'd composed myself enough to be able to speak, I called my brother. I was not in the habit of asking my very emancipated brother for help. I figured he'd made a clean escape from the mess I was living in and I didn't blame him if he wanted to steer clear. Which he did, most of the time. The other unusual thing about the phone call was that the first words out of my mouth after I heard his "hello," were: "I need help. Mom's drunk. She says she's going to kill herself and I don't know what to do."

This was the first time ever that I'd said anything at all to my brother about my mother's drinking. I'd never so much as hinted to him that it was a problem. I wasn't sure now that he was going to believe what I was telling him. I hardly believed it myself, that she was threatening to kill herself if I left her alone. That she'd called me a "gutter tramp."

"Wow," Dick said after I'd told him the details. "It's gotten really bad. Tell you what, can you still get to the theater before the play starts?"

"Yes, barely."

"Then you go. Sandi and I will come over and keep an eye on her. Don't talk to her, don't say anything at all. Just go. Forget about it and go have a good time."

I did as he told me. At the theater, I somehow managed to escort people to the proper seats, in spite of the tears that kept collecting in my eyes, in spite of the way my mind was running my mother's words over and over and over. *Cheap. Don't come crying. I'll be dead. Gutter tramp.*

During intermission, when my friends and I had finished selling Cokes and 7-ups, and the audience was filing back inside to watch Act Two, I pulled my friend Alice into the girls' restroom. I told her what had happened and what my mother had called me. I don't know how I looked, but I felt as if I was confessing a crime that I, not my mother, had committed. So much shame. It was hard to get the words out.

When I was finished Alice's eyes were round with surprise. Then she burst out laughing.

"A gutter tramp?! She called you a gutter tramp?! You, of all people! You're practically a saint, compared to me. Your Mom's nuts. Where'd she get that word? From one of those movie star books she's always reading?"

My mom was nuts. Yes. That was right. I believed Alice. I was not a gutter tramp and my mom was nuts. As I let these thoughts soak into my brain, the world righted itself.

My mother didn't die that night. In the morning she was her "good-mom" self. We ate French toast together and watched Saturday morning cartoons. I don't think my father ever knew about that night. Once I asked my mother, when she had been sober for at least ten years, whether she remembered calling me a gutter tramp. She laughed and said she didn't remember it at all. She gave me a skeptical look, as if she didn't believe she could ever have done such a thing.

Now, in the car all these years later, I felt really sad, for both of us. It was hard to reconcile the sober person she'd been in the recent past with the woman she'd been when I was a teenager, especially during that year, my senior year in high school, when I was so lost and off-balance. At the time I kind of realized that my mother was even more lost and off-balance than I was, and on some level, I felt responsible to keep her safe, as if there'd been some secret thing I should be doing for, or about, her that would have changed her, steadied her, and made her be the mother I wanted, needed, her to be. For me.

As I drove home now I felt that old feeling again: that it was my job to protect and repair my mother and, despite everything I'd learned since being a teenager, I still had no clue how to do it. Or how to forgive myself for not knowing how.

38

Bewildering Changes

"A stroke is an injury to the brain. It can
cause difficult and bewildering changes in
a person's emotions and behavior."

— "STROKE," my.clevelandclinic.org

MY FATHER AND I went together to the Title 19 office and applied for
funding, which was quickly approved. My mother, still unable to walk,
feed herself, talk clearly or sit up straight without straps and trays holding
her, was delivered to her new home, The Shores, in an ambulance.

I arrived there shortly after she did. It was late November. The wind
was cold and very strong. It spun a pile of dead leaves into a whirlpool
and pushed them hard against my chest as I walked up the small incline
to the entrance. I pulled on the handle of one of the glass doors; the door
didn't move. The wind whipped my hair into my eyes. I pulled on the
door handle a second time, harder, and this time was able to slip my body
inside just before a gust slammed the door shut again. It bumped against
my back. Not an easy entrance. How in the world, I wondered, would
someone in a wheelchair or using a walker be able to get in or out of this
place? How was my father going to be able to do it?

The air in the lobby was overly warm, redolent with the smells of Lysol and urine and an unnamable sourness. I breathed through my mouth

while I waited at the reception window for directions to my mother's room. Room 107, I was told. Take the elevator down.

The elevator doors swung open on neon-lit corridors where I was sure no natural light had ever entered. The linoleum floor was polished to a slippery-looking gleam. An aide in the nurse's station informed me that I should go "straight down the hall to the dining room."

The dining room? My mother's room was in the dining room? Puzzled, I followed signs with arrows pointing to "Dining Hall" and came upon a large room with big windows. In full daylight, these windows might add a little cheer to this room, but right now, at five o'clock, it was as dark as night outside. The windows were big squares of blackness, coated with condensation. I would later see that they looked out onto a sunken patio with one lonely picnic table. Inside there were eight long wooden tables edged with steel-legged plastic chairs. A large-screen TV with the volume turned up high blasted the room with the local news. Four slack-jawed people in wheelchairs were facing away from the TV.

I found the closed door of room 107. Room 107 and its neighbors, 108, 109, and 110 opened right into the dining hall. I knocked and my Aunt Jeanne's voice invited me in. The room was even hotter than the dining hall and the lobby. Its two sweating windows faced a window well that was half-filled with dry leaves and dark shadows. My mother lay on top of a dull brown bedspread on one of two single beds. The other bed was bare, its linens folded neatly at its foot beside an unopened suitcase. On the dresser beside the unoccupied bed was someone's purse and a large picture frame containing photographs of someone else's grandchildren. With the two beds, two dressers and two nightstands, there was barely enough room for me to walk in. I couldn't imagine how anyone could maneuver a wheelchair in this space.

Jeanne stood in a one-foot square spot next to the dresser. She was writing Mom's name into the collar of a shirt with a permanent Sharpie. As if my mother was a child going off to summer camp.

"Hi, Mom," I said.

She opened her eyes and stared dully at me for a few seconds. She opened half her mouth and yawned, the stroke-impaired side drooping in the opposite direction. "Oh, it's you," she said at last. "Look, Jeanne, Judy's here to spring me from this rat-hole."

"I wish I could, Mom." I sat on the unmade bed and set my purse on the floor. I hated this room. I hated this whole place.

"You *have to* get me out of here. This room is terrible."

"It's not so bad," I lied.

"It's a hell hole and you know it!"

"It is a little hot," I admitted. I spotted the round bump of a thermostat near the doorway. "What's the heat set on?"

"It's off," Jeanne said. "And the window only opens an inch or two. It's as far open as I could get it. We're next door to the kitchen. An aide told us it's always hot in here and there's nothing they can do about it."

"Well, let's see what we can do to make the room prettier, then."

"I thought that would be good too," added Jeanne. "Remember, Mary? We were talking about bringing in some of your needlepoint pictures to hang on the walls?"

"Someone will steal them," my mother responded. "I need to go home."

"Mom, I'm afraid this is it for a while. Just for a while. Until you can walk again."

My mother's eyes filled up with tears. "What good are you then?"

Jeanne and I organized and put away and did our best to make Mom comfortable. Which was not possible. The air in the room was motionless and scorching. My mother complained that her immobilized leg hurt all the time and that she was exhausted. The noise from outside the room— the blurred din of television voices, the occasional wailing of a resident, the aides shouting to penetrate someone's deafness—all made it impossible to be comfortable. My mother was right: it was a hellhole.

Jeanne was closing my mother's now-empty suitcase when my mother asked, "Where am I?" and then five minutes after I'd answered, "At The Shores, Mom, in your new room," she said, "Where am I?" again. I didn't know if she'd forgotten that she'd asked or if she just wanted a better answer. She asked the same things over and over for the next twenty minutes. "Where am I? Why aren't I in my house? I want to be in my own room."

Jeanne and I varied our ways of answering her.

"You can't be home yet, Mary. You need to get better here for a while," Jeanne said.

"You need to stay here for now, Mom. You wouldn't be safe at home," I told her. The next time she asked I added, "Dad can't take care of you alone."

This hit an old nerve, and she changed her approach. "Stupid old man. Why not?"

I explained to her again about the stroke, about her limitations and his.

"Oh yes," she said, as she'd said many times before in this frustrating exchange. "Oh yes, I remember now." And then, "I hate this place. I don't want any roommate. Why do I have to have a roommate?"

"I'll see if I can get them to give you a room alone, Mom. You'll have to be patient for a little while. We'll make this as comfortable for you as we can."

"Where am I? I don't like this place."

"Mary," said Jeanne, sharply. "Stop it. You know damn well where you are and why. Just stop it."

I was startled. I'd never heard my aunt talk to anyone like this. She was always polite and sweet, too much so. I kind of liked seeing this part of her. And it worked.

"Oh," my mother said. "Yes. I'm in a stinking nursing home. I have to stay here and then later I can go home."

Jeanne looked up from the shirt she was folding and met my eyes. She looked exhausted and sad. "Sorry," she whispered to me. "I've about had it."

I sent Jeanne home. I stayed for three more hours, reading the paper to my mother, helping her into a wheelchair and taking her for a very short outing along the hallway. After only five minutes she complained of tiredness and nausea and wanted to go back and lie down.

I brought her back to her stifling room. I unfastened the gait belt, the strong canvas belt that held her upright in her wheelchair, wrapped it around her back and it under her arms and held the ends tight in one hand. I braced her curving, useless left foot in its white slip-on Ked, against my patent-leather blue Dansko clog, and pivoted her to sit on the bed. Then I tipped her gently onto her side and took off her shoes. She closed her eyes and moaned; the corners of her eyes were wet.

"This is all so awful," she moaned.

I didn't know what to say then. She was right; it *was* awful. Not just her landing in this hot room, but everything she'd lost on her way here.

What do you say to a person sitting in the rubble of their whole life? I wasn't about to chatter platitudes at her. "The darkest hour is just before the dawn." "God never gives us more than we can handle." Or the AA phrase, "Let go and let God," that was on the rear bumper of her car.

I finally left around eight thirty. The cold wind smacked me in the face the second I stepped outside. My eyes teared up, from the wind, from the whole sad situation. When I reached my car I put the key in the ignition but didn't turn it. I rested my head on the steering wheel, thinking *This is intolerable and there's nothing I can do to change any of it.*

When I went to bed that night, Chris held me while I told him about my mother's impossible room, her inability to remember where she was and why, her pain and restlessness. How not herself she was. He made sympathetic noises and kissed the top of my head before he fell asleep.

I lay staring up at the ceiling, my eyes wet with tears. For a few minutes then I was five years old, my face pressed against the front window in my family's living room, watching the taillights of an ambulance disappear as it turned a corner at the end of our block, carrying my mother away. No one had told me she'd be back by morning, that this was just one of those brief epinephrine treatments for her asthma. I remember the sick feeling in my stomach. As if I was watching her leave me forever. She did come home the next morning but it was too late: I'd already decided I'd seen the future: any day my mother might be spirited away in an ambulance and never return. I both dreaded and expected it until I grew up and left home and learned, with difficulty, how to let go of my damaged mother.

Timmy, my most reliable comforter, wiggled his way in between Chris and me and licked the tears from my face. I'd let my mother go, yes, but here I was again, feeling helpless and guilty as I lay snuggled in bed with my dog and husband while my mother lay alone in that hot room, as scared and confused as an abandoned infant.

❦

My mother lived out the rest of her life, nearly five years, at The Shores. She stayed only a week in that first, tiny room next to the overheated dining hall. In response to my increasingly urgent requests, the nursing director moved her to a larger, much quieter room on the third floor. Although this room was a double and Medicare required it to be occupied by two people, my mother never had a roommate. She was noisy, the staff told me. She didn't sleep well, she pushed her call light frequently, and shouted for an aide if no one came right away. And at night she often cried. Her first and only roommate, the one who'd shared the hotbox room, could testify to the fact that rooming with Mary meant never sleeping. Neither Medicare nor Title-19 would pay for a single, so the nursing director put Mary into a double, billed it as one-half of a double, and just never filled the other bed.

The new room was pleasant, with two large windows that looked out over a lawn, a freeway, and a high school. The walls were pink, bordered with a pink and blue wallpaper strip at the top. There was a thermostat that actually worked on the wall near the door and the windows could be opened to let in fresh air. I'd brought in some Country Garden Potpourri air freshener. My mother enjoyed watching the freeway traffic, the high school soccer practices, and the sunsets over the trees of the subdivision beyond the high school. And she enjoyed watching reruns of sit-coms and quiz shows turned up loud on her small black and white TV.

In the beginning the panic attacks she'd had in the hospital returned full force. She cried more days than not. Her doctor told us these were common post-stroke symptoms and would probably get better over time. Whether because of the tendency of even brain-injured human beings to adapt or the liberal use of anti-anxiety medication, my mother's depression and agitation eventually subsided. She was "oriented;" she knew where she was and what time it was. She even made a couple of friends.

And every single time anyone in her family visited her, she asked to be taken home.

We all adapted, too. Each of us figured out our own way of explaining to Mary why she couldn't go home and why The Shores was the best option for the time being. (Even though it was our unanimous opinion that The Shores was barely adequate; we all wished there were more and better Title-19 facilities. There were not.) We set up a visiting schedule. Bert came every day. Jeanne came on Wednesday afternoons, Dick came on Mondays and once on the weekend. I came Tuesdays, Thursdays, and once or twice on weekends.

Hanging out with this new version of my mother wasn't ever easy for me. She was so like the sick mother of my childhood, the drunk mother of my teen years. Frail, self-centered, irrational. And—now more than then—innocent. Destroyed.

I always wished I could do more for her. Chris frequently reminded me that no way could I do more. That what my mother most needed was a ton of money to allow her to live at home with 24/7 help and not one of us had that kind of money.

At times I felt grateful that the demands of my work and my family made it impossible for me to do more. I didn't actually *want* to take care of my mother; I just wished that *someone* would.

The stroke wrecked more than just her life; it had landed smack in the middle of mine, requiring me to spend hours with my mother every week, hours that I didn't have to spare. I was seeing twenty to twenty-five therapy clients a week, consulting at a runaway shelter, trying to write, and parenting an eccentric son who was struggling and failing to fit in with his peers. Chris was working fifty hours a week; there were two dogs to walk and a household that needed me to run it. I resented the damn stroke. Despite my ancient habit of believing it was my job to take care of my mother, I didn't *want* to have to make time for her in my crowded life. My lack of generosity of spirit made me feel small and mean. Which stressed me even more.

Over time the predictable rhythm of my nursing home visits, three or four of them every week, each an hour to an hour and a half long, reshaped my relationship with my mother. I never loved visiting but eventually it felt like an ordinary task, like cleaning the bathroom or showing up for boring work meetings. I let go of most of my internal pressure to be my mother's savior, her all-giving angel. I did what I could do and I mostly stopped feeling guilty about what I couldn't do. In place of the guilt, I felt this heavy sorrow for the impossibility of either of my parents having a decent end to their lives.

Finally, eighteen months after my mother's first stroke, my appetite returned and I began to feel centered again. I'd dropped down to 110 pounds, what I'd weighed during my senior year in high school and also after all those weeks in the hospital in 1990. Finally, food looked good again, my normal curves began to fill out, and I was able to sleep full nights. My life felt manageable again. Often overly packed with responsibilities but equally as often joyful.

During my mother's nursing home years, my father's way of dealing with essentially having lost his wife (or at least the wife he'd been used to) was to visit her at The Shores every single day. He was seventy-four when my mother's stroke occurred. He was tethered to the barrel-size oxygen tank when he was at home and to the smaller, portable one that he carried with a shoulder strap when he went out. The portable tank was hard for him to carry. It took him fifteen minutes to lug it and himself down the basement steps to the indoor garage where he kept his car parked by the basement door. He would sit for a few minutes behind the wheel and catch his breath and then drive the five miles to The Shores. When I drove him it would take us about seven minutes; when my dad drove alone it took close to thirty. He'd always been a very cautious driver. Now that his reflexes were slow, he told me, he felt more in control when he moved slowly, walking or driving. He even talked more slowly these days. But the other reason he drove so slowly was that he couldn't see. Macular degeneration. He'd actually failed his last driver's license vision test, he told me, but somehow or other he still had a valid driver's license. Shocked, I asked him how in the world he made that happen, and he said, cryptically, "Your old dad still has a trick or two up his sleeve."

When my dad arrived at The Shores he always sat in his car for a little while to catch his breath and psyche himself up for the uphill walk to the door. Then he shuffled painfully, slowly, to the heavy door and struggled to open it until someone heard him and opened it for him. He sat and rested for five more minutes in the lobby before undertaking the rest of the journey to Mary's room. When he got there, he dropped his skinny body onto the one chair and panted loudly, "uh, uh, uh," for another five minutes.

I got used to everything about The Shores, as if it were simply my mother's new neighborhood. I learned its layout quickly—the PT-Rehab area, where to find a cup of coffee, the social worker, the nursing director. I also learned what I could and couldn't expect from the aides who provided all the hands-on care. I learned which ones lied and which ones were rough. Which ones would respond to friendliness and which ones seemed unreachable.

My mother told me every day that the staff were trying to kill her. When asked why, she answered, "It's because they think I'm a spoiled white lady." Or "I'm onto them; I'm the only one here who's with it enough to notice what they're doing." Or "they're all lazy, don't want to be bothered and I bother them too much."

She might have been right about some of that. She pushed her call light button a lot and got ignored a lot. I'd witnessed it myself. There was no intercom system at The Shores. This had always struck me as strange, perverse, even cruel. You would think that here of all places, where people couldn't get up and go get the help they needed, there should be a two-way intercom system. If a resident was having chest pains or felt dizzy, they'd have to hit the call light and wait for someone to notice that the light over their door had turned on or that a tiny panel with their room number on it on a display in the nurse's station had lit up. Keep in mind that, often as not, no one was even *in* the nurse's station.

Sometimes when I was visiting we would wait for half an hour for someone to come help my mother use her commode or get into her wheelchair. Sometimes it was even longer. I'd filed formal complaints with the Milwaukee County Department on Aging about the lack of cleanliness at

The Shores and about these long wait times. The regulation, I'd learned, was that a call light had to be responded to as soon as possible and never longer than fifteen minutes. In fifteen minutes someone could die from a heart attack or from mucus stuck in his or her windpipe. I could reach my mother's bedside from my own bedside in fifteen minutes. Fifteen minutes should have been plenty of time to answer a call light requesting help, but the nursing aides often took a lot longer.

Sometimes, when I got tired of waiting with my mother I'd go down to the nurse's station and remind them of the regulation. "It's been thirty minutes," I would say. "This is inexcusable. You could lose your license for this."

The responses I got were all pretty similar: "We're understaffed today." "I'm moving as fast as I can, ma'am." Or, once from an aide who was more honest than the rest: "Your mama acts like everything is an emergency, like she's gonna die or something, when all she wants is one of us to reach her a tissue. She shrieks like she's in terrible pain. I never be knowin' if what she wants is important or not."

To which, I said, "It's all important to her. At least let her know you're on the way, even if you can't get there for a while." And, to that same aide on another similar occasion, "Yeah. I know. It drives me crazy, too. Be patient. She's like a child." I didn't say, "Believe me, I know. I grew up with her." But I wanted to.

I caught these little glimpses now and then, of how it was between my mother and these overworked, underpaid women who didn't like or understand her. The women who thought my mother was "difficult" and "demanding." I understood why they might be slow—or even a little rough at times. And in a way their bad behavior was a help to me. A reminder to me to be kind even when it cost me. A reminder that if my life lacked just one of the crucial parts that kept me mostly steady, like my good husband or the safe neighborhood we lived in, I too might treat my mother with too much force.

There were several aides who seemed to actually care about my mother. Geraldine, a woman in her fifties, was one of these. Geraldine clued me in about how things ran, who to trust and who to avoid. She also told me all about her errant daughter, her beloved granddaughters of whom she had custody, and some of the good and the bad men in her life.

I also got to know some of the other long-term residents of The Shores. Some had obvious disabilities, like the quadriplegic young man who manipulated his wheelchair by puffing into a tube. The majority of the people at The Shores were elderly, victims of strokes or dementia or a conglomeration of failing body systems too numerous to fall into any one diagnosis. Old. Just very old.

At the start of every visit I walked down the hall to my mother's room passing through patches of distinct smells, just as you do when you walk through a neighborhood in summertime. But here, the smells were disinfectant rather than new-cut grass; Glade air freshener and dying floral arrangements instead of blooming gardens; the lukewarm, gray smell of cafeteria food instead of fried chicken or burgers on the grill. And always, here, no matter what they layered over it, urine. Still, it all contributed to an environmental identity, a character. As did the people I passed. I'd pause and exchange a sentence or two with the ones who could both hear and speak: "Hi, Sheila," I might say. "How's your sore foot?" Or "Did your daughter have that baby yet, Ernestine?" And they'd ask me "How's that little boy of yours?" Or "How's your daughter like being at that college she's gone to?"

Whatever time of day I arrived, my mother was lying on her bed, gazing at the TV, always the TV, with its volume way up and its picture wobbling in and out of focus.

The staff tried to get her up into her wheelchair and out of her room a few times every day, but she resisted. They didn't have the time, the patience or the investment it would take to force the issue. So my mother got away with eating all her meals in bed in her room, thereby avoiding her decrepit neighbors at mealtime. "They all drool or shout or cry or fall into their food," she told me.

Because of her loud television, my mother wouldn't hear me when I arrived. I'd have to shout, every time, "Hey! Mom! Turn that thing down!" Then she'd finally look over at me, hit the "off" button on the remote, and say, "You finally came?" As if I didn't operate on a predictable schedule, coming around the same time on the same days every week, for years, as reliably as the sunsets she watched out her window every afternoon or evening, depending on the time of year.

39

The Sun Shifts Forever

"When your father dies, say the Armenians,
your sun shifts forever.
And you walk in his light."

　　　—DIANA DER-HOVANESSIN, "Shifting the Sun"

FROM 1992 'TIL 1997, my parents, each in their own way, slid in slow motion towards their deaths. Their companions on this journey consisted of a couple of doctors, a generally unresponsive nursing home staff, their son who was working fifty-hour weeks, their retired sister/sister-in-law who was nearing seventy herself, and their overstretched daughter. A thin team, a listless team, with little knowledge and few resources. We were, in a word, inadequate to respond to the multiple and enormous issues. We made little impact on my mother's sad confusion or my father's suffocating fear. We tried. We bought Bert's groceries, accompanied him to doctor appointments, brought magazines and videos for Mary, sat in the nursing home's "malt shop" with her and discussed the weather, updated her on what Jessie, Rebecca and Nic were up to. We called the nursing director when the staff was screwing up. It was never enough.

By November of 1995, my father wasn't getting enough oxygen, despite the supplemental tanks he was always hooked up to. He now had difficulty thinking clearly, walking faster than a shuffle, talking without gasping, getting enough air to be able to chew and swallow. Yet, like his aging car—which, defying all odds, continued every day to squeak, bounce and rattle on the roads between my parents' condo and my mother's nursing home—my father, too, kept on functioning.

That he did so joylessly was not surprising. You could never have described my father as a joyful person. I didn't ever know much about his childhood but Jeanne had told me my father had always been an odd duck. His intelligence and social awkwardness were evident as early as Kindergarten. Jeanne couldn't remember him ever having a friend. Nor could she recall that anything special had been done to feed his enormous appetite for learning. He read a lot," she'd told me. "And he liked to run." His family had never expected he'd marry and have children.

In the last three years of his life, my father lived primarily on the Hungry Man TV dinners and miniature Snickers bars he had me buy for him every week. Not exactly a balanced diet. The emphysema had weakened him but being malnourished weakened him even more. In his youth, he'd been skeletally thin, Frank Sinatra, Fred Astaire thin. He was that thin again, except not so lanky and elastic. Now he looked brittle and starved. Jeanne, horrified, had told me he was drinking Southern Comfort in his bed at night. She'd seen the bottle on the floor when she'd gone to clean his house for him. She wanted me to talk to him about it. She wanted me to warn him of the dangers of getting drunk and falling down, lying alone on the floor in his condo unable to get to the phone. No one knowing.

So I talked to him. I told him we were worried. "I use the booze," he told me, "to make it through the long evenings without your mother." He told me that Southern Comfort was a good name for it because it was the only comfort he had when he felt so anxious he wanted to jump out of his skin. And it worked for him. He drank only in bed. He wasn't going to fall out of bed. "Tell my sister to mind her own beeswax," he said. I didn't bother him about the drinking again, even though Jeanne still called me from time to time fretting over it.

My father developed pneumonia several times after his emphysema diagnosis. A particularly bad bout of it in the early eighties, years before my mother's stroke, was what had finally convinced him to quit smoking for good. My mother had been driving him to the hospital when he'd stopped breathing. This time, on the way, she pulled over and flagged down a passing ambulance (strange luck!) whose driver resuscitated my dad so they could continue on to the hospital.

Now, in the spring of 1995, he developed pneumonia again. He drove himself to the hospital where he was immediately admitted and put on higher concentrations of oxygen.

"I think I'll be here a few days," he called to tell me. "Come visit your poor old dad."

I went first thing the following morning. I was prepared for my father to look ill; he'd been ill for so long but I wasn't prepared for this additional diminishment. He looked like a skeleton lying under the white hospital blankets, the ever-present nasal cannula across his cheeks, its two nubs resting in his nostrils, feeding him oxygen. His arms, bent at the elbows crossed against his abdomen, looked like sticks.

"Hi, Dad. We've got to stop meeting like this." I tried to sound light. He snorted. Wheezed. Chuckled a little and then coughed and coughed, his painful, emphysema choking cough. I sat beside him until he caught his breath. I shook my head at him, tears in my eyes. He reached for my hand.

His doctor, the portly Dr. Jones, showed up soon after and asked me to come out in the hallway to talk. My father was asleep.

"Your father's blood oxygen level is seriously low," the doctor said. "Normal blood oxygen is over 85. Your father's is between 65 and 75 even with the extra oxygen. He might not make it through the night tonight. You should call your family in to say good-bye."

So we gathered, my brother Dick and I, our spouses and our kids, and Jeanne. We hovered around Bert's bed for most of the night. He roused from time to time. Once he lifted his head, looked around at all of us, noticed his grandchildren sitting on the floor against the wall, and said, "Oh. this is it, huh? You're all here to see the old man die? Okay. Okay. That's okay." and lay back again, asleep or unconscious, I didn't know which. Towards dawn, his oxygen levels rose somewhat and he opened his eyes again. "My mother was here," he told me. "Did she go home?"

Relieved—because of the better oxygen level—we all went home to sleep. When I came to see my father the next day Dr. Jones told me that he was improving. It looked like he might be going to recover from the pneumonia. "But," cautioned the doctor, "It's only a matter of time now. His tests show such an advanced stage of emphysema that I don't understand how he's keeping himself alive, much less walking around and driving a car."

"It's because he thinks he has to stick around to take care of my mother," I told Dr. Jones.

"That's nuts," said the doctor.

"Yeah. I know."

"Surely he can't be of much help to her at this point."

"He doesn't see it that way."

"He shouldn't be driving."

"I know."

"And he can't go back home to live alone. Is there any family member who doesn't work, who could take him in? He needs people to keep an eye on him."

"There isn't anyone who can do that." As bad as I felt saying this, it was still the truth.

"Then, I'm going to recommend a health care facility."

"My father," I informed Dr. Jones, "is a very stubborn man. I can't imagine him agreeing to go into a health care facility, although, God knows, it would be a huge relief to the rest of us."

We decided we needed to have a family meeting in my dad's hospital room.

Dr. Jones, Dick and his wife, Sandi, Chris, and I gathered around my father's bed. Dr. Jones told Bert he would discharge him only if he'd agree to go to Laurel Oaks, a rehabilitation center located halfway between my father's condo and The Shores. It was a good, clean facility, the doctor said, and comfortable. Medicare would cover it for three months since it was rehab and not just residential.

"I'm going home to my own condo," my father said angrily. "I don't need any goddamn nursing home."

Dr. Jones listed for my father, for all of us, the reasons that as a responsible physician he could not release him to his home. "You aren't getting enough oxygen. You could pass out on the toilet, getting up from your chair. If you fall, you will break a bone. There will be no one there to help you. Or an equally likely possibility: you might develop a mucus plug in your bronchial tubes; you would need help immediately or you would die."

"I keep the portable phone next to me at all times," my father said. "I'm going home. Whether you approve it or not."

"How will you get there if none of us take you, Dad? You need to be at Laurel Oaks." I tried to say this in a light tone but my voice sounded flat and uncompromising.

My father paused for a beat. I think my disloyalty surprised him. And then he was even angrier. "Who needs you?! I'll call a cab. Who needs the whole bunch of you?!"

This is so wrong! I thought to myself. *I never tell my father what to do and my father never yells at me.* I wanted to erase what I'd said, replace it with something like, "Okay, I'm sorry, you're right. I'll drive you home right now. You'll be fine." But I knew he wouldn't be fine. I was always worrying about him alone in that condo, with its two flights of stairs, its sharp-edged tables and slippery bathroom floors. Dr. Jones was right.

My father pushed the blankets off his hairy, scrawny legs. He pulled the nasal cannula off his face and sat up as if he was going to leave right this minute. He swung his legs over the side of the bed, caught himself with his hands just before he would have wobbled over and onto the floor. The limp hospital gown gaped open at the back and hung loosely over his bony chest and narrow hips. He looked like an awkward, angular bird, with his head thrust forward, all cheekbones and nose. Dr. Jones stepped forward and wrapped an arm around him, easing him back down on the bed.

"Mr. Marks," he said. "I mean you no disrespect. I know you to be an intelligent and sensible man. You have to make your own decision and I have to make mine. Why don't you talk this over with your family? I'll check in with you this afternoon."

My father was breathing hard from his failed attempt to escape, from frustration, too, I imagined, and anger. His face was flushed, his eyes closed.

The next day he called me to pick him up and take him home. He couldn't breathe well enough to complete a sentence without pausing to gasp.

"Dad, what happened about Laurel Oaks?"

"I don't need that damn place."

"Dr. Jones said you did."

"No, he didn't. You heard that wrong."

"We all heard it. You can't go home alone. I'll take you to Laurel Oaks whenever you're ready to go." He hung up on me.

Finally, my father was made to understand that if he left the hospital against medical advice and without a discharge signed by Dr. Jones, his insurance wouldn't pay for his expensive, week-long inpatient hospital treatment. My father didn't want to be stuck with a big hospital bill. So, he caved. He went to Laurel Oaks in an ambulance.

He was angry and unhappy, and, though he would never say so, he was scared. The first couple of nights he was there he was nasty to the staff. He called me or my brother, one or the other, every hour during the day and until he fell asleep at night. During one of my visits to his very clean, cold, and sterile room there, I begged him to give the place a chance. I was exhausted, I told him, tears in my eyes, from trying to balance work and kids and Mom and him. If he was somewhere safe, it would at least relieve some of the burden on me. I meant this sincerely, and I expected his concern for me would override his rebellion. I didn't tell him how scared I was that I was going to get sick again if something didn't let up pretty soon. But that was true, too. I was eating now and was slowly regaining weight but I was operating on less than enough sleep, constant anxiety about both my parents, and guilt about how little time I was spending with my kids.

He was furious. "I don't give a goddamn about your burden," he shouted at me. "You try living in this place! You try it for one day!" I was stunned into silence. "Okay, Dad, okay," I said and made up some reason I had to get home.

"Don't worry about me," he said as I picked up my purse and dug for my car keys. "I won't be here much longer. I have a plan."

"What do you mean, Dad?"

"Just that. I'm leaving this joint." He wouldn't tell me more.

The next morning I had a call from Laurel Oaks informing me that my father had slipped in his bathroom, fallen, and broken his hip. He'd been taken to the hospital. When I reached him in his room there, he chuckled, "See? What'd I tell you? I'm out of that place."

"You fell on purpose?"

"That's between me and the fencepost. I'm out of there and I'm not going back." He sounded very pleased with himself.

My father had hip replacement surgery that afternoon. Amazingly, it went well. He had little post-surgical pain and was breathing fairly well, receiving oxygen, as always, through his nasal cannula. In the night, however, he woke up and didn't remember where he was or why. In a moment of panic at 2:00 a.m., my father picked up his phone and called 911. "Help me!" He begged the 911 operator. "I'm locked in a room here and they're going to kill me." So, in the middle of the night, two EMTs, in full firefighter gear—heavy boots, jackets and helmets—had shown up at my father's bedside, a nurse trailing behind them. After ascertaining that my father's life was in no danger from the people he'd claimed had kidnapped and imprisoned him, the EMTs and the nurse worked to make my father understand where he was. They failed. The nurse had to sedate him.

In the next several days, my father got crankier and crankier, not with me or with any of his other visitors, but with the nursing staff. He'd call me up and regale me with tales of how he'd told off the poor woman who'd brought his food tray, sworn at the person who came to draw his blood, threatened to fire the kind Dr. Jones. Who was this creature living in my father's wreck of a body? This was not the same man who brought those warm washcloths for my infected eyes when I was little, not the one who cooked Saturday hamburgers or mixed Manhattans for my mother.

And this was not, it turned out, the truth. My father's primary nurse laughed when I apologized to her for his bad behavior. "He's not nearly as bad as he's telling you," she told me. "He gets frightened and he's a little brusque sometimes, but we understand him. He usually has a reason to be upset when he says he is. I listen to him and I believe him. That takes the wind out of his sails. We get along fine, he and I."

From the hospital, my father was released to a different, and he thought, better, rehab facility. He was still anxious to get back home, but since he was too weak to walk without a walker, he accepted the necessity of a brief stay at Bradford Terrace. He was there only a week when his oxygen level fell dangerously low again. He was rushed back to Columbia Hospital, unconscious. As soon as I had a break between therapy sessions, I went to see him. When I reached his room, I found him surrounded by medical people; I couldn't see my father at all. Dr. Jones glanced at me over his shoulder and abruptly told me to leave the room, go wait in the visitors' lounge.

I didn't go to the lounge. I went to the nurses' station. This floor was an intermediate care floor, just one step less vigilant than intensive care, and I knew that all the patients' vital signs were monitored on a screen inside the nurse's station. I'd noticed it on my last visit. Now I identified a square on that screen that had my father's room number on it. His blood oxygen, the screen told me, was 50. No wonder there were so many people hovering around his bed.

Dr. Jones found me a few minutes later leaning over the counter of the nurse's station, trying to get a better angle on the screen. The 50 looked like maybe it had changed to a 60, then maybe a 70; the numbers were blurred and I couldn't be sure.

Dr. Jones confirmed that, yes, my dad's blood oxygen level *was* improving. His lung had collapsed a little while before I'd arrived. Damage from the long-term effects of emphysema. Dr. Jones had just now finished inserting a chest tube, without which my father would have died right around the time I'd arrived at his room.

"I was at my daughter's school when I got the page," he told me. "I hurried to get here, because I had to, because that's my job and because I like your father. But it might have been better for him if I hadn't made it in time. I've probably just prolonged his suffering. You can go visit him now," he said as he turned and walked away, slump-shouldered, sad.

My father was in the hospital for three more weeks as his oxygen levels fluctuated on any given day from alarmingly low to almost decent and back down to low again. Most of the time his numbers were barely high enough to sustain life. Most of the time he was unconscious.

One day, a week after his lung had collapsed, my father, barely conscious, had ripped out his IV, pulled off his nasal cannula and tried to sit up in his hospital bed. A nurse heard him gasping and panting, half-in and half-out of the bed, unable to speak. She got him plugged back into everything and calmed down, apparently still asleep. But when she came to check on him ten minutes later, he'd pulled his IV out again. She had to strap his hands to the bed frame to keep him safe.

"Dad, Dad, Dad. I'm so sorry you have to be here," I whispered to him the first time I came to his room and found him strapped down. Seeing him like that was unbearable. *What harm would it do,* I thought, *to unstrap his hands for the time I'm here in the room with him?* He seemed peaceful right then, no sign of struggle. I unstrapped his right hand and then the left. I rubbed his wrists where the straps had left pale red marks. As soon as I let go of his right hand, he used it to reach for the IV needle that was embedded in his left wrist. His eyes were still closed. He grunted. His right hand flailed in the air over his wrist unable to make contact. I captured the hand and tearfully strapped it down again. The left one, too.

He didn't open his eyes but spoke in a hoarse whisper. "I need to get home."

"Is that why you were trying to unhook yourself?"

"I need to get home. It's Abby's dinnertime. She'll be wondering why I'm not there."

He looked thinner than the day before. His cheeks unshaved and sunken. His face full of shadows. I glanced over at the monitor that showed his fluctuating blood oxygen saturation level, currently at 70.

"I have to feed Abby. Would you feed Abby for me?"

"Abby's not alive anymore, Dad. No one needs to feed her."

"You know where her food is?"

"Yes." It seemed cruel to argue with him.

"She was here just a little while ago. She wanted me to feed her. You'll do it?"

"Sure, Dad."

"Is my mother still here?"

"What do you mean?"

"Oh. No. I guess not. She was right over there in the corner. I guess she had to get home to make dinner."

"Your mother came to visit? Why was that?" I asked, thinking I knew the answer. This was the way a brain acted when it was dying, wasn't it? That's what I'd read, that our brains shut down in a particular way that caused hallucinations. That's why people saw dead relatives and tunnels with white lights at the end of them. But maybe it was real? Could Abby and Gram have come to guide my father to the next phase? I wanted to believe he wasn't just hallucinating. I liked the idea of spirit guides. It appealed to my aesthetics; it appealed to my heart.

"Joojy?" My father used his old nickname for me. I hadn't heard it since the day of my mom's stroke. Before that, not since I was ten. It sent a peculiar jolt through me.

"I'm here, Dad." I slid my fingers under his on top of the covers. The canvas strap around his wrist made it hard for him to lift his hand. I squeezed it but he didn't squeeze back.

"Joojy, bring that bottle of Southern Comfort back with you when you come, will you? It's on the floor next to my bed, on the side facing the wall, that's a good girl."

"Sure, Dad. Happy to. Anything else?" But he'd fallen asleep again or wasn't conscious.

I wasn't going to bring the bottle. I knew he wouldn't remember asking for it. But when I told Dick about our father's request, he said, "What the hell. Let's bring it to him. In fact, I'll pick up a new bottle for him and bring it myself. What harm can it do?" That whiskey bottle sat unopened, tucked between his hospital bed and bedside table. It was never opened.

A few days later my father was moved back to Bradford Terrace nursing home. I visited him once there, but I don't think he knew it. He was rarely awake now. His hands were strapped again and he was, I was told, lightly sedated. I didn't stay long. I kissed the dry flaky skin on his forehead before I left. "Bye, Dad," I whispered and his eyelids fluttered. "I'll take care of Mom for you. You do what you need to do. It's okay." He lifted the fingers of one anchored hand but didn't speak. I kissed him again and left.

He died two days later. I got the call that he was "being worked on" while I was in a session with a contentious couple whose endless arguments made my stomach hurt. I ended the session as gracefully as I could (they were sympathetic, far nicer to me than they ever were to each other). I drove to Bradford Terrace as fast as I dared but my father was dead by the time I arrived. He'd been alone in his room. By the time a nurse thought to look in on him his lips were blue and he couldn't be revived.

My dear friend Barbara had been babysitting Nic while I was at work, when the first call from the nursing home had come to my house. As soon as she understood that Bert was dying she asked her sister to watch Nic and rushed to see what she could do. She'd been fond of my father and also was watching out for me. My father was already dead when she got to him but I wasn't there yet, so, because no one at Bradford Terrace had thought to clean up the room or my dad's body, Barb closed his eyes, removed the IVs and the nasal cannula, and washed his face. She scooped up empty syringes and tossed them in the sharps container. Bundled up the stained bedding and asked for a new clean blanket.

"I didn't want you to see him the way they left him," she said, when I finally arrived. Then she closed the door softly behind her, leaving me alone in the tiny cell of a room that had been my father's final home. There was hardly enough space to walk around the remaining medical equipment to get to his bedside.

I noticed his hands had been freed from their restraints. "Good," I said out loud. "No more straps. We hated those straps, didn't we, Dad." Then I leaned over, kissed his cheek, and said, "I love you." His skin was cool and whiskery against my lips. I'd always thought kissing someone dead would be creepy. It wasn't creepy at all. It was my father, a colder, unmoving version of my father but still my father. It didn't feel like he was gone. I expected him to jump back into his body at any moment, open his eyes, and ask me to feed Abby.

I picked up one of his hands. His long thin fingers, so familiar, were limp and soft. I studied the ropy veins that lay flatter than usual on the back of that hand, then set it down gently, as if I didn't want to wake him.

I looked around for a chair so I could comfortably hang out with him for a while longer, but there was no chair in the room and no space on his bed, so I leaned against the wall. I stood there watching him for at least half an hour. He didn't seem settled, not quite at peace despite his stillness. There wasn't anything specific that made me think that, no visual evidence of violence. It was more something that lingered in the air. A sense of aftermath, the kind of quiet startledness that, for example, comes immediately after the noise of a car crash. Despite Barb's efforts to protect me from how my father died, I knew it had to have been terrible, a thrashing, panicked fight for breath. The knowledge made me hugely sad, a sadness I still carry.

As I stood there looking at my father's body I was filled with sorrow about his whole life. Did he know, I wondered, that I'd seen how difficult the last ten years of his life had been? Did he have any idea how much I appreciated everything he'd done for me? I'd told him a few times in bits and pieces over the years: How he'd been the one sure thing in my childhood. A source of reason and unwavering love no matter what happened in our house or in my life after I left home. I'd even told him once that I wasn't entirely sure I would have survived without him. But I don't think he believed me or understood what I was talking about.

As he lay in that narrow white bed in that small room, I could almost believe he was hearing me. "Thank you," I said out loud, "for everything. For being the one who would always come when I had a nightmare. For the homework help. For holding onto my two-wheeler bike just long enough and then getting out of my way. For expecting more from me than I did myself."

I talked that way, out loud, until I felt something shift in the room. It was as if the air smoothed out and quieted down. The light seemed brighter. Which was not possible since it was night and the room was lit by overhead fluorescent bulbs that had been on the whole time.

"Bye, Dad," I said, pausing in the doorway. "Good-bye."

My brother Dick had already gone to bed when our dad died and hadn't heard his phone ring. He got the news from his answering machine the following morning. He and I went together to the nursing home to tell our mother. We rarely visited her together and never in the morning, so right away she knew something was up.

She was sitting in her wheelchair, watching television; she turned and stared at us. "Something's wrong. It's Bert, isn't it?" she said. "He's gone, isn't he? I knew it. I had a feeling last night. It was last night, wasn't it?" She didn't cry. She asked us to tell her what happened, then cut us off in the middle, saying she couldn't stand to hear any more.

"What happens now?" she said. Then, plaintively, "What's to become of me?"

We reassured her that nothing would change, that Dick and I would still look after her the same way we'd been doing. We didn't tell her we were going to have to sell the Cherrywood Village condo. When it sold four months later, Dick and I thought about keeping this hard truth from her but it seemed kinder—and would spare us a lot of uncomfortable lying—if we told her about it. So we did. But, we never told her, and she never asked, about her furniture: we sold everything at auction but there was no need for her to know about that.

She seemed satisfied with that. She left all the funeral arrangements to us. Geraldine, her favorite caregiver at The Shores, later told us that she'd cried, quietly and not for long, every time she was alone that week and the next.

My father had told us he wanted to be cremated, "as cheap as possible," with a small service led by a minister, with only family attending. "No gawkers." So that's how it was. A minister who hadn't known my father said some prayers and some good Christian life-after-death words and Chris read a short eulogy. We went out to lunch with my mother and Aunt Jeanne afterwards. Jeanne said, "Wasn't the minister comforting? He said all the right things."

"I couldn't hear anything he said," my mother complained.

"Maybe you need hearing aids, Mary," Jeanne said.

"Maybe I didn't *want* to hear him," my mother answered.

My father's box of ashes were placed in a small marble-fronted vault at Wisconsin Memorial Park, near Aunt Jeanne's husband's ashes and beside the empty space that waited for Mary.

I still sometimes find myself reviewing the facts of my father's death, searching for a different outcome, a gentler dying. His hands were tied to the bed rails to stop him from pulling out his IV. But that also meant he couldn't reach his call light or the suctioning device he'd used in recent hospital stays to clear his own airway. He was all alone and rarely conscious, so, even if he'd had enough strength and air to call out loud enough for someone to hear, he might not have thought of it. I have no idea how long it takes to suffocate when your airway is blocked but it must have been a terrifyingly long struggle. No one should have to die like that. He should have lived his last days with a caregiver at his bedside 24/7. Then he could have died a few days later, peacefully, as Dr. Jones had told us he would, breathing less and less, not conscious of the approaching end. Slipping away. No distress. Medicare was paying for his rehab stay at Bradford Terrace but it didn't cover 24/7 care either at home or in a nursing home, and no one in our family had anything close to the $3000 per week that extra care would have cost. I suppose if we'd realized what the dangers were my brother and I might have been able to take shifts, but for how long? I couldn't have afforded, financially or for my own health, to care for my dad longer than a couple days. And, really, would it have made any difference?

❦

A month later, Timmy, our steadfast golden dog, developed a malignant tumor. It happened suddenly; one day he seemed fine and the next day he couldn't walk or eat. I held him in my arms while he was given the injection that ended his life. It was a sad but gentle end. I was struck by the difference between how Timmy died with peace and dignity, with his family all around him, and how my father had had to thrash his way through weeks of pointless suffering and had died horribly and alone, in a nursing home.

How is it we are allowed to release our dying pets but not our dying parents?

I told seven-year-old Nic that Timmy had gone to join Grandpa, to keep him company. Nic looked at me as if I'd lost my mind and said, "You don't really believe that, do you?"

"I'm not sure," I told him. "It makes me feel better when I think it's true."

"Grandpa is dead," seven-year-old Nic said in his ultra-rational voice. "He's ashes. He's gone. And he was the only one in my family who understood higher math."

"You could have had a lot of fun together, Nic."

"I hate cigarettes and I'm never going to smoke."

40

She Had Always Wanted to Escape

"I felt as if she had always wanted
to escape and now she escaped. Then she turned,
slowly, to a thing of bone,
marking where she had been"

—SHARON OLDS, "Last Hour"

August 31, 1997

GERALDINE, MY MOTHER'S PRIMARY caregiver at The Shores called while I was in a therapy session. Doris taped a pink "While You Were Out" slip on my office door: "Your mother was taken to the hospital this morning. Her back hurt and she was sleepy." When I reached Geraldine, she repeated her message and added. "Your mama, she don't look right to me this morning." I cancelled my next two clients and drove to Columbia Hospital's ER. Again.

On the way there, I tried to count how many times I'd been in this ER in the past ten years. There had been so many visits: Jessie's broken foot, the time I cut my finger with a power trimmer while pruning a mock orange bush, Chris's sprained ankle, my mother's stroke, at least five visits with one or the other of my parents after that, and, of course, two visits that were because of my fevers and inflamed colon. One was that first night Chris made me go, when my temperature was 105; the next, weeks later, was the night I thought I was dying and Betty called the EMTs. I expected I'd know the first names of most everyone working there this afternoon.

But not this time. The unfamiliar young nurse at the intake desk asked if she could help me.

"I'm here to be with Mary Marks. She was brought in from her nursing home a little while ago?"

She checked her computer monitor. "Mrs. Marks," she told me, eyes still on the screen, "is in x-ray."

I found my mother lying on a gurney waiting her turn for a chest x-ray. I had expected her to be panicky as she had been when she had her stroke. I had intended to hold her hand but she looked cheerful and relaxed. She smiled when she saw me and said, "Well, look what the cat dragged in. You came to keep me company?" Her voice was quiet, tired, threadbare, her face small and pale against the white hospital pillow.

"I'm yours for a few hours if you'll have me," I told her.

"All I'm doing is waiting here. Not much for you to do."

"Why are you here. Mom? Do you know?"

"They said a chest x-ray. But I think maybe it's because of my leg?" she said.

My mother was not here because of her leg, which was in a knee-high cast. She'd had the cast for over a month. Her physical therapist at The Shores should have been giving her exercises all along to help her maintain the muscle tone in her paralyzed left leg and foot. That hadn't happened. Her muscles in that leg had weakened and her left foot was sickling inward and could no longer flatten. In order to correct this my mother was having a series of casts to gradually return her foot to its functional position. She hated the casts, of course. Just when she'd begun to get used to a cast, when it wasn't causing any aching anymore, they'd replace it with another one and the aching would return. The process reminded me of what it was like to have my teeth straightened when I was in grade school.

"I see you still have your little plaster friend," I said. "But I don't think you're here because of that."

My mother didn't seem to hear me. There was a fair amount of background noise, voices floating out of distant speakers, footsteps, conversations in rooms up and down the hallway, telephones ringing. I walked closer, looked directly into her face, and asked again.

"What did they tell you about why you're here?"

"I don't remember. I guess because I don't feel well."

"Geraldine told me that your back hurt and that you seemed sleepy."

"Oh. No. My back doesn't hurt. I just don't feel well. A little short of breath."

I waited outside the door while an x-ray technician took pictures of my mother's chest.

An hour later a doctor joined us in the ER and informed us that my mother's lungs contained fluid. Her heart wasn't pumping efficiently. He didn't know why. She also had too much digoxin in her blood—the heart medication she'd been taking since she had her mitral valve replaced with a pig valve eight years earlier. The digoxin was probably causing her sleepiness. He would admit her for further tests and try to stabilize her medication level. I woke my mother up to tell her she would be staying in the hospital.

"Good," she said, and fell back asleep.

I drove back to my clinic, called my brother, saw a few more clients, went home and had dinner with Chris and the kids.

I returned to the hospital around seven carrying a bouquet of yellow daisies, my mother's favorite flower. When I entered her room, three nurses were in the process of moving my mother's semi-limp body onto what looked like an extra thick mattress. Someone had just given her a sponge bath.

"How are you doing, Mom?" I set the vase on her bedside table. The nurses bustled out of the room.

"A little tired. Glad to be out of that joint. I don't think I'll go back, do you?"

"You might. Hard to say at this point. Do you know where you are now?"

"Well . . . they tell me I'm not at Home Depot. I thought I was for a while but I don't see any hammers or anything so I guess I'm not." She laughed quietly. "No. I know. I'm at Columbia Hospital."

"Do you remember why?"

"Of course I do. I had a stroke," she answered, with some defensiveness. "Your father was upstairs. I was eating toast and I fell."

"Actually, Mom, that happened a few years ago. You haven't had any strokes lately. You were very tired and didn't seem to feel well. The doctor says your heart medication is out of balance. They need to keep you here to fix it."

"Oh, okay. Has it stopped snowing?" She looked over at the large window, which was filled with bobbing green leaves, tree limbs and pieces of blue sky.

"It's July, Mom. Here. I'll open the curtains wider. See the leaves? It's summertime. It must be ninety degrees out there."

"Oh," she said and closed her eyes. She seemed to have gone to sleep again. I went out into the hallway, saw her chart on a rack next to her door, picked it up and read as much of it as I could understand. An admitting doctor had written that a cardiologist had been called in to assess my mother's heart functioning. I wrote a note to the cardiologist and left it in the chart: "Please call me."

I was tucking the chart back into the rack beside the door when my brother arrived.

I filled him in.

"Are her no-code instructions in that chart?" Dick asked. He was referring to the decisions we'd made for her about whether or not she should be put on a ventilator or a stomach tube after she had the original stroke. After she'd recovered enough to think about such things, she had confirmed those decisions: Do not prolong her life through artificial means; no ventilators or stomach tubes; do not resuscitate.

"Yes," I answered. "I checked. You know, I think she's going die really soon. I think she wants to."

Dick nodded. "Can't blame her. I wouldn't want to hang around if I were her."

The next day when I got to my mother's room, Dr. Johnson, the cardiologist, was just leaving.

"Are you the daughter?" he asked. "I was just going to go call you. Let's talk a spell. Come on down to the lounge."

We sat across from each other at a round card table covered with a partially completed jigsaw puzzle. Battered children's toys littered the floor.

"From the pictures we took yesterday," Dr. Johnson said, "it looks as if your mother's replaced heart valve has worn out. I see from her records that it's only eight years old. It shouldn't have worn out this soon."

"Why did it wear out? Any guess?"

"An infection, maybe. Something nobody caught. Hard to say." He looked squarely at me. "We can't fix it at this point. I don't think she'd make it through the surgery." He was speaking carefully, with kindness, as if he expected me to cry. As if he thought this news would be hard for me to hear.

"That means she's going to die soon?" I asked.

Dr. Johnson looked startled. "Well," he said. "Well, well. I didn't think we'd get to that question so quickly. Okay. Yes. That's right." He looked at me curiously. "She might live another two months but I doubt it."

I felt a need to explain myself. "I'm not surprised," I told him. "And not really sad either. She's been dying for a long time, more than five years, since she had a stroke. I'm used to the idea."

"Ahhhh." He nodded. "I understand that."

"Plus, I think my mother's decided it's time to go."

"You know, it's funny you say that," Dr. Johnson replied, "because I told a colleague just this morning when I was discussing your mother's case, that it seemed like she had decided not to fight this."

The next time I visited my mother she assured me that she still knew she wasn't at Home Depot. And she knew it wasn't snowing. "That," she announced, "was a side effect of my digoxin level being too high." She remembered medication names and the names of syndromes better than I did even when she couldn't remember if she'd had breakfast or not. I explained to her about her heart valve and her slim chances without having to simplify anything. She seemed to understand. She was unperturbed. In fact, she wasn't much interested.

"I wouldn't want surgery even if they said I should have it," she said. "I guess I don't have to go back to that awful Shores place." She sounded bored and sleepy. Then she brightened, turned her head to the right, reached her hand through the bars of the bed rails, and made a motion with her fingers.

"Hello, precious," she murmured. Her fingers curved and made scratching motions at the air.

It took me a second to recognize what she was doing. Dog ear-scratching. It couldn't be anything else. "Mom, is Abby here?"

"Well, yes, of course." She smiled. "Abby has come to take me home."

I didn't know what to say. Abby was my mother's last dog, the beloved collie who'd died several years ago while my mother was in the hospital having her left knee replaced.

"Oh. Okay. Abby's here." I tried to sound non-committal. Just because I couldn't see Abby didn't mean she wasn't there, did it? My father had seen her too.

My mother continued to pat and scratch at empty space.

"Did you know, Mom, that Abby visited Dad too the last time he was here?"

"Did she? He told me his mother came." Scratch, scratch. Whispered endearments: sweetie-face, dearest angel.

"His mother came, too." I watched my mother flatten her hand and run it down an invisible skull, a silky, aristocratic collie muzzle. I could almost see Abby there myself. There was silence between us for maybe five minutes while my mother patted and scratched.

"Do me a favor," she suddenly said, between caresses.

"Sure. What?"

"I want my ashes to be next to your dad's."

"That's the plan, Mom. You told us that and it's all been taken care of."

"But I want to be in the mountains too. Can we do both? Is that allowed?"

"I'd be glad to do that for you. Does it matter which mountains?"

"*My* mountains. You remember."

I did. Every time we'd taken a summer vacation when I was a child we'd gone somewhere in the Rocky Mountains. And always, on the first day of our stay, my mother would sit weeping in a rocking chair on the porch of whatever cabin we'd rented, accumulating a mound of damp, wadded-up Kleenex in her lap. When one of us would ask her what was wrong, she would invariably reply that nothing was wrong . . . *for once.* She was just relaxing.

I'd watch her with fascination, the way I'd have watched a snake shedding its skin. I knew that when the process was finished the mother I loved the best would emerge. The mother who sang while she sat rocking and knitting; who'd go to the horse corral with me to pet the horses, sharing with me the pleasure of their horsey smells; the one who packed lunches and took us on day-long hikes up to waterfalls or alpine meadows. My mother had always been happiest in the mountains.

"Yes, of course I remember," I told her. "I'd be delighted to take you back to your mountains, Mom."

My mother's eyes closed. Her hand went limp. I watched her chest to see if she was still breathing. She was.

When her face was relaxed, like now, the paralyzed left side matched the right side and she looked almost normal. She looked almost like that mother in the mountains. Not the perennially resentful one, not the sick one or the angry or the drunk one. The one who used to love to dance and sing. I pictured how she was back in the days when she liked to go out with my father to the Fireside Lounge, where the piano player invited the customers to sing. I was six then and she was thirty-one. It was before her drinking was a problem or before I knew her drinking was a problem. I'd hear her singing at home sometimes, while she washed the kitchen floor or ironed our clothes, the hiss of the iron a soft percussion under her voice. She sounded like Ella Fitzgerald, her voice mellow and rich. *Try a little tenderness. She may be weary, women do get weary.*

I remembered how she looked on the nights when she and my father went to the Fireside Lounge, after the babysitter came and they were ready to leave. Her dark brown hair gleamed in a freshly unrolled shoulder-length pageboy. Her lips and nails were painted in matching shades of Frankly Scarlet. Her black stiletto heels, three inches high, clacked against the floor and her thin nylon-stockinged legs made a whoosh, whoosh sound. She smelled of Arpège cologne and Revlon face powder.

"How do I look?" she'd ask me as she twirled before me in the small bedroom she shared with my father, her mid-calf skirt swooping around her in a moving sculpture of cotton and tulle.

"Oh Mommy," I would say. "You look beautiful! Like a movie star."

I'm pretty sure my mother was trying to make her life match a scene from a 1950s film, like the Fred Astaire Ginger Rogers movies she loved, those movies with their sleek, leggy, red-nailed women, everyone holding a cigarette. The men were sleek and thin too, and everyone drank a lot and smoked and never got liver or lung diseases. No children in those movies either unless they were off to one side somewhere, adorable and occasionally witty, tended to by a nanny. The many Manhattans I later learned my mother drank at the Fireside Lounge were, in the beginning, one more prop for the movie scene. She seemed so happy on the mornings after those nights. She sang over breakfast and off and on for the whole following week. It was only after many years in AA that she talked about those nights with guilt and shame. I could never quite reconcile in my own mind how something that made her sing like that could be something bad, something to be ashamed of.

Now I sat in a chair across from her bed, looking at the frail being she'd become and felt sad that she hadn't gone right on singing every single day through all of it, the good years and the bad, the drinking and the sobriety and the relapsing in between, the warm wonderful summer family vacations, the happy Christmases, the disappointments, the losses. It seemed utterly unfair that her road to this day had held so much sorrow, guilt, confusion, and pain. As if life was ever fair.

Nine days later she was well enough to be discharged. Which was not to say that she was well. Only that her lungs were nearly clear and her digoxin levels were back to normal. Dr. Johnson told me that in spite of her failing heart he was going to have to send her back to The Shores the following day. Medicare rules. I explained this to my mother. Strangely, she didn't seem to care.

"Okay, if that's what they think," she said. "Raise my bed, would you?"

I pushed the button on the control and the upper part of the bed tilted up. No sooner had I put the control down than she picked it up and lowered it back down. Then she raised it. Then she handed me the control and asked me to lower her. Then to raise her up. Then she wanted the controls back in her hand. Then a nurse came in. My mother held out the control to her. "Put me down, please."

"Now, Mary," the nurse scolded, "we've talked about this. Your head needs to be up to help you breathe. Remember?"

Mary pushed the down-button herself. The nurse took the control from her hand, raised the head of the bed, repositioned the pillows, and placed the control out of my mother's vision and reach. "And who is your visitor today?" she asked, tilting her head towards me.

"That's Abby, my collie."

The nurse looked confused for a moment.

"Her dog has come to visit," I explained. "She's taking a nap over there." I pointed to the space under the round table in the corner of the room.

"Oooooh, I see," said the nurse. "No, Mary, I meant this *person* sitting here talking to you."

"I know who that is. Do you people think I'm crazy?" She sounded annoyed. "Always asking me stupid things. Do I know what day it is, do I know where I am. I'm at Columbia Hospital, and it's some day in . . . November . . . I think." It was still a hot July day.

"Okay, well, if you know this person, who is she?" the nurse challenged.

"They tell me," wicked little smile, "that's my daughter."

"Is she?"

"Sure, that's what they say . . ."

The nurse caught my eye and raised her eyebrows. I shrugged. I was pretty sure my mother still knew who I was. When the door closed behind the nurse my mother made a sound, a quick snort, like a laugh. I looked at her questioningly, but she'd closed her eyes and drifted off to sleep.

I sat and read a book for twenty minutes. Then my mother suddenly opened her eyes and said, "Hey!" in an angry voice.

"What is it, Mom?" I was on my feet and at her side.

She stared in the direction of the round table at the opposite side of the room. "Hey!" she repeated sounding offended. "Who is that growling at my yellow flowers?" Her eyes had the hard glittering look that I recalled from her drinking days. A reflex of revulsion shot through me. I made myself look at her drawn, seventy-four-year-old face, her thinning gray hair, her dark-rimmed sad eyes. The glitteriness shifted to a myopic suspiciousness.

"Is it Abby, Mom?"

"No," she said, irritated. "Are you blind? Abby's sleeping over there." She pointed to the opposite side of the room. "Did you invite that person? Who is that?"

"Beats me, Mom." Before I could figure out how to deal with my mother's new vision she changed her focus.

"And what are these spinning, green things doing on my bed?" She was outraged. "Get them out of here right this minute. Did you think I wouldn't notice these? Get them off." She brushed frantically at the clean white blanket covering her legs.

"I don't see them, Mom. But I believe you do."

"Of course I do. I'm not blind, you know."

"No, you're not blind. Neither one of us is blind." What was the sense in arguing with her? But then, what was the point of playing along? I chose a neutral stance.

"Are they still there?"

"Yes," she answered, closed her eyes, and seemed to sleep. A second later, she opened them, found her bed control, and used it to lower the upper part of the bed several more times. I tried to distract her.

"Mom, since Abby has come," *and*, I was thinking, *spinning green things and growlers*,

"maybe Dad will come visit you, too."

"I can't think why he'd want to do that." She stopped playing with the bed control and focused her attention on me.

"To take care of you. He always tried to take good care of you."

She considered this for a moment. "Yes . . . I guess that's true. He did take good care of me."

"He did."

She was silent for a few minutes, staring at the wall. Thinking about Bert, perhaps. Then, because there didn't seem to be anything better to do, I asked her if she wanted me to put some polish on her toenails. This was something I'd done from time to time ever since she'd started living at The Shores. Brought her souvenirs from the real world like Godiva chocolates, peonies and lilacs from my garden, an aromatherapy device that plugged into the wall, and nail polish.

Today I'd brought clear nail polish with silver glitter floating in it.

She opened her eyes again and said, "Yes . . . I'd like that."

While I worked on her toenails her supper tray was delivered, filling the room with the smell of something warm and salty. I removed the metal plate cover: meatloaf and mashed potatoes.

"You can just cover that right back up," my mother muttered.

"You don't want any? I'll help you with it."

She shook her head. "Not hungry." She closed her eyes again.

"How about some Jell-O? Looks like green jell with carrots in it. No? How about these canned peaches? I could cut them up into small pieces for you."

"I guess a few of those would go down okay." I knew she was agreeing just to please me. As I pulled the tab to open the small can of peaches, a nurse walked in to check my mother's vital signs.

"Mary, you shouldn't eat in bed," the nurse warned as she pumped up the blood pressure cuff. She pushed the call button and asked for help "to transfer the patient to a chair." While my mother waited with a thermometer strip in her mouth, the nurse turned to me. "Your mother hasn't been swallowing very well. We've been having her sit up in the chair when she eats. It's safer for her."

It took four people, three women and one man, to lift my mother into the recliner beside her bed. Once seated she listed more to the left in a way I hadn't seen in a couple of years. The male nurse pushed her into a more upright posture while one of the women wrapped a gait belt around her middle and then buckled it tight around the chair back to hold her in place. The team left and I began feeding my mother bits of diced peaches, the same way I'd fed my kids when they were babies. She obediently opened her mouth for the slippery spoon and chewed slowly, grimacing as if she were eating dog food or grass. After three or four spoons full she shook her head.

"Enough," she whispered. She took a quavering, wheezing breath. And began to cough.

"Are you choking?"

She shook her head, but a gurgling sound accompanied her next breath. She squirmed and coughed again.

I hit the call button, asked for immediate help, and within seconds the team of four was back in the room. I moved out of their way, still holding the spoon and the container of peaches. Feeling responsible. Feeling as if I might have just killed my mother. The nurses lifted her back into bed with the head raised to a sitting position. They clamped an oxygen mask over her face for a few seconds, then removed it and instructed her to cough. A young man, the attending resident I assumed, ran into the room, his stethoscope flopping against his white coat. They made a space for him. He felt for her pulse. He spoke loudly into her face: "Take deeper breaths, Mary. Slow down. Deep breaths. We've got you; we've got you now."

As if she were falling down a deep mine shaft. As if they could stop her falling.

I found myself wondering if Abby *was* nearby, waiting for my mother to slip out of her body and come scratch her ears. Waiting to guide my mother out of her body and into whatever was next.

Suddenly my mother sat straight up, leaned toward me, staring at me around the doctor's elbow. "I'm dying, you know," she told me in a clear, matter-of-fact voice. She flopped back against the bed, coughing and wheezing.

I didn't know what to do or say, so what came out was another automatic, stock therapist-type question. "How do you know that, Mom?" I asked.

She stopped coughing and put her one functioning hand over her heart. "Oh, we know these things, that's all." And then her breathing slowed and her heart rate stabilized. The white coats breathed a collective sigh and stepped back from the bed as my mother drifted off, not into death but into sleep.

"No more food for a while," the doctor said before he left.

"No problem," I answered.

I stayed and watched my mother sleep peacefully for fifteen minutes. Then I kissed the top of her head and said good-bye. I didn't expect to see her alive again.

The next morning the phone rang at five thirty. It was a nurse. My mother had died ten minutes before.

Chris came with me to the hospital. We walked into her room together. My mother was lying on her bed, covered with a blanket, staring up at the ceiling. She looked as she'd often looked when I arrived at The Shores and found her watching TV, her eyes open and dull and her jaw slack. She did not, of course, turn to greet me when I sat down in a nearby chair. There was no "They're trying to kill me here," or "When can I go home." Only unmoving silence and a look of deflation, as if someone had pricked her and let out just enough air to sink and soften her body the tiniest bit. Barely noticeable but unmistakable. I remembered my father's body having that same look of deflation, despite the roughed-up air in his room.

This room felt peaceful and warm, like a room where someone had been reading a good book or talking with a well-loved friend. My mother's face looked peaceful too, despite its frozen expression.

"She was okay at the end, I think," I said to Chris. "She wasn't in pain."

Chris nodded. "Would you like to be alone with her?"

"Yes. Just for a few minutes."

"Should I close her eyes before I go?"

"Thank you."

Chris placed an index finger on each of Mary's eyelids and gently pushed them shut. He kissed her forehead and he left the room.

I lay my hand on her bare arm. Her skin was warm. I remembered how a few days ago I'd massaged her arms and hands with the Madame Rochas lotion she'd always loved, running my hand down her arm from her elbow to her knuckles with long, smooth strokes. Now I held my hand still on her warm lower arm.

"Good-bye, Mom. I'm glad you don't have to go back to The Shores." A few tears slipped down my cheeks.

This was my last chance to see my mother's face, the last time I would see her other than in my mind. Was there anything left to say? I thought about it, but, really, there was nothing. And there was no one left in this body to talk to anyway. I didn't need to linger as I'd done in my father's room, waiting for everything to settle down. Waiting until I felt like my father had taken his leave. Everything here was settled. My mother was gone.

As I left the room I ran into my mother's primary nurse. "I'm so sorry for your loss," she said. "I was with your mother when she passed. I thought you would like to know that her last few minutes were easy."

"I know," I said.

"Her breaths," the nurse continued, "just got further and further apart until there weren't any more. She never seemed scared. She wasn't struggling for air or anything like that."

"Yes. Good. Thank you for telling me. That's very nice of you."

She nodded and left. My brother and his wife arrived. We called the funeral parlor. Her body would enter the crematorium with glittering silver toenails. It was a fitting end.

41

We Can Live. And We Will.

"I want to love more than death can harm. And I want
to tell you this often: That despite being so human
and so terrified, here, standing on this unfinished
staircase to nowhere and everywhere, surrounded by
the cold and starless night—we can live. And we will."

—OCEAN VUONG, "The Weight of
Our Living: On Hope, Fire Escapes,
and Visible Desperation"

NIC WAS HAVING A slumber party. There were two extra nine-year-old boys in the house, and despite Nic's usual sedentary nature the boys were running around, being noisy. Seconds after their running-around stopped, the TV began blasting the background music for Nic's Super Mario videogame.

It was April 15, 1997, seven years after that frightening summer of high fevers and organ inflammation, two years after my father died, three months before my mother would die. I was tired and didn't feel quite right. I asked Chris to take over supervising the raucous little boys and I went upstairs to the room that used to be Jessie's bedroom. She was in her sophomore year at Colorado College and had been gone for over a year. I hadn't had the heart to change her bedroom. It still had a mattress on the floor under a leaded glass window that looked out on the neighbor's house and garden. There were glow-in-the-dark stars all over the walls and the slanting ceiling over the bed. When you were in that room at night it felt like being caught in a swarm of fireflies, all those tiny glowing lights. The room still smelled like Jessie, some cologne I've forgotten the name of.

I lay down on Jessie's mattress by the window and pulled the comforter up. I was feeling worse by the second. Shivering. Wanting to close my eyes and sleep whatever this was away.

And then it hit me. This was not the beginning of something ordinary, a cold or the flu. I recognized the unique fatigue, a heaviness of body and mind, the rising heat in my face. I didn't want to overreact. I'd been working at not overreacting since 1990—trying not to think that every mild symptom was the start of the disease that almost killed me and ruined one whole summer. If there had been a time for my symptoms to return you'd have thought it would be during those hard years when my parents were both still alive but terminally ill and I was trying to balance my own newly reclaimed life and their enormous needs. During the five years my parents were sick and dying, each of my kids had also suffered in each of their own ways: my daughters had argued and cut each other to shreds with silences. Nic was miserable, as he told us, and hated the therapist we found for him. Chris and I had some struggles too. And I hadn't gotten sick.

But now I felt it beginning again: the shivering and then the waves of unbelievable heat. I knew that if this really was the same disease (Still's, although no one was sure of its name at this point), I would have a rash. I cautiously lifted my shirt. There they were, the tiny red dots, the itching just barely beginning. It would be gone by morning, I told myself.

But I couldn't talk myself down from my fear. I woke up repeatedly all night long, scared, sometimes crying a little. Finally I asked my father and Dick Olney—both alive in the spirit world or maybe just in my mind (who knows?) to please help me with this. *Help me know what to do. Help me bear it if it is in fact Still's. Help me be well enough to go hiking with Jessie.* I missed her a lot. And I missed the mountains. I'd been so happy when she called to ask if I'd come for her spring break and go hiking with her in New Mexico. I was supposed to fly to Colorado in two days to pick her up and then we were going to drive down to New Mexico; the weather there was more likely than the Colorado mountains to be springtime warm.

When I woke up in the morning my temperature was normal. The rash was still there but it was only a little scatter of red dots around my waist. I was tired. I didn't feel totally okay but maybe, I thought, this would be minor. A small bout of fatigue. It would be gone by tomorrow. I kept my appointment with Kathleen, my intuitive, nearly magical body-worker friend.

"You're sick," she told me when she laid her hands on my feet.

"I'm trying not to be," I told her.

"But you are sick," she repeated. "You're going to be okay but it's the same thing, isn't it, that happened before?"

And yes. It was. I knew it was.

"I don't want to miss this opportunity to be with Jessie," I told her.

"Go," Kathleen said. "It's going to be okay. You're going to remember this trip forever."

So I went. Sitting on the airplane as it circled the landing field in Colorado Springs, I knew I was in a full-blown flare-up. I'd dozed during the flight, hoping I could sleep away the rising fever, dimly aware each time I woke that I was a little sicker than when I'd last closed my eyes. By the time the plane landed I guessed my temperature was at least 104, maybe 105. It was hard to think straight but I knew I had to. No one was going to take care of me. No one was even going to meet me at the airport. Jessie was in class. I was going to meet her for dinner that evening.

While I waited for my turn to leave my airplane seat, I noticed that the man sitting next to me was holding a brilliantly colored walking stick. It looked hand carved. I needed something other than my physical discomfort to focus on even if just for a few minutes, so I asked him about his stick. "It's beautiful," I told him.

"Yes," my seatmate said. "It was a gift. Look, it's a series of animals. A lion, a bear, a zebra, a parrot. The man who made it told me it had protective powers."

For a moment I felt unaccountably safe. This stick had nothing to do with me. But it was impossible to look at it, at that bear in particular, and not think about Dick Olney, how he'd taught me to identify my spirit animals: the rabbit and the bear. I remembered my prayer a couple of nights ago, and the bear, the stick, the owner of the stick, all that seemed like some kind of response to that prayer.

"Can I touch it? Would you mind?"

"Touch the animal you like best," he said.

I reached out and stroked the bear's chiseled fur. And for a moment, I sensed Dick Olney's presence. As if he were standing beside me, watching me stroke that wooden bear.

I looked over at the cane's owner as he stood up to leave. He looked nothing like Dick Olney. He was tall, thin, grey-haired. Plus he had a South African accent.

"Powerful thing, isn't it?" he said as he stepped out into the aisle.

Before I could think of another thing to say, he was out the door, walking down the metal steps onto the tarmac. I hated to see him go.

In the terminal everything in me wanted to stop moving, to lie down, to close my eyes. Instead I started coaching myself, as I'd done during that hot run so many years ago when my illness was just beginning to be that almost-fatal flare-up. *Keep your eyes focused on the edge of the road. One foot, the next foot. Breathe deep in your belly.* "I can do this," I told myself. One thing at a time. *Find the car rental counter. Get the car. Drive to the ER.*

It was 1997 so of course I still didn't have anything like a cell phone or a GPS. I thought the hospital might be beside the Colorado College campus and it was. I found it. I told the receptionist in the ER that I was very sick, that I had a high fever and needed medication. She looked at me skeptically but took my insurance information and set me up with a triage nurse.

"I have Still's disease," I told the nurse, thinking she would take me more seriously if I named an actual illness (not just a fever) even though I wasn't sure at this point that Still's was the right name for what I had. When I'd been discharged from the hospital seven years ago the working diagnosis had still been ulcerative colitis, even though I had almost every symptom I'd read about in that frightening article about Still's that the doctor gave me. It would take several additional doctor visits in the coming months, after the hiking trip with Jessie, to confirm the Still's diagnosis.

At any rate, saying I had Still's didn't help at all. The nurse didn't believe there was anything seriously wrong with me. I'd walked in on my own two feet and was speaking clearly. The ER doctor was skeptical too, until he took my temperature. My fever was 105; the doctor talked about admitting me. I asked to use a phone. It was mid-afternoon by then (and an hour later in Wisconsin) and I hoped Dr. Randall, the GI doctor who helped me during the worst weeks of my 1990 hospital stay, would still be in his office and would be willing to somehow get a prescription sent to a drugstore in Colorado Springs. Whatever the proper name for this illness was, I knew what it could do to me and I knew I needed Prednisone.

Dr. Randall took my call right away and talked to the ER doctor and within twenty minutes I had the medication. I went directly to my hotel, let myself into the room, and took the first dose—it was a double dose for a kick-start. I lay down on the bed, tears in my eyes, and talked again to my father and Dick. *Okay,* I said. *This is it, another bout of the disease. Help me do the right things. Help me somehow be able to spend this time with Jessie. Help me keep functioning even if I'm not 100 percent.* I fell asleep feeling surrounded by my father's and Dick's love even though I had a burning head, an aching chest, a rash that now reached my neck and my feet. It was everywhere except my face.

I woke up three hours later without a fever. At least I thought I didn't have a fever. I'd picked up a thermometer in the drug store where I'd bought the prescription. I stuck the thermometer in my mouth and waited. My temperature was 99. Not perfect, but damn good. And the rash was gone. I could hardly believe it. It was like the morning after Dick Olney's second hospital visit when I woke up without colon symptoms. Could I trust it to last?

I probably cried again. I must have. That's what I do with big feelings; I can't help it. I learned to curb it most of the time when therapy clients told me sad things. But once in a while I even cried with a client.

I went for a walk, testing the reality. Was my mind actually as clear as it seemed inside the hotel room? Yes, it was, mostly. I was still tired and feeling odd. But no fever, no rash.

I met Jessie and her current boyfriend at a restaurant. During the meal I felt that old depersonalization feeling, like I was separate from everything. I suppose it was partly the aftermath of being so frightened by the return of the disease. I was having trouble focusing on the conversation, wondering every minute if I was going to stay well or not. And I was tired, spent. I didn't talk very much although I tried.

I didn't want Jessie to know what was going on with me. When I was most sick in the summer of 1990, Jessie, who was then twelve years old, had been at a French immersion camp in northern Minnesota for two weeks. I'd sent her cheery letters, telling her I was getting well when in fact I was getting sicker and sicker. When she got home, walked in the door, and saw the EMTs carrying me out the door to take me to the hospital, my lie became obvious.

It seemed to me that ever since then she'd been uncomfortable about illness. Mine, at least. Even when I mentioned something minor like a cold she'd go silent, look irritated, and I'd change the subject. So no way was I going to tell her my disease was back. Or that it had been back that morning. That it might be coming back again; I didn't yet know. And, if Jessie didn't know I was sick again, maybe I could forget about it myself.

I also didn't like that boyfriend. He seemed cold, didn't know how to talk to someone my age and wasn't listening to Jessie either. (She broke up with him shortly after that night.) I went back to my motel and to bed as soon as I could politely extricate myself.

I was supposed to take the Prednisone every day at the same exact time. I soon learned that this mattered. I woke up the next morning still free of fever and I didn't get the pill into my mouth until eleven. It was supposed to be taken at ten. At eleven thirty the rash popped up on my lower legs and chest. Two hours after I swallowed the pill it was gone. It would go like that every day for six more months. When I was even a little late taking the pill, symptoms would start up again.

Prednisone is a weird drug. I don't remember a thing about our hike except that I was slow and Jessie teased me about getting old and that the hike was somewhere in the desert in New Mexico. We drove down there from Colorado Springs the morning after I'd arrived and spent three days there. I remember I had to go to bed early every night during our trip because I'd used up all my energy by eight pm. I also remember that we both got tattoos at the Route 66 Tattoo Parlor in Santa Fe. On the way there I mentioned to Jessie that I wasn't sure I should get a tattoo while on Prednisone. By then, since I was doing just fine—or appeared to be—I'd told Jessie I'd had some symptoms but that the Prednisone was working and all was under control. So when I worried out loud about the safety of getting a tattoo she got annoyed. "Either do it or don't, Mom," she snapped at me.

Well. Okay then.

"Yes. I'm in," I said.

I was. But it did feel like a big risk. A tattoo on my ankle while in the midst of a camouflaged flare-up of whatever I had. I went ahead anyway. I got a black medicine bear scratched onto my right ankle. He was about an inch from snout to butt, with a green arrow shooting through his body. I'd read about the possible meanings of the bear symbol. According to various Indian nations he was a symbol of protection, courage, and physical strength. The green arrow running through him was commonly seen as a symbol of the life force or of spiritual strength.

A strong brave bear and an arrow of spiritual strength seemed a perfect choice for a person trying not to be sick.

Despite the pain of the vibrating tattoo needle, I came through the tattoo process just fine. Jessie however fainted in the middle of getting a large tattoo—a blue and green fish together in a yin yang symbol, a design she'd drawn herself—on her back. Quite beautiful. I kept her company as she submitted to the tattoo needle. When she turned pale and silent and passed out I thought, *Oh God, this is my fault. What a bad mother I am to expose my daughter to this damage! What am I going to tell her father?* But there was no need to worry. The tattooist brought her two cold cans of Coke, one for her face and neck and one to drink. They took a fifteen-minute break after which she was fine. Her tattoo was much prettier than mine. And better done. I think the tattooist was more interested in decorating my lovely nineteen-year-old daughter's back than my forty-nine-year-old ankle.

Did that bear on my ankle help me get well? Did the totem bear on my seatmate's cane help? Or the spirit of Dick and my father? All of that maybe.

But probably it was mostly the Prednisone. It was wonderful to have it work so well, sending most of my symptoms back into a basement closet, but it wasn't perfect. On day two of the Colorado trip, which was also day two of taking Prednisone, I developed pleurisy: inflammation of the lining around the heart. Very painful. Dr. Randall told me to up the dose from 40 milligrams to 60 milligrams. The increase in the medication calmed down my chest pain in a few days.

I had to stay on that high dose for six months. Every earlier attempt at weaning off failed; the rash and fever would slip back in and I'd have to return to the high dose again. The drug made my face grow moonlike in shape and I gained weight. That didn't happen when I took it seven years before, or maybe it did and I didn't notice because I was so ecstatic about getting well. This time my stomach got rounder and I was thicker all over.

And then there were the hallucinations. They were entertaining. The auras around the new blades of grass in our front lawn, the way I imagined birds were speaking to me, the rippling motion of certain patterns in cloth, carpets, sidewalks. I think my few adventures with LSD in my twenties helped me relax and enjoy the weirdness. It was kind of fun. Not sleeping more than a few hours a night, another side effect of the

Prednisone, not so much fun. After six months I was finally able to wean off the drug.

Early on during the flare-up I decided I needed to get a better handle on this powerful illness. What should I call it? What could I expect from it? I thought the Still's diagnosis might be right but I wasn't sure. It didn't seem likely that ulcerative colitis was the right diagnosis: I hadn't had a single diarrhea attack since 1990.

After I got back from Colorado I made an appointment with Dr. Randall, in part to thank him for taking the ER doctor's call and prescribing Prednisone so quickly when I was in the hospital in Colorado Springs, but also to ask him if he still thought I'd had ulcerative colitis. He told me he'd presented my case at a medical conference, showing colleagues the images of my colon taken when I was having that terrible bloody diarrhea. They all thought his diagnosis, ulcerative colitis, was probably right but that it was a very unusual presentation for colitis.

Dr. Randall himself had concluded that I never had colitis in the first place. He thought perhaps the colon symptoms were a bad reaction to the Indocin, the drug they gave me at the end of my first week in the hospital. That seemed plausible. The timing was right—I started getting bleeding and diarrhea right around the time I was on Indocin. I hated that drug; it made me feel *muzzy*—disconnected and weird. Dr. Randall suggested I see a rheumatologist at the Medical College of Wisconsin. Which I did. She confirmed my suspicion: I had Still's disease. I'd had almost every possible symptom, both times. She also said I was very fortunate to have recovered as much as I had and that I could expect another bad flare-up or two in the future. Or, equally possible, I might have small recurrences of the disease that weren't as bad as the previous ones. She referred me to the Cleveland Clinic for more tests.

The doctor at Cleveland Clinic was both a rheumatologist and an osteopath and was knowledgeable about alternative healing, including Native American healing rituals. Sweat lodges. Shamanic journeying. I'd read a book about blending shamanic healing with western medicine, and I was intrigued. Maybe there were ways for me to stay well other than taking pills. I told the doctor about my experiences with Dick, how he'd visited me twice in the hospital when my illness was at its worst, how he'd used hypnosis to take me deeply into myself and after the second experience I'd recovered almost overnight. Dick seemed somehow to be connected with my ability to heal.

After a battery of tests at the Cleveland Clinic—extensive blood work, echocardiogram, colonoscopy—the rheumatologist/osteopath and I sat in his office discussing the results and my diagnosis. My colon was fine, he told me. I actually knew this already because I'd been only mildly sedated for the procedure and had watched the travels of the mini camera through my colon, projected onto a large screen over the table I was lying on. This colonoscopy was so different from the one I'd had seven years before. No pain at all this time and very interesting. As opposed to seven years ago, when the colonoscopy had hurt so much I'd cried through the whole thing and Dr. Randall had said the inside of my colon looked like it had been dragged along a gravel road. This time there was no sign of past or present inflammation or damage of any kind.

The Cleveland Clinic doctor told me my daylong exam had revealed nothing other than my current good health. "This," he said, "was a bit like closing the stable doors after the horses got out."

"What do you think caused all my symptoms before?"

"You have adult-onset Still's disease," he said. "No other diagnosis fits. But I don't think you need to worry about the name of it. Live your life. Do what makes you happy and if the disease shows up again, call your healer friend. What was his name?"

"Dick Olney."

"Call Dick Olney."

❖

Dick Olney. I'm always going to remember his visits to my hospital room the summer of 1990. During the first visit he asked me to get in touch with a time I'd felt strong, told me to go back as far as I needed to find it. I went back to 1986, to the Grand Canyon, that life-changing hike with my friend Ginny. I went back to that blazing sunlight, the swooping ravens, the ancient secret-keeping rocks, a pink rattlesnake slithering on pink sand. I still remember the images from that first hypnosis session.

The second time he came he didn't talk to my mind, he talked to my body; he ordered it to mend. And that was all I remembered from that session. I'd tried to tape record it but later, when I listened to the tape, I heard nothing but murmurings and hisses. Only Dick's words at the end were clear: "Your body is healing more and more rapidly. Your colon is already returning to its normal healthy state. You are going to be completely well so quickly that your doctors will be amazed." And they were.

It was glorious to get well after that first terrible bout of Still's disease. For months afterwards I remained hyper-awake, all my senses at 100 percent reacting to an ant on the sidewalk, a shadow cast on my bedroom wall, the gold flecks in Timmy the dog's otherwise dark eyes, hawks migrating right above me in a bright blue sky. No one gets to keep that kind of full awake-ness. It slipped away. Maybe not all the way away. It's in me somewhere and sometimes it still surprises me.

But I couldn't stay wide awake like that when dealing with my failing parents. I turned down the volume on my own needs, turned it way down, but not without resentment. I was angry on some level that my parents' declines were darkening my sky, encroaching on my new intermittent awake-ness. Selfish, yes. Cold, not really.

I cared deeply about my parents' suffering. I'd worried about both of them forever. When I was nineteen, the only way I knew how to hold onto myself was to mostly stop talking to them, stop helping them in any way, and stop asking them for anything they couldn't give (like money, sound advice, help to get back to college). I had no choice when they both got so sick the year after I recovered from Still's. Maybe someone who was more evolved than I was could have managed to stay awake and alive in the face of impossible demands; I'm sure some people do it. Pema Chodron could do it. Roshi Joan Halifax could do it. I couldn't do it.

Two years after my mother's stroke and three years after I'd gotten well, I attended a hypnosis training weekend in Taos, New Mexico, with Dick Olney. It turned out to be about shamanic journeying and hypnotic trance induction. At the end of the weekend Dick shared with us that he'd recently done a vision quest alone in the mountains of New Mexico. On his third day without food or water he'd met a little green man, a demon. He swore the demon seemed as real as any of us in the class. When he'd returned from his quest—shaky, hungry, dazzled—he worried he might have somehow offended the green man. He wondered, too, if he had made him up. He discussed these concerns with his shaman after he returned from the quest.

"Are demons real?" Dick asked the shaman.

"You bet your life they are!" the man replied.

"Can they harm me?"

"Only if you let them."

⊰◇⊱

Dick's story about his green demon makes me think about the demons I met during my illness and a few years afterward. Were any of my demons real? The ones from childhood nightmares, the ones who came to me in dreams during my illness. Could they harm me? Did I let them harm me? Or were they there to save me?

I remember meeting a demon about five years after my mother's stroke, right before she died. I was learning sand tray therapy to use in my own therapy practice. It's a technique where you ask a client (most often a child client) to create scenes in a small sandbox. The therapist provides the props: small people, animals, fences, plastic plants, utensils, tiny toys. During my first lesson, the teacher asked me to use the sand tray to show her my childhood. I quickly chose a small house, trees, toys, a teeter-totter, a dog, a bird in a tree. A mommy, a daddy, a boy, a girl. And then I selected a crouching monster, a demon, and placed him behind a plastic bush.

"Is that it?" the psychologist asked me. "Your childhood?"

"I think so, yes." The sand tray showed it all: the shelter, the toys, the garden, the dog. The many pleasures of my childhood, but also, always there: the hidden danger. The threat. The things I sensed and couldn't clearly see. They colored my whole life. The underlying cracks in my world. The demons.

The demons who came to me when I was ill all seemed to carry messages about survival.

In the story Claire told me during one of my brief breaks from being in the hospital, this young monk has to move through a crowd of demons who embody his deepest fears in order to reach the door behind which waits his heart's desire. These demons aren't real but in a way they are. He has to move through them, not let them stop him. They harass him mercilessly as he walks toward the door. Through this trial he learns two important skills: Keep moving no matter how scared you are. Keep your eye on the door.

Then there was the demon that visited my friend Marty and told him that he, the demon, was wrecking Marty's colon to teach him to embrace his life, to come back to the things that brought him joy: poetry, rock and roll, drinking whiskey. Smoking. (Some studies have shown smoking reduces the inflammation of ulcerative colitis.)

I had two demon dreams when my fevers were 105 and 106. Both involved molten lava that surged toward where I stood on a dark street. I began to run but I couldn't outrun the lava. In the distance, a demon beckoned: *Come to me, I am your only hope.* I woke up before I could decide whether he meant to save me or destroy me. The other dream also involved lava and a demon and was even more vivid. A volcano erupting, spewing fire, a demon surrounded by orange and red flames rising up out of the earth, extending an arm to me and calling out, as the first demon had, *Come, I will save you.* Before I could run or wake myself up, he caught hold of my shoulder and pulled me down with him into the fire. I was terrified. I fell through a fiery whirlpool, then a cool mist began to fall all around me. The demon disappeared and the bright orange and red light faded out.

Both these dreams, I think now, were about accepting what was happening to me, accepting it and keeping on moving through my fear. When I was pulled down into the fire in the second dream, the fire actually died. Maybe both dreams were prompting me to trust that I would move through the sickness, through the fevers, to the continuation of my life. Maybe they were suggesting that the heat of the fevers would transform me along the way.

The fevers could have killed me. Their ferocity, intended by my body to eradicate some bacteria or virus that didn't exist, could have destroyed my brain, my heart, my other organs. Instead my fever demons forced me to stop trying to control the illness, to control everything. And when I surrendered to my symptoms another kind of energy rose up in me, a faith that I would come through the flames. I didn't know what would come after the fire. There was no need to know. No way to know. I was not exactly transformed by the alchemy of my fevers. By my demons. But I was returned to myself. Returned from hell to heaven, to everything I loved, to being alive.

In my many sessions with Dick Olney, even before I was ill, I'd learned this same lesson but I will always need to relearn it: The importance of being where you are right now, being there 100 percent. It's the only way through anything overwhelming or terrifying, even if you think you can't survive it; you can. Do what that young monk had to do: Don't let fear stop you. Move into and through it. Dive deep. Feel it all.

42

The Mountains are Home

"Mountains are giant, restful, absorbent. You can heave
your spirit into a mountain and the mountain will
keep it, folded, and not throw it back as some creeks
will. The creeks are the world with all its stimulus and
beauty; I live there. But the mountains are home."

—ANNIE DILLARD, *Pilgrim at Tinker Creek*

THREE MONTHS AFTER MY mother died I flew to Colorado Springs with
nine-year-old Nic and a box containing half my mother's remains. The
other half had been placed in a small marble-faced niche beside my father's similar one in the columbarium at Wisconsin Memorial Park. At
my mother's request, the other half of her ashes were set aside in a sturdy
cardboard box with my name on it. To take to the mountains.

I chose Colorado, not just because it contained more than enough
mountains to please my mother but also because Jessie was still at Colorado College in Colorado Springs. She'd had lots of opportunities to ex-
plore the mountains that filled the sky to the west of her campus. She'd
found, she told me, a great place to leave Grandma.

On the morning of my first day in Colorado Springs, I walked out
to my rented car in the Holiday Inn parking lot, preoccupied with taking
Jessie and Nic out to breakfast, not thinking about mountains. I hadn't

seen mountains last night when I got in after dark and I was startled when I looked up and saw them there, filling half the sky, monstrous and beautiful. The sky itself was a miracle of turquoise. The massive peaks of the Front Range lay against all that blinding blue. Sunlight flowed over them, sinking into the rock faces, making the white patches of snow glow. And there was Pikes Peak, 14,000 feet high, just a little taller than its mighty comrades: Cheyenne Mountain, Mounts Manitou, Rosa and Arthur, Eagle Mountain and Cameron Cone. I remembered their names from some brochure I'd read last year, although I couldn't remember anymore which one was which.

Nic and I picked up Jessie and the three of us drove for about an hour, west on Colorado Avenue, through Manitou Springs, up past Pikes Peak Highway, through Woodland Park and Crystola, to a dirt road thirty-eight miles outside of Colorado Springs. There was a small sign by the turn-off: "Eleven Mile Canyon."

The dirt road led us almost immediately into a pine forest and along a series of sapphire blue lakes. Words like "crystalline" and "pristine" sprang to mind. When we were nearly at the canyon Jessie asked, "Is Grandma in the trunk?"

"Yes," I said.

"Weird. Did you have her in your suitcase?"

"No, my carry-on bag."

The road we were on came to an end at a small parking lot beside a picnic area. Two other cars were parked there and four climbers were crawling lizard-like high up on a nearby rock face. There were a few wooden tables accompanied by grills on posts. Pine trees and aspens encircled the picnic area and rose up the slope beyond it. A narrow, roiling river flowed alongside the road. A brown national park sign identified the river as the South Platte.

"This is it," Jessie said. "I know it looks kind of public but if we walk just a little way in, I don't think anyone will see us."

"This is fine," I told her. "I like it."

I opened the trunk and pulled out the cardboard box that held my mother's ashes. It was surprisingly heavy. A label pasted on the outside contained the following warning: "The remains inside contain fine ash, and bits of bone and tooth. Scattering these remains would best be done by someone other than a close family member as the reality of those hard bits among the ashes could be emotionally upsetting."

I pried open the top of the box. Packed inside were layers of wadded-up paper towels, as if to keep something from breaking. As if my mother's ashes couldn't tolerate a little bouncing around. I pulled out the towels and then a clear plastic bag that contained what looked like gray, grainy dust. Sure enough, among the fine, sand-like ashes I could see tiny flecks of hard-looking white. Not a big deal but good to be forewarned.

"I want to do the scattering," Nic told me, running to my side, his hands reaching out. "I'll do it all. Jessie doesn't get to do any of it."

"We'll each have a turn, Nic," I told him.

We began to walk up the steep trail beside the picnic grounds. We were soon surrounded by trees and giant-sized rocks.

"This is it," I announced. The air was clear with a soft but steady breeze. Sunlight fell in patches through the pine needles above us, warming the ground and releasing the smell of drying and decaying leaves. The river roared below. The only other sounds came from nearby birds calling out to each other and the distant rock climbers doing the same thing.

The three of us sat cross-legged in a circle, the bag of ashes in the middle. "Nic, would you like to read?" Jessie asked. Nic took the book of essays that Jessie had brought along and began to read a mythical story by Terry Tempest Williams, about a woman dancing in the night with Bear, Raven, and Wolf. Nic read very well for a nine-year-old, but he didn't understand what he was reading. He read too fast and gave up quickly. "Stupid," he said, and handed the book back to Jessie.

"It's about being one with the wild things," Jessie explained. Her brother made a face. He poked at the hard ground with a stick, drew a circle and began etching math problems inside it. At least he was quiet.

Next I read a few lines from a poem called "Hands"[1] by Mark Turcotte. The poem ends with these words: "May the Grandfathers give you feathers, all is forgiven down here."

"May the Grandfathers give you feathers," I repeated.

"Whose grandfathers are we talking about?" Nic asked.

"It means the great spirit, I think, Nic. Or God," Jessie said.

"All is forgiven down here," I said to myself again while Nic rattled on about how his grandfather didn't have feathers and there wasn't really a god.

"All *is* forgiven down here," I said out loud. I could see Jessie had some idea what I meant. Nic didn't care.

---

1. Turcotte, "Hands," 35.

I handed him the bag of ashes. He pulled out a fistful of grey ash and swung his arm in a small arc, abruptly opening his hand. The ashes dribbled onto the ground. The hard white bits made a pattering sound. Rather like scattering gravel on a driveway.

"Hmm," I said. "This isn't quite what I had in mind."

"Maybe," Jessie said, "we need to be up higher." She looked up at the boulder towering above us. "That looks like a better ash-throwing place."

"I don't think I'm up for a climb," I told her. The boulder was surrounded by smaller rocks but all of them looked slick and sharp-edged. And I was feeling a little shaky.

"How about Nic and me going up?"

"Sure. Okay." They weren't shaky. They'd be fine.

Jessie took Nic's hand, and before he'd had a chance to object she'd jollied him up to the very top of the boulder, some fifteen feet above my head. I shaded my face with my hand and peered up at them. Jessie was gripping the back of her little brother's shorts as he wobbled in his slippery sandals at the edge of the rock. One of his hands had remained inside the plastic bag of ashes while he'd slid and trembled his way up the rocks, as if he were holding onto his grandmother for safety. I watched my children from below and tried not to picture them toppling over the edge to their deaths.

"You know, Nic," Jessie said. "You can just pour that stuff out of the bag. You don't have to keep touching it."

"I want to touch it. I like it." Nic pulled his fist out, drew another arc in the air with his arm, and opened his hand. The wind caught the dust this time and lifted it sideways, creating a gauzy curtain that hung motionless for an instant. The thin October sunlight picked out the white bone particles and made them sparkle as they twirled and then fell out of the dust cloud, which thinned a moment later and then fell too onto the hard dirt, into my hair and all over my clothes.

"Hey, look!" Nic shouted. "It's raining Nana on you!"

"Mom," Jessie called down. "Do you want us to keep doing this? Is this okay with you?"

"It's fine," I called back up. "More than fine. I like it and Nana would have liked it too."

And she would have, I thought. She would have loved all of it: her grandchildren planting these tiny pieces of her into her beloved mountains, the pine needle smell, the sound of the river, our laughter, the way the bits of bone rattled against the dry soil and the granite boulders, making a sound like falling rain. She'd have loved the way the air came clear after the ash cloud settled. The quiet that followed.

"Save the last little bit," I called up to Nic. "I think we should put some into the river."

The kids climbed down off the boulder. We followed the sound of the river, climbing slowly, sideways, down the steep slope, and then sat on some medium-sized rocks beside the river. The water was dull green and frothy. A true mountain river, created from snowmelt and nearly as cold as ice. I wouldn't want to put a toe into it, I thought. But my mother would have. It was what she always did when meeting up with a river like this: found a way to get to its edge and dip her toes into the water.

I pictured her on some family trip we'd taken—to Wyoming, maybe, or the Black Hills in South Dakota. In my mind she was young again, her dark hair pulled back with a twisted red bandana, a pair of big round sunglasses, red lipstick, rolled-up jeans. I saw her taking a giant step out onto a huge flat rock surrounded by foaming rapids. She sat down, pulled off her shoes and plopped her feet into the frigid water. And kicked and splashed, laughing, sending sprays of icy drops onto her jeans, her t-shirt. I imagined my father calling her, once, twice, again, until she finally heard and with obvious reluctance left the river and returned to the car.

If she were here, I thought, she would have had her shoes off long ago. She'd be sitting right here, splashing. Looking up into this amazing sky. Filling her lungs with the fragrant air. She'd be absorbing these mountains, drawing them in through her eyes and making them part of every cell of her body. Carrying them away with her. Taking them home.

"I'll do this part," I said. Nic handed me the nearly empty bag and I poured what was left of the ashes into the water. "There you go, Mom," I told her in my head. "Now you don't ever have to get back in the car."

The ash mixture vanished the second it hit the water, the heavier pieces sinking to the river bottom. From there, I imagined, they'd be pulled downstream, worn down to silt, lodging eventually against the river's banks, joining up with the soil, getting sucked up by the roots of trees and grasses. Ending up in water lilies and reeds. Ending up in the bellies of fish and the gizzards of birds.

The sun was sliding down below the line of the mountain ridge, casting its shadow along the slopes, across the road and the river, to where we sat. The temperature was dropping. I shivered.

"Time to go," I said and stood up.

That night I had a dream. I saw my mother and Geraldine, her favorite nursing assistant from the nursing home where she'd lived her final years. They were walking together across the parking lot at the Colorado Springs airport, heading for the terminal. This was not the Mary Marks of the past five years, the woman who'd suffered a devastating stroke that had destroyed her ability to walk and to think like an adult. This was Mary in her sober mid-fifties. Her eyes were clear; she walked with energy and determination. She and Geraldine were talking animatedly and laughing. Mary flipped open an old cell phone without missing a step. The wind was blowing her dark brown hair across her eyes. She pushed it back with one hand and pressed the phone to her ear with the other.

"I'm going to the mountains," I heard her say through the cell phone that had suddenly appeared in my hand.

"But Mom," I said. "You can't do that. You're dead."

"Silly girl," she said, with a laugh. "I'm already there."

She clicked off her phone, tucked it into her purse and, without looking back at me, kept on walking.

Bibliography

Barnes, Julian. *Nothing to Be Frightened Of.* New York: Knopf, 2008.

Brown, Chip. *Afterwards You're a Genius.* New York: Riverhead Hardcover, 1998.

Broyard, Anatole, et al., *Intoxicated by My Illness and Other Writings on Life and Death.* New York: Fawcett, 1993.

Dillard, Annie. *Pilgrim at Tinker Creek.* New York: Harper Perennial Classics, 2007.

Endicott, Jean, et al., "Anxiety and Dissociative Disorders." In *Diagnostic and Statistical Manual of Mental Disorders.* 3rd ed. American Psychiatric Association, 1980.

Manguso, Sarah. *The Two Kinds of Decay.* New York: Farrar, Straus and Giroux, 2008.

Price, Reynolds. *A Whole New Life, An Illness and a Healing.* New York: Scribner, 1994.

Reginato, Antonio J., et al., "Adult onset Still's disease: experience in 23 patients and literature review with emphasis on organ failure." In *Seminars in Arthritis and Rheumatism,* Volume 17, Issue 1 (August 1987): 39–57.

Sontag, Susan. *Illness as Metaphor.* New York, Farrar, Straus and Giroux, 1978.

Thomas, Dylan. "Fern Hill." In *The Collected Poems of Dylan Thomas.* Edited by Dylan Thomas. New York: New Directions, 1971.

Turcotte, Mark. *The Feathered Heart.* East Lansing, MI: Michigan State University Press, 1998.

Wikipedia Contributors. "Depersonalization." In *Wikipedia, The Free Encyclopedia,* March 28, 2022. https://en.wikipedia.org/w/index.php?title=Depersonalization&oldid=1079829802.

Yeats, William. In *The College Anthology of British and American Poetry.* Edited by A. Kent Hieatt and William Park. Boston: Allyn and Bacon, 1964.

Made in the USA
Columbia, SC
02 January 2023

75366269R00157